Daoist Master Changchun's Journey to the West

Daoist Master Changchun's Journey to the West
長春真人西遊記

To the Court of Chinggis Qan and Back

Li Zhichang, Compiler 李志常

Translated by
Ruth W. Dunnell, Stephen H. West, and Shao-yun Yang

OXFORD
UNIVERSITY PRESS

OXFORD
UNIVERSITY PRESS

Oxford University Press is a department of the University of Oxford.
It furthers the University's objective of excellence in research, scholarship,
and education by publishing worldwide. Oxford is a registered trade mark of
Oxford University Press in the UK and in certain other countries.

Published in the United States of America by Oxford University Press
198 Madison Avenue, New York, NY 10016, United States of America.

© Oxford University Press 2023

Library of Congress Cataloging-in-Publication Data
2023915080

ISBN 978-0-19-766837-5

Printed by Sheridan Books, Inc., United States of America.

Contents

Acknowledgments vii
Table of weights and measures of the late Jin period viii
Table of Dynasties ix
Lunar years of the Xiyouji *by stem and branch and by animal of the zodiac* x
Finding list of Qiu Chuji's poems xi
Maps xiv
Introduction xvii

DAOIST MASTER CHANGCHUN'S JOURNEY TO THE WEST 1

PREFACE 3

BOOK I, RECORDED BY HIS DISCIPLE MASTER ZHENCHANG,
LI ZHICHANG 7
   In Shandong 7
   Departing Shandong 9
   At Yanjing 11
   Through Juyong Pass to Stay at Longyang Monastery 17
   To the Camp of Great Prince Otegin at Hulun Buir 35
   Across the Mongolian Plateau to the Qatun's *Ordo* 39
   To the City of Chinqai and into the Yinshan (Tian Shan) Range 45
   Through the Yinshan (Tian Shan) Range to Samarkand and the Imperial
      Camp 55
   With the Qan in Afghanistan, Samarkand, and Central Asia 85

BOOK II, RECORDED BY HIS DISCIPLE MASTER ZHENCHANG,
LI ZHICHANG 91
   Return to the East 107
   Return to Yanjing 125
   Death and Apotheosis 149

Endnotes 159
Additional Note 171

Appendices

  1. Chinggis Qan's Rescript Requesting Qiu Chuji to Journey to the West 175
  2. Qiu Chuji's Request to Remain in the Yanjing and Dexing Area 179
  3. Chinggis Qan's Response to Qiu Chuji's Request for Delay 183
  4. Chinggis Qan's Sagely Directive to All Officials 187
  5. Chinggis Qan's Sagely Directive Delivered by Alixian 189
  6. Imperial Edict from Chinggis Qan Conveyed by Jia Chang 191
  7. Shimo Xiandebu (Sendeb) Invites Qiu Chuji to Take Charge of Tianchang Monastery 193
  8. Wang [Juchuan] Invites Qiu Chuji to Take Charge of Tianchang Monastery 195
  9. Shimo Xiandebu (Sendeb) Invites Qiu Chuji to Reside Permanently in Tianchang Monastery 199
  10. Disciples Who Accompanied the Master 203
  11. Four Mongols Ordered to Escort and Protect the Master 205
  12. *Record of the Felicitous Encounter with the Mysterious Wind of Daoism* 207
  13. Excerpt from *A Disputation of Contrived and False Records of the Zhiyuan Era* 229
  14. Wang Guowei's Preface to His Edition of *Changchun's Journey* 231

Abbreviations for Oft-Cited Texts 237
Bibliography 239
Index 251

Acknowledgments

The seed for a new translation of *Changchun zhenren Xiyouji* was planted early in Ruth's career when she was teaching classes on the Mongol empire at Kenyon College. That seed sprouted in 2019 (the year she retired from Kenyon), by which time Shao-yun Yang, her colleague at nearby Denison University, had offered to collaborate and to prepare a digital map of Qiu Chuji's journey. Ruth and Shao-yun were immensely fortunate to recruit Stephen West of Arizona State University, another retiree, to the project in 2020 and quickly discovered that three brains (and sets of eyes) were always better than one. With his experience in translating Chinese literature of the era, Steve rendered the heretofore dismissed and untranslated poems peppering the account, to fully express Qiu Chuji's shifting attitudes about the trip. This complex text fully required the combined skills and expertise that its translators marshaled to render its many treasures accessible to a modern audience. We three are grateful for such a rich and fruitful collaboration that provided a heady learning experience for all of us while we brought this project to completion.

The numerous unnamed reviewers who read versions of the manuscript along the way performed an essential service in moving us closer to our goal. We are also grateful to Chris Atwood for his ready willingness to offer counsel on all questions relating to Mongolian and other personal names, place names, terms, and usages. A special note of thanks goes to Wen Zuoting, who prepared the Chinese text of the account. The Hsu-Tang Library's OUP editorial team has been a joy to work with—ever thoughtful, patient, encouraging, attentive, and supportive. Wiebke Denecke, Stefan Vranka, Kathleen Fearn, Lucas Klein, Eleanor Goodman, Daniel Gill, Isabella Furth, and others not named here lent their time and talents to perfecting our imperfections. Any remaining flaws must be borne by the authors alone.

Ruth W. Dunnell, Chicago, Illinois
Stephen H. West, Tempe, Arizona
Shao-yun Yang, Granville, Ohio
August 15, 2022

Table of weights and measures of the late Jin period

Capacity or dry volume

1 *dan* (*shi*, "bushel")	= 10 *dou* or 67 liters (about 17.7 gallons)
1 *dou* ("peck")	= 10 *sheng* or 6.7 liters (about 1.77 gallons); increased to 9.5 liters (about 2.5 gallons) under the Yuan (a US peck is equivalent to about 9 liters)

Length

1 *li* ("Chinese mile")	= 360 *bu* or 180 *zhang* or 0.56 kilometers (about 0.34 of a mile)
1 *zhang* ("ten-foot")	= 10 *chi* or 3.12 meters (about 10.24 feet)
1 *bu* ("pace")	= 5 *chi* or 1.56 meters
1 *chi* ("foot")	= 10 *cun* or 31.2 centimeters (about 1 foot)
1 *cun* ("inch")	= 10 *fen* or 3.12 centimeters (about 1.2 inches)

Weight

1 *yi* (1.25 *jin*)	= 20 or 24 *liang*, or 800 or 960 grams (about 1.76 or 2.12 pounds)
1 *jin* ("pound")	= 16 *liang* or 633 grams (about 1.4 pounds)
1 *liang* ("ounce")	= 10 *qian* or 40 grams (about 1.4 ounces)

Area

1 *qing*	= 100 *mu* or 5.73 hectares (about 14 acres)

Sources: Pu Huiquan 2008 and Luo Zhufeng et al. 1994

Table of Dynasties

Note

SHANG ca. 1300–1046 BCE

ZHOU ca. 1046–256 BCE
    Western Zhou ca. 1046–771 BCE
    Eastern Zhou 770–256 BCE
    Spring and Autumn 770–481 BCE
    Warring States 481–221 BCE

QIN 221–207 BCE

HAN 206 BCE–220 CE
    Western Han 206 BCE–8 CE
    Eastern Han 25–220

THREE KINGDOMS
    Wei 220–266
    Shu-Han 221–263
    Wu 222–280

WESTERN JIN 266–316

EASTERN JIN 317–420

NORTHERN AND SOUTHERN DYNASTIES 420–589

SUI 581–618

TANG 618–907

FIVE DYNASTIES 907–960

SONG 960–1279
    Northern Song 960–1127
    Southern Song 1127–1279

LIAO 916–1125

JIN 1115–1234

YUAN 1271–1368

MING 1368–1644

QING 1636–1911

Lunar years of the *Xiyouji* by stem and branch and by animal of the zodiac

LUNAR YEAR ACCORDING TO WESTERN CALENDAR	STEM AND BRANCH	ANIMAL OF THE ZODIAC	
1219.01.18–1220.02.05	*jimao* 己卯	*tu* 兔	hare
1220.02.06–1221.01.24	*gengchen* 庚辰	*long* 龍	dragon
1221.01.25–1222.02.12	*xinsi* 辛巳	*she* 蛇	snake
1222.02.13–1223.02.01	*renwu* 壬午	*ma* 馬	horse
1223.02.02–1224.01.21	*guiwei* 癸未	*yang* 羊	sheep
1224.01.22–1225.02.08	*jiashen* 甲申	*hou* 猴	monkey
1225.02.09–1226.01.29	*yiyou* 乙酉	*ji* 雞	chicken
1226.01.30–1227.01.18	*bingxu* 丙戌	*gou* 狗	dog
1227.01.19–1228.02.07	*dinghai* 丁亥	*zhu* 豬	pig
1228.02.08–1229.01.26	*wuzi* 戊子	*shu* 鼠	rat

Finding list of Qiu Chuji's poems

Classical poetry *shi* 詩

1. "Responding to Pacification Commissioner Wang Juchuan" 13
2. "Inscription for Yan Liben's 'Painting of the Most-High Lord Leaving the Pass'" 15
3. "Sent to Gentlemen of the Way in Yanjing" 17
4. "Roaming Mt. Chanfang and First Entering Defile Pass" 19
5. "Inscribing the Artesian Spring at Longyang Monastery in Dexing" 21
6. "Written after the *Jiao* Ceremony at Longyang Monastery in Dexing" 21
7. "Two Quatrains Written at Chaoyuan Monastery in Zhangde" I 25
8. "Two Quatrains Written at Chaoyuan Monastery in Zhangde" II 27
9. "Celebrating the Artists' Completion of Wall Paintings in the Lineage Hall of the Chaoyuan Monastery" 27
10. "Written on the Southward Return to Longyang, to Show to My Companions in the Way" 29
11. "Using a Poem to Inscribe the Western Corridor of a Hall at Longyan Temple" 31
12. "Two Poems to Send to My Companions in the Way in Yanjing" I 31
13. "Two Poems to Send to My Companions in the Way in Yanjing" II 33
14. "Another Poem Sent to Companions of the Way in Yanjing" 33
15. "Using a Poem to Relate the Facts as We Pass the Mingchang Boundary" 35
16. "A Poem on Passing Yu'erpo" 37
17. "Traveling Again along the Yu'erpo Post Road for Ten Days, Relating the Facts in a Poem" 41
18. "Recording This Portion of the Trip with a Poem" 47
19. "Sighing over My Life" 49
20. "Three Quatrains" I 51
21. "Three Quatrains" II 53
22. "Three Quatrains" III 53
23. "Written on the Road While Passing through a Desert" 55
24. "A Rainstorm at Night, a Large Tree Outside the Garden: Another Piece for the Group" 57
25. "For the Student Li Boxiang" 59
26. "A Poem to Record the Journey from the Jinshan (Altai) Mountains to the City of Almaliq" 63

27. "A Poem Occurred to Me West of Where We Gazed on the Great Snowy Mountains" 69

28. "A Poem upon Reaching Samarkand (Xiemisigan)" 73

29. "Two Poems Written on the Walls of the Old Palace" I 75

30. "Two Poems Written on the Walls of the Old Palace" II 77

31. "Roaming West of the Outskirts, I Write a Poem" 79

32. "Two Poems to Show to My Fellow Wanderers" I 79

33. "Two Poems to Show to My Fellow Wanderers" II 81

34. "Composed on the Twenty-ninth Day of the Third Month" 83

35. "Two More Poems on Coming Out of the Defile" I 87

36. "Two More Poems on Coming Out of the Defile" II 87

37. "Another Poem on Returning to Samarkand (Xiemisigan) after Being Summoned by Rescript" 89

38. "His Excellency Imperial Envoy Li Goes Eastward, and I Send a Poem to Friends of the Way in the East" 91

39. "Writing a Poem on Passing Hezhong to Record Its Facts" 95

40. "Two Quatrains" I 95

41. "Two Quatrains" II 95

42. "At Mid-Autumn I Offer a Poem to the Medical Officer of the Third Prince" 97

43. "Writing Out Words of Instruction to Show to the Congregation" 113

44. "Imperial Envoy Sir Yu of Fengzhou Brings Fine Paper to Request Calligraphy" 115

45. "Two Poems on Roaming Outside the City on the Eve of the Seventh" I 117

46. "Two Poems on Roaming Outside the City on the Eve of the Seventh" II 117

47. "Presented to the Elite of Yunzhong" 117

48. "A Poem on Chaoyuan Monastery in Xuande Prefecture" 119

49. "Two Poems Written at Longgang to Express My Feelings" I 123

50. "Two Poems Written at Longgang to Express My Feelings" II 123

51. "Two Poems Written in Qiuyang Monastery in Jinshan" I 123

52. "Two Poems Written in Qiuyang Monastery in Jinshan" II 123

53. "Roaming in Spring" I 129

54. "Roaming in Spring" II 131

55. "Climbing to the Peak of Mt. Shoule" 133

56. "To Show to Chen Xiuyu" 133

57. "The Yellow Register *Jiao* at Mt. Pan Finished, a Poem to Show to the Congregation" 137

58. "Repeating the Rhymes of Great Minister Wu Deming, Four Poems" I 139

59. "Repeating the Rhymes of Great Minister Wu Deming, Four Poems" II 141
60. "Repeating the Rhymes of Great Minister Wu Deming, Four Poems" III 141
61. "Repeating the Rhymes of Great Minister Wu Deming, Four Poems" IV 141
62. "Inscribed on Zhi Zhongyuan's 'Portrait of the Three Transcendents, Deyi, Yuanbao, and Xuansu'" 143
63. "A Quatrain for an Adept" 143
64. "Written at Midnight on the Thirteenth Day of the Eleventh Month, to Show to the Congregation" 145
65. "Roaming in the Eastern Hill Cloister after the Rains, a Quatrain to Show to the Group" 147
66. "After Lesser Heat, a Poem to Show to the Group" 147
67. "An Hymn Left Behind in the Afternoon of the Ninth Day of the Seventh Month" 151

Lyric poetry *ci* 詞

a. To the tune "Celebrating the Sagely Dynasty" I 23
b. To the tune "Celebrating the Sagely Dynasty" II 25
c. To the tune "The Phoenix Perches on the Parasol Tree" I 73
d. To the tune "The Phoenix Perches on the Parasol Tree" II 75
e. To the tune "Resenting That Joy Is Slow to Come" 135
f. To the tune "The Phoenix Perches on the Parasol Tree" III 137

Hymn poetry (*gāthā*)

The First *Gāthā* 15
The Second *Gāthā* 15
The Third *Gāthā* 33
The Fourth *Gāthā* 121

Encomia (*song* 頌)

"Four Encomia to Show to Daoists from Afar" I 127
"Four Encomia to Show to Daoists from Afar" II 127
"Four Encomia to Show to Daoists from Afar" III 129
"Four Encomia to Show to Daoists from Afar" IV 129

Maps

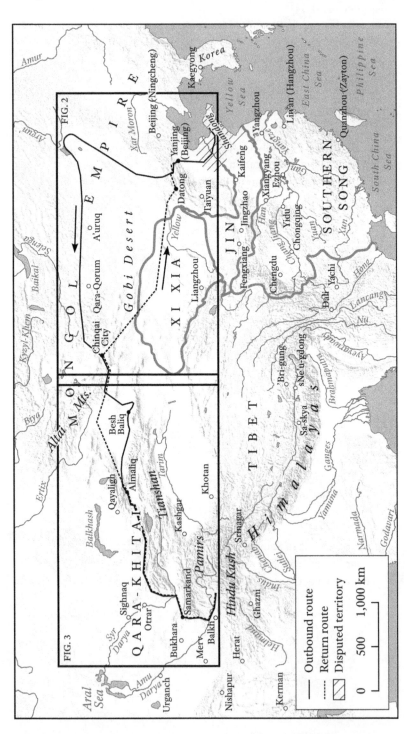

FIGURE 1 Route of Changchun's journey

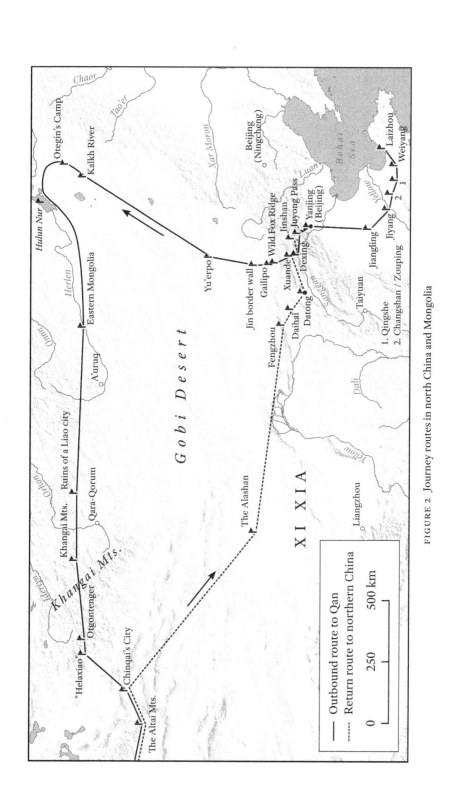

FIGURE 2 Journey routes in north China and Mongolia

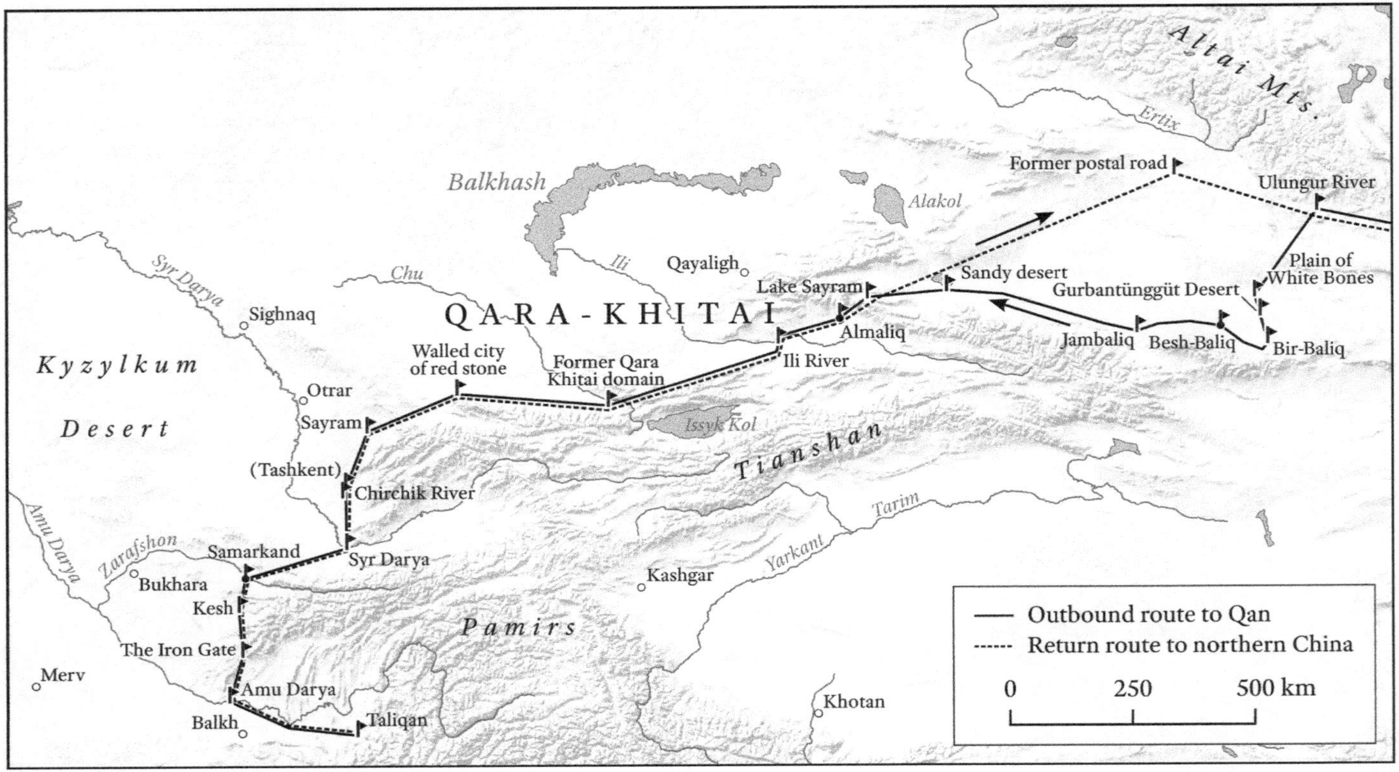

FIGURE 3 Journey routes in Central Asia

Introduction

In a monastery near the coast of Shandong at the beginning of 1220, an aging Daoist master received an unusual guest bearing an invitation. When he accepted that invitation, Qiu Chuji (1148–1227) changed the course of history for the Quanzhen (Complete Perfection) sect that he headed, and for the social and religious landscape of north China.[1] The guest, Liu Wen 劉溫 (ca. 1190–1230), called by his byname Zhonglu 仲錄 in the text, was an envoy from Chinggis Qan (1162?–1227), who was then prosecuting a war against his enemies in Central Asia.[2] The imperial invitation directed Qiu to travel to the Qan's camp and deliver up the secret of long life. Qiu set out with eighteen disciples a few weeks later, lingered in Yanjing (today's Beijing) and northern Hebei for a year, departed north China in 1221, and returned to northern Hebei in the latter part of 1223. Thanks to special favors that Chinggis granted them to reward Qiu's loyalty in answering his summons, early in 1224 the Quanzhen leaders took up residence in the Tianchang Monastery in Yanjing and established new headquarters. There they kept busy administering to growing congregations of followers throughout north China, and there Qiu Chuji died in August of 1227, a few days before or after the death of the Qan, with whom he had forged a fateful relationship.[3]

The diary of their epic trek and relocation to Yanjing, the capital of Mongol-occupied north China, was published in 1228 under the precise title *Changchun zhenren xiyouji* (Account of the Perfected Eternal Spring's Journey to the West). "Eternal Spring" was Qiu's Daoist name, and "Perfected" (*zhenren*), his Daoist title, denoted both his status as an accomplished adept of the qualities propounded by the Quanzhen sect

---

1   His actual birth name is unknown; his selection of Chuji 處機 for his given name is related to his byname Tongmi 通密. Chuji means "to reside in the exigency of change," and his byname, Tongmi, means "to penetrate to the mystery of the Way."

2   See Huang Taiyong 2016. Liu was a medical specialist, evidently of Parhae descent. Parhae (Bohai in Chinese), a polity encompassing the northeast Korean peninsula and northeast Manchuria, was absorbed by the Liao state in the early tenth century. See Sloane 2014a.

3   On the date of Chinggis Qan's death, on which there is some disagreement between sources, see Pelliot 1959, 305–309; de Rachewiltz 2004, 979–981.

over which he presided as well as identifying him as a lineage master. In our translated title, *Daoist Master Changchun's Journey to the West*, this term is more simply rendered "Daoist Master."

Traditionally, Li Zhichang 李志常 (1193–1255), one of Qiu Chuji's disciples and a member of the travel party, is credited with authorship of *Changchun's Journey* (which we shall call the work for short).[4] We understand this to mean that Li Zhichang was the primary compiler and editor of the account, written in Yanjing upon their return and based on the recollections and/or notes kept by all surviving members of the travel band. He thus played the role of shaping the narrative voice of the record to serve the purposes of the Quanzhen sect and its leaders (see below for a discussion of narrative voice).

Historical and cultural significance of the text

The early thirteenth century was a major watershed in the history of all Eurasia. The rise of the Mongols under Chinggis Qan (r. 1206–1227) dramatically reconfigured the political, economic, demographic, and cultural landscapes of Eurasia, even in those parts that the Mongol imperial enterprise did not directly subsume or invade. Not surprisingly, communication played a crucial role in shaping these events, and travelers of all sorts emerge as important if often obscure witnesses and agents of the changes unleashed in the process. The best known Chinese accounts include *An Embassy to the North* (*Beishi ji* 北使記), preserved by Liu Qi 劉祁 (1203–1259), detailing a Jurchen mission to the Mongols in Central Asia in 1220–1221. *A Comprehensive Record of the Mongol Tatars* (*Mengda beilu* 蒙韃備錄) recounts the visit of the Southern Song envoy Zhao Gong 趙珙 to the Mongols' headquarters in north China in 1221. *A Sketch of the Black Tatars* (*Heida shilüe* 黑韃事略) was a joint compilation of reports by Peng Daya 彭大雅 and Xu Ting 徐霆, who separately traveled from Song China to the camp of Ögödei (r. 1229–1241) in 1235–1236. *Notes on a Journey North of the Mountain Ranges* (*Lingbei jixing* 嶺北紀行) by Zhang Dehui 張德輝 (1195–1275) (Yao Congwu 1971) depicts his journey to the Qaraqorum region in 1247. *An Embassy to the West* (*Xishi ji* 西使記), by Liu Yu 劉郁 (ca. 1200–1260) (Chen Dezhi 2015) chronicles the 1259 journey of Chang De 常德 to Prince Hülegü, younger brother of Möngke (r. 1251–1259), who was then completing the conquest of the Abbasid Caliphate in Baghdad. Chang De was a revenue officer in Hülegü's appanage territory in

---

4 Li Zhichang, byname Haoran 浩然, Daoist name Master of Perfect Constancy (Zhenchangzi 真常子).

Hebei. Contemporary with Li Zhichang's account is *Record of a Journey to the West* (*Xiyou lu* 西遊錄), by Yelü Chucai 耶律楚材 (1190–1244), published in 1229.[5]

Of all the Chinese travel narratives extant from the Unified Empire period of Mongol history (1206–1260), *Changchun's Journey* is the first and possibly only unofficial account of travel across the Mongolian plateau (on the outbound leg) and into central Asia. It stands out from other accounts in length, quality, and thoroughness of detail, and it allows historians to better identify, date, and locate the movements of Mongol armies and the Mongols' domestic and military infrastructure across northern and western Asia at the time. For its geographical, historical, and cultural value, *Changchun's Journey* is often compared to the *Great Tang Account of the Western Regions* (*Da Tang Xiyuji* 大唐西域記), the Tang dynasty account of the 629 to 645 journey to India and back by the Buddhist pilgrim Xuanzang 玄奘 (602–664).[6]

Equally vivid is how *Changchun's Journey* gradually unfolds the worldview of the travelers, as Chinese and as Daoists, as they move across an alien environment beyond anything they had ever experienced. Much of this worldview comes through in the poems that Qiu wrote along the way, inserted later by the compilers but omitted from the previous English translations of Emil Bretschneider and Arthur Waley.[7] As in all travel memoirs, the value of the narrative lies as much in what it tells us about the authors as in what they say about the places through which they traveled. In this translation the poems receive our full attention. Our translation is also accompanied by line maps as well as a digital StoryMap created by Shao-yun Yang, to help readers move through the landscape along with the travelers; the latter can be accessed at https://arcg.is/1vC1Pvo.

Changchun's Journey documents a key period in the history of Daoism in China, a period that saw the rise of the Quanzhen sect under the Jin dynasty (1115–1234) and its rivalry with northern Buddhists, as both struggled to secure patronage and protection under the new Mongol rulers and their local representatives. The Quanzhen sect, founded in

---

5   See Zhao Gong 1968; Peng and Xu 2014; de Rachewiltz 1962; Yao Congwu 1971; Chen Dezhi 2015; Yelü Chucai 1981; and Liu Qi 1983. For English translations of Zhao Gong, Peng Daya and Xu Ting, and Zhang Dehui, see Atwood 2021. Shao-yun Yang has created a digital StoryMap with new translations of *An Embassy to the North* and part 1 of the *Record of a Journey to the West* (see Shao-yun Yang 2018).

6   See Xuanzang and Li Rongxi 1996.

7   Bretschneider 2001, 35–108; Waley 1931. Bretschneider's translation is abridged and focuses on history and geography.

the mid-twelfth century by Wang Zhe 王嚞 (1112–1170), a charismatic practitioner of "inner elixir" (*neidan* 內丹), later counted the Seven Perfected Ones among Wang's followers, of whom Qiu Chuji became the most famous.[8] In the late twelfth and early thirteenth centuries, Wang's successors built an enduring and innovative religious organization across north China distinct from those of other Daoist and Buddhist sects, one that welcomed a broad range of lay participants, including women, encouraged relief work, and offered a set of readily accessible teachings that drew from the three major intellectual and cultural traditions of China: Buddhism, Daoism, and Confucianism. The alchemical elements of Quanzhen Daoist cultivation, which drew the attention of earlier writers such as Arthur Waley, absorbed considerable influence and terminology from Chan Buddhism. But what really distinguished Quanzhen practitioners was their successful development of a large-scale, widespread, and locally rooted organization.

Furthermore, Quanzhen leaders managed to parlay the resources they tapped from their lay supporters into approval from a suspicious but cash-strapped Jin court. In this effort, it appears that Qiu Chuji showed himself to be particularly astute. His fame as an adept brought an imperial summons to the Jin court in 1188, and by 1197 he had secured state recognition of the new order.[9] As a result, Quanzhen leaders, their lay congregations, and monasteries emerged as the principal source of support and order for the populace when Jin authority collapsed in the early thirteenth century, shattered by natural disasters, a needless war provoked by the Song state to the south, and invasions by the newly unified Mongols from 1211 on.[10]

China in the early thirteenth century

By the year 1219, when this narrative opens, China had been divided into two rival states for nearly a hundred years. The Jurchen Jin dynasty in the north had displaced the Song dynasty (960–1279), whose court lost the northern plains and its capital at Kaifeng in 1126–1128 and retreated south

---

8   Wang Zhe: byname Zhiming 知明, religious name Chongyang 重陽 (Double Yang), founder of the Quanzhen sect and Qiu Chuji's teacher. In the *Journey* he is commonly referred to as Chongyang. On Wang's life and role in Quanzhen, see Komjathy 2006, 33–52. For the history of early Quanzhen, see Goossaert 2001; Marsone 2001; and Jinping Wang 2018, chap. 2.

9   EOT 815. Goossaert calls Qiu the brains behind the "corporate" leadership of the emergent religious organization (EOT 810).

10 See Franke 1994, 245–265 and Allsen 1994, 357–364 for the last decades of the Jin dynasty and early Mongol operations in north China.

to Jiangnan (the lower Yangzi River valley), establishing a new capital at Hangzhou (renamed Lin'an, or designated as *xingzai*, "the emperor's temporary stopping place"). A mixed hunting and agricultural people from the forested mountains of Manchuria, the Jurchens adapted Song bureaucratic institutions, ideology, and personnel to rule the Chinese lands they occupied, while keeping features of the Kitan Liao system, including their five multiple capitals. By the early thirteenth century, most northern Chinese had come to identify themselves as subjects of the Jin dynasty, whereas many educated Song Chinese, particularly those originally from the north, looked upon their lost territories with regret and revanchist hopes. Thus, when Mongol armies first came thundering through Jin defense lines in 1211, the Jin court confronted an existential threat. When the news reached Hangzhou, many Song officials, in contrast, saw another opportunity to exploit after their failed 1206 campaign to "recover the north."[11]

From at least the early 1190s, Jin authorities were aware that the tribes along their empire's northern perimeter were jostling for power and attempted to bolster their frontier defenses, but to no avail. By spring of 1214, a Mongol blockade of Zhongdu (the Central Capital, Yanjing) had forced the Jin ruler to negotiate with the new steppe power and surrender a ransom in gold, silks, slaves, horses, and the obligatory Jurchen princess for Chinggis Qan. She was the "Princess Qatun," whose camp the Daoist travelers later visited along their route.[12] The Jin court quickly abandoned the exhausted city and relocated to Bianliang (modern Kaifeng) on the south bank of the Yellow River, the former Song capital. Mongol armies soon renewed the siege of Zhongdu, forcing the remaining inhabitants to surrender in May 1215. Yanjing thereafter became the headquarters of Mongol operations in north China, and effective control over the north slipped out of Jin hands and into those of local strongmen, acting sometimes in concert with the Mongols, sometimes with the Song, and often on their own behalf. We meet several of these warlords at the beginning of the travelogue.[13] For the masses of commoners, those left alive in the wake of Mongol operations across large swaths of the north China heartland between 1211 and 1216, life was precarious at best.[14]

At the local level, Qiu Chuji's base of activity in 1218–1219 lay in Laizhou on the northwest coast of the Shandong peninsula. Qiu had

11 See Garcia 2012 and Sloane 2014b.
12 See YS 1:17. *Qatun* is the Mongol word for a *qan*'s consort, or empress, of whom Mongol *qan*s had many. She was the daughter of the recently murdered ruler, Prince Shao of Wei (r. 1209–1213). See vol. 1, n. xli of the translation.
13 See de Rachewiltz 1966 for information on these men.
14 Jinping Wang 2018, "Introduction," offers a vivid picture of the times in affected areas.

returned to his native village in Qixia County in 1191, east of Laizhou, after a period of ascetic training and teaching in Shaanxi and a visit to the Jin court in Yanjing in 1188.[15] In 1211 on the eve of the first Mongol invasion, apparently Qiu made another trip to the Jin capital at the invitation of the ruler Wanyan Yongji, known posthumously as Prince Shao of Wei (r. 1209–1213).[16] On that occasion Qiu may have sensed the precariousness of Jin fortunes. The feckless monarch was violently deposed in 1213, just before the first Mongol siege of Zhongdu. Given the hazards of travel in conditions of war, Qiu refused subsequent invitations from both the Jin and Song courts, remaining in Qixia with his followers until 1218, when he moved to Laizhou, where Liu Zhonglu found him. Qiu departed Shandong in February of 1220, never to return.

Shandong was a pivotal and unstable coastal province on the border between the rival Song and Jin regimes. In 1193–1194, repeated Yellow River flooding, a perennial feature of the north China plain, ravaged Shandong and Hebei. From about 1204, border hostilities with the Song began escalating. Mounting disasters disrupted life for thousands of people, crippled the northern regional economy, and seriously undermined the Jin court's ability to respond effectively to new threats. Shandong's sufferings thus long predated the first Mongol invasions. Besides Daoist recluses, refugees, and rebel groups like the Red Coats, Shandong harbored armed Song loyalist groups seeking to take advantage of Mongol inroads into Jin territory to seize control of Shandong on behalf of the Song court. In these years, Qiu put his followers to work organizing shelter and food supplies for displaced people.

In sum, the rise of the Mongol empire and its expansion outward frame the larger context for the Daoists' journey. Within a China bisected by rival regimes and with the Jin experiencing a weakening social and political fabric, the growth in the north of an innovative Daoist sect under a charismatic leader in the late twelfth and early thirteenth centuries helped Qiu Chuji and his followers achieve widespread notice.

The Mongols and religious specialists

The Mongol empire was born when Temüjin was acclaimed Qan with the name of Chinggis in 1206, after unifying the nomadic tribes on the Mongolian plateau. The Mongol polity was a highly adaptive, flexible, and hierarchical organization. Its ideological basis lay in the conviction that Chinggis had been chosen by Heaven (Tengri, the Mongol sky deity) to

---

15   EOT 808–811.
16   ISTK 211; de Rachewiltz writes that Qiu on this occasion even traveled north to Dexing, near the Jin frontier, just as Mongol armies were about to cross the mountains.

rule all the "peoples of the felt-walled tents," which at some later date became the "world." Those who stood in his way did so at their peril and in violation of Heaven's will. The Mongols' earliest campaigns targeted nomads who resisted incorporation and fled the plateau. To their south, the Tangut Xia state (between the Jin and Central Asia) stood accused of harboring such rebels, and to their southeast, the Jurchen Jin state had harassed and insulted Chinggis's ancestors for decades while managing its own frontiers.[17]

Finally, in the winter of 1218–1219, during Mongol diplomatic exchanges with Sultan Muhammad of Khwarazm, a new expansive realm in Central Asia, the Sultan's governor in Otrar (Utrar) put to death a large Mongol trade caravan heading to Samarkand, the Khwarazm-shah's capital. Commerce was vital to Mongol imperial priorities, and the baseless murder of merchants and diplomats launched Chinggis Qan's Western Campaign. An enormous invasion force began marching southwest into Central Asia in the summer of 1219 to punish the perfidious Sultan.[18]

Chinggis's true genius, however, lay less in battle than in scouting for talent and cementing the loyalty of those recruited to his mission. As well as mighty warriors, the Mongol leadership needed technicians of every stripe: people adept in languages, trade, culinary science, weaponry and siege craft, medicine, mining, and communicating with the forces of the unseen world, to name a few. Whatever their social origins, people with practical skills could carve out a new career, even a lucrative one, under the new imperial polity if they were positioned to make that choice. Qiu Chuji was so positioned, and by 1220 he understood that earning the Mongol Qan's favor was not a choice easily turned down.

From the beginning, the Mongols had shown an openness and curiosity about different religious practices and personnel that has been generally misinterpreted by Western scholars as a kind of religious tolerance.[19] It was both more and less in that it was an ecumenical outlook natural to multicultural conquerors who came to see themselves as world rulers with a mandate from Heaven, as well as a calculated policy of harnessing the divine and material assistance of any person or institution available to render it unto them.[20] Hence, clergy of the various religious groups encountered by the Mongols received preferential

---

17 For accounts of the Mongols' origins, see Allsen 1994; Biran 2007; Dunnell 2010.
18 The (in)famous Otrar Incident was even made into a Kazakh film in 1991, *Gibel Ortrara* (The Fall of Otrar), directed by Amirkulov Ardak. On early thirteenth-century Central Asia, see Biran 2005 and Barthold 1977.
19 See Atwood 2004b and Jackson 2005.
20 On the Mongols' personnel policies, see Allsen 1997.

treatment as specialists in communicating with Heaven, the source of the Mongol *qans'* legitimating authority. The Mongol policy of granting tax exemptions, administrative privileges, and generous patronage, in exchange for prayers for fortune and long life, began with Qiu Chuji and spread to others. It represented a marked divergence from previous Chinese policies toward religious groups. In some ways, the Mongol and the Quanzhen enterprises shared some important common ground. Emerging at about the same time around charismatic leaders, the Mongol polity and the Quanzhen sect both developed expansive, dynamic, and inclusive organizations that appealed to and incorporated diverse groups of people, though for rather different purposes.

For decades following the travelers' return to north China, the Quanzhen leaders overshadowed their Buddhist peers. Protected by Chinggis's decrees that granted tax exemptions to the Quanzhen sect and gave authority over religious affairs in north China to Qiu Chuji personally, the sect and its leaders repurposed Buddhist temples and lands, avoided taxation and enslavement, and sheltered or liberated staunch supporters, including former Jin literati and officials, from slavery. This was all carried out at the expense of their resentful rivals.

Yet by the time that Qubilai Qan (r. 1260–1294), founder of the Yuan dynasty (1271–1368), came to power in China, the Mongols' Buddhist subjects and sympathies were tilting the balance of patronage and power against the Daoists. In 1281 Qubilai issued a ban on all Daoist texts apart from the *Daodejing*.[21] While this edict led to the destruction of the Daoist canon printed under Quanzhen auspices in Pingyang (Shanxi) in 1244, it is unclear what further impact the ban had on the ground throughout north China.[22] The influence of Buddhists, especially the Tibetan Buddhist clergy, superseded that of the Daoists, as Tibetan Buddhism became the preferred rite of the Mongol royal family. Yet in the post-Qubilai era (after 1294), both groups, it has been argued, found common ground against the Christians and Muslims.[23] In any case, Quanzhen became the dominant form of Daoism in China and remains so to this day.

Yelü Chucai, Qiu Chuji, and Li Zhichang

How did Chinggis Qan hear about Qiu Chuji in the first place? According to Yelü (Yila) Chucai, the personal (Chinese) secretary and prognosticator for the Qan, Liu Zhonglu submitted a memorial to Chinggis claiming

---

21 Known in the West as either *Laozi* or *The Way and Its Power*.

22 Jinping Wang 2018, 74–78.

23 Atwood 2016.

that Qiu Chuji was three hundred years old and had secret techniques for preserving life. Both Yelü Chucai and Liu Zhonglu were recruited to the Qan's entourage in 1218 on the eve of the Western Campaign. Chucai was the son of a wealthy Jin official who traced his family's descent from the Kitan ruling clan. Having themselves been conquered by the Jurchens a century earlier, many Kitans under Jin rule, including Yelü clan members, had already rallied to the Mongol cause. In the text we meet two other prominent Yelü clansmen, the brothers Tuhua (younger) and Ahai (elder). Both brothers participated in the so-called Baljuna Covenant, when nineteen men joined the future Chinggis Qan in his struggles against his patron and rival, Ong Qan of the Kereit, at the turn of the thirteenth century. We first encounter Tuhua as the regional military commander of Xuande Prefecture (Hebei), and Ahai as the governor of Samarkand.[24] The careers of these two men testify to the significance of Kitan influence on the early Mongol conquest establishment.[25]

The younger Chucai lived through the Mongol siege of Yanjing in 1214–1215, an experience that propelled him into a period of intensive Buddhist study, before receiving the call to serve Chinggis.[26] Both Zhonglu and Chucai traveled to Central Asia with the Qan. Chucai supported Zhonglu's recommendation of Qiu Chuji, hoping that the Daoist master might temper the Qan's thirst for battle with the teachings of the Chinese Confucian, Daoist, and Buddhist sages. He probably drafted the first imperial summons to Qiu Chuji and tells us that he composed the second (see our Appendices 1 and 3).

Although Yelü Chucai was thus a key intermediary in communicating between Chinggis and Qiu Chuji, and although he spent most of his time in Samarkand while in Central Asia, befriending the Daoists during their stay there, he is never mentioned in *Changchun's Journey*. For his part, Chucai became disenchanted with the Quanzhen mission. In early 1229, probably after reading the account published by Li Zhichang, he published his own version of Qiu's visit to Chinggis, in a text titled *Record of a Journey to the West* (Yelü 1981). Though prefaced by a brief travel account and ethnography, this work, written in the spring of 1228 upon Chucai's return to Yanjing, is primarily a polemical attack on the

24 On Yelü Tuhua, see YS 149.3532–3533; on Ahai, see YS 150.3548–3550. ISTK 112–121, speculates that Ahai died early in 1223. See also QXYJ02 A.10a; and Biran 2015, 163–164. On the Baljuna Covenant, see Cleaves 1955, 404–406.
25 See Buell 1979.
26 Unlike Liu Zhonglu, Yelü Chucai went on to become a prominent figure in the early Mongol ruling establishment. See his biography in ISTK 136–175.

Quanzhen sect. In it the author attempts to explain his role in mediating Qiu Chuji's meeting with the ruler and accuses Qiu of making a naked grab for power and privilege, requesting exemptions and insignia of authority from Chinggis, in order to take over Buddhist temples and lands in north China.[27] Chucai went on to play a prominent role in shaping (or trying to temper) Mongol fiscal and other policies in north China in the 1230s, and was honored upon his death in 1243. His efforts to curb the power of the Daoist clergy, however, did not meet with much success.

Influential in his own way was another newcomer on the scene, the putative author of *Changchun's Journey*, Li Zhichang. Raised in western Shandong and educated as a classical scholar (*ru* 儒) in his youth, Li joined Qiu Chuji in 1218, shortly before his master received the imperial summons from Chinggis Qan.[28] He accompanied Qiu on the journey to Afghanistan, although he remained behind at Chinqai City, in western Mongolia, with seven other disciples to build a monastery, and so was not with Qiu during the master's sojourn in Samarkand and did not meet Yelü Chucai.[29]

It becomes evident, however, that by the end of Qiu's life in 1227, Li had emerged as a central figure in the Quanzhen leadership, one whose literary skills were marshaled to compile *Changchun's Journey*. Li maintained a cordial relationship with Chinggis Qan's successors and played instrumental roles in establishing a school in Yanjing for the education of talented Mongol youth in Chinese studies, as well as a Daoist monastery in the new Mongol capital of Qaraqorum, under Ögödei Qan (r. 1229–1241). In 1238 Li Zhichang became the seventh Quanzhen patriarch, a post he held until his death in 1256, shortly after losing a debate with Buddhists in Qaraqorum in the presence of Möngke Qan (r. 1251–1259), whose high regard for the Quanzhen leader apparently remained untarnished. Li's career as a Quanzhen leader and liaison with the imperial court thus serves to justify his authority for compiling this work, though the construction of the travel narrative exposes a kind of literary ventriloquism, in which he speaks on behalf of numerous actors.[30]

Narrative and poetic voice in *Changchun's Journey*

This text is several things at once. It is a travel and poetic diary, as well as a hagiography, in the full sense of that term: both an idealization and

---

27 De Rachewiltz 1962, 28–29; Yelü Chucai 1981, 15. For the travel account section, see also Shao-yun Yang 2018.

28 On Li Zhichang, see Guo Wu 1998.

29 See Book 1, n. xlviii, of this translation.

30 On Buddhist accusations against Li Zhichang, see Appendices 13 and 14.

an adulation of Qiu Chuji. It invites us to speculate on the choices that
Qiu and those around him make under duress, on how they use new
opportunities to advance their personal and organizational missions,
and on how they articulate their actions and motives to a wider audience. While structured by an underlying linear diachronic pattern, the
text remains a concatenation of events and voices, each speaking at a
particular time and in a particular way. And except in the case of dialog
or poetry, these voices are difficult to identify.

Li Zhichang, the compiler, spent over half the journey in the Abuhan
Mountains, the location of Chinqai City, to supervise the construction
of a monastery there. Thus, the text of *Changchun's Journey*, or at least
the portion between late August 1221 and midsummer in 1223, was a
corporate product, assembled by Li Zhichang sometime between the
group's return in 1224 and 1228. This fact is acknowledged by Qing historians and bibliographers, who often use the term *shu* 述 to describe
the production of the text. *Shu* does not mean "to write," but "to tell the
story of," "describe," or otherwise "relay information" to the reader. In
his notes to his compilation of book titles from the Yuan period, Qian
Daxin 錢大昕 (1728–1804) wrote, "Li Zhichang narrated the affairs of
Qiu Chuji [on this journey]."[31] It became a general rule among later bibliographers that this story "was recounted" (either orally or in writing,
presumably), and there are clear indications that the text took on its
present shape only after Qiu's death, but before its circulation in 1228.
Thus, it probably was a mixture of different kinds of accounts written
along the journey, recalled memories, and judicious intervention by
editorial hands, seeking to rectify, ameliorate, or enhance not just the
memory of Master Qiu, but also the status of the sect.

Narrative voice is thus extremely difficult to identify in this work
for several reasons. For one, Classical Chinese regularly and insistently
dispenses with the use of personal pronouns, unless perhaps used re-
flexively. Apart from a directly quoted speech, the narrator or narrators
of this linear story do not identify agency or voice. Of course, English
demands pronouns as agents of description. We also know that, however ambiguously represented, an implied pronoun always lies behind
the production of any statement in Classical Chinese, or indeed in any
language. After all, someone must utter or write the words we encounter.
In this text, we understand the voice to be that of an omniscient narrator
speaking in a recognizable status as first-person agent. This narrator can
freely move between speech communities, real and imagined.

31 See Qian Daxin 1989, 29.528.

As a good example, in one scene the narrator describes a conversation to which he could not possibly have been party. When preparing to cross the Plain of White Bones, a dangerous stretch of desert, Chinqai, the Mongol general and minister, describes the difficulties that Qiu Chuji will face on this leg of the journey: "Ahead we will come to the Plain of White Bones, where the earth is all black stone. After another two hundred *li* we will arrive at the northern edge of the desert, which has plenty of water and grass. Still further on we cross about one hundred *li* of a large desert, so wide from east to west that no one knows how many thousand *li*." But prior to describing these difficulties to the Master, the text recreates a private conversation between Chinqai and Liu Zhonglu, the Imperial Envoy Plenipotentiary, held before they went to meet Qiu: "The Imperial Envoy deliberated with Chinqai, saying, 'This place is the most difficult part of the journey. What does the Minister advise?' His Excellency Chinqai replied, 'I have long been familiar with this land.'" Here the text slips into a mode of exposition that we most often encounter in fictional works: filling in background information from a presumed source to set the stage for delivering news. While the narrator may perhaps have known that a prior conversation had taken place through a report or even a simple guess, we should accept that his account of the conversation is an imaginative reconstruction. It is not likely that the narrator would be privy to such higher-level discussions among those responsible for looking after Qiu.

In other cases, the omniscient narrator slips into commentary, levying judgments, criticisms, or praise on the words or actions that he describes. For instance, as they pass over the Wild Fox Ridge, north of modern Zhangjiakou, the narrator describes the dividing line between Chinese sedentary life and the nomadic north:

Ascending the heights, we looked southward and had a bird's eye view of the various peaks of the Taihang mountain range (which mark the boundary of the east China plain). Under clear skies the mist-shrouded mountains looked particularly enchanting. Turning north, we saw only cold sands and sere grass as far as we could see. Here marked the end of the sights and habits of the Central Plain. Yet the heart of a Daoist is at home anywhere.

While the main portion of the paragraph is both descriptive and emotional, the last sentence is judgmental. In the context of the emotional look backward to the warm and mist-shrouded land of the Central Plain and the turn of the head toward a land of cold sand and dying grasses, the final line reveals a presumption of fortitude among the group. But it also points to the narrator's claim to an authority to judge. Daoism teaches one to transcend the bounds of physical engagement and emotional entanglement, to spiritually soar or travel beyond the world of phenomena in what Daoism describes as "free wandering," a mental state that should fortify the travelers for the long journey. Simultaneously, this belief implies that the journey's descriptions, like the description of the journey over the Central Plain, will stem from just such a view that observes the physical world with detachment. It promises that we can rely on the narrator for an objective relating of events that occurred on the trek—a subtle gesture, to be sure, but enough to secure our trust in the reliability of the narrator.

Our narrator or narrators also keenly observe the physical world around them, describing in detail agricultural practices, unfamiliar plants and animals, strange landscapes, and the customs and habits of the people they encounter. The narrator tends to expand the narrative in these descriptive passages when communities of Chinese are encountered on the journey, sometimes accompanied by a desire to make that place "real," in the sense of embedding it within Chinese culture and texts, both of which would be a way of communicating. For instance, when the group reached Besh-Baliq, they met a large group of Chinese. who, when asked about local customs, relate to them the following:

"This was the Tang-period Beiting Protectorate. In the third year of the Jinglong era [709], His Excellency Yang He was the protector general. His governance was just, and all the barbarians willingly submitted. The legacy of his benevolence has carried on for generations, and it serves us even to this day. In the Longxing West Monastery there are two inscribed early stelae still extant that verify the transformative nature of his virtuous accomplishments. The temple also houses a set of Buddhist scriptures. Many frontier towns of the Tang period still remain: Several hundred *li* east of here is a prefecture called Xiliang."

This paean to the otherwise unknown Yang He has language reminiscent of that found in funerary inscriptions, historical writing, and historical geography. What is related might very well have been fact, but stemming from a request for information on "local customs," it is remarkable that this was the sole conversation recorded and that it was constructed in this way. In this case, one might presume that, some eighteen months after leaving Shandong, the disciples would be searching for something, anything, familiar. As such, the report stems from a familiar shared linguistic environment (they are conversing in Chinese) and highlights the historical Tang dynasty, the last major imperial dynasty to push far into the Western Regions from the Chinese heartland. Surely, in context, this passage means to say, "Our people have also been out here and have created a stable and long-lasting cultural influence that has lasted five hundred years or more." The juxtaposition of this endurance with the swift and brutal Mongol assault on the western regions betrays an anxiety on the part of the speakers that is both personal and cultural. The information in the report may be reliable, but the rhetorical flourishes in its written presentation argue for the deft hand of a compiler familiar with literary Chinese and its rhetorical touchstones. It surely is not an actual record of their conversation, which would have been carried out in the vernacular, since it lacks a conversational tone and vocabulary. What it does betray, however, is an autistic chauvinism on the part of the compilers.

Perhaps nowhere is narrator authority less reliable than in the description of the lead pilgrim, Qiu Chuji. This unreliability is most apparent, of course, in the frequent references to his ability to command weather and dispel spirits. Canopies of clouds formed to shield congregants from the heat upon his ritual performances; he had the power to summon rain through the efficacy of his ritual acts, and equal power to quell the thunder god. He confronted the Mongol belief in animistic spirits and wights with the concept of the "upright person" (*zhengren* 正人). This notion implies a person who understands a priori laws about reason and ethics, drawn by theoretical induction from a particular belief system that is true and "upright" (*zheng* 正).

Quanzhen Daoism is remarkable for a dogma that unites the three teachings of Confucianism, Daoism, and Buddhism into one (*sanjiao heyi* 三教合一). The supposition within the school was that there exists an ethical and material rationality in the cosmos (although in most cases only partially perceived) consisting of distinct laws on which to model behavior and action. What is unperceived is due to a lack of refinement or to early stages of evolution within the perceiver's own ethical or spiritual progress. Thus, the baleful influences in life are not due to preternatural spirits, but to a lack of knowledge (*zhi* 知) of the correct and upright Way of the cosmos.

Qiu himself was an unwilling traveler. At seventy-three he demonstrated little interest in a seven-thousand-mile round trip through modern Inner Mongolia, Mongolia, Kyrgyzstan, Uzbekistan, and finally to Chinggis's camp in the Hindu Kush. Even after his grudging acceptance of the trip, he petitioned twice at various stages to be allowed to remain in place and wait for Chinggis's return to the east. Both petitions were denied. But as he progressed on his journey, we can see in his poetry different stages of emotional response. *Changchun's Journey* includes some seventy of Qiu's poems of various kinds, including classical verse (*shi* 詩, called "poems" in our text), musical lyrics (*ci* 詞, called "lyrics" in our text), religious hymns or *gāthā* (transliterated into Chinese either as *jiatuo* 伽陀 or 偈陀 or as *jiasong* 伽頌 or 偈頌) and encomia (*song* 頌).[32] At the beginning and end of *Changchun's Journey*, the poems are mostly social exchanges with Daoist and literati friends as he was leaving and reentering his native land, as one would expect. On the journey itself there appear two major inspirations for poems: immediate reactions and reflections on experience. But something happens in moments of inspiration of both types as he makes his way to the snowy alps of modern Kazakhstan and Afghanistan. The religious element of his poetry is challenged, or even shaken, by unexpectedly brutal or beautiful moments, and his own belief system no longer predetermines how he situates himself as a conscious being perceiving the natural or human world. There is no direct and incremental change clearly visible as the poems move through time, only sporadic moments of difference that display contingent moments of anxiety or displacement from what he understands by experience and belief to be normative reactions to the temporal and material world.

For instance, in poem 15, "Using a Poem to Relate the Facts as We Pass the Mingchang Boundary," written on the first major leg of his journey, he talks about the long, seemingly endless road, the abundance of salt beds and stagnant ponds, and the utter lack of people in touch with the isolated salt makers. He describes the inhabitants as having no grains to eat, but only "curdled milk," who still, dressed in hides and living in felt tents, "beam with happiness." In terms of his religious beliefs, he has encountered a people who, free of the oppressive weight of institutions and ethical rules of the Confucian sages, are able to act in a completely spontaneous way that Daoists identify as the "heart of a child" or as an "uncarved block." This simple lifestyle calls to mind the utopian village of *The Way and Its Power*, where villages are self-contained, isolated units that are self-sustaining and joyful, and lack the hierarchies of control and obligation that Confucianism would impose. At a later stage of his travels, however, he describes a similar scene in poem 17, "Traveling

---

32 *Gāthā*, pronounced *kaetha* in thirteenth-century Chinese, and derived from Sanskrit *gāthā*, is a term introduced into China by Buddhism, especially Chan Buddhism. Qiu's use of this genre is an example of Quanzhen syncretism.

xxxii DAOIST MASTER CHANGCHUN'S JOURNEY TO THE WEST

Again along the Yu'erpo Post Road for Ten Days, Relating the Facts in a Poem." The verse begins like the prior one, talking about the endlessly vast landscape, but then moves to a section that begins to betray how he rationalized his experiences:

> Endless mountains and streams as far as the eye can see,
> Wind and mist without break, streams formed unceasingly.
> Why, when the Shaper of Things formed Heaven and earth
> And reached this place, did it make these people herd horses and
>   cattle?
> They drink blood and eat meat with the fur on, just as in high
>   antiquity,
> And wear high hats and braid their hair differently from the
>   Central Regions.
> Here sages and worthies were unable to pass down the
>   transformative power of culture,
> So through the ages these people have been free to do exactly as
>   they please.

We can see here a subtle destabilization of Qiu's trust in the phenomenal world as explained by Daoist notions of the creation of materiality. He ascribes the differences of life, food, clothing, and hairstyle to something he cannot know about, the Shaper of Things, the force of the Way that creates materiality. The last couplet seems an ambivalent attempt to reconcile this scene with what he knows from his own experiences and beliefs. Unlike the earlier poem, which grants the inhabitants a spontaneous joy, here he seems to suggest that this world is also tinged by a barbarism that flourishes in the absence of the fundamentally shared ways of a Chinese world based on a culture created by the Sage Kings of antiquity. We can never know, of course, if this awareness made him realize that the presumed universal values of the Way held only if expressed within the culture of the Central Plain, or if this was a moment in which he questioned the omnipotence of the Shaper of Things in creating the entire material world. He reveals here only the difficulty of placing this rough nomadic and subsistence lifestyle within what were generally understood to be the material and cultural manifestations of the Way. Seeking models comparative to his own lived experience, he understands both the desirable and undesirable nature of a life that allows one to live as one pleases without the constraints of the ethical values inherent in culture and the Way. This brings to the fore a question about how much Qiu could truly learn about a foreign world. Although he lived for two years in this foreign world, perhaps, like some learners of second languages, he was unable to escape the idiom of his own culture to become fluent in another.

The two most significant changes to his worldview happened as he neared Samarkand and when he went on his two journeys from Samarkand to Chinggis's camp on the western piedmont of the Hindu Kush. In the latter instance, it was his first real encounter with the violence of war. He was somewhat shielded from the remnants of war while in residence in Samarkand. In the first part of his journey, he passed through several sites—the old site of a Jin-Mongol battlefield, the "Plain of White Bones" of the Naiman-Mongol battle—strewn with skeletons, but without the stench of battle. When he returns from his initial visit to Chinggis, though, he is faced with the rotting corpses of men and animals:

35. *"Two More Poems on Coming Out of the Defile" I*

The Iron Gate route seemed passable north of the river,
But the stony gorge on the south was unbearably alarming.
On both sides precipices held up the towering sky,
And the chilly surge of a mountain stream debouched and roiled
    over the ground.
People covered their noses because of corpses strewn about the
    narrow path,
But it was the long-eared asses drowned in the stream that
    sickened my heart.
War has raged for ten years and over huge distances,
But in the end, armies will go back and peace will be restored.

Certainly, monastery life in Shandong had also shielded Qiu from such scenes left on the field of battle by the Song, Jin, and Mongols. The trials of his westward journey had also been ameliorated by his time in Samarkand, given over to eating, bathing, and strolling through the gardens with other Chinese literati. Smell, surely, is the most potent perceptual phenomena and, like hearing, it cannot be avoided. While one can choose not to look at skeletons, the stench of the rotting dead was overpowering and inescapable.

The unease that we notice above in poem 17 becomes something of a signature in Qiu's poems in Samarkand. There he was confronted not only by the human world, but also by the natural world. A culminating point of his journey through the Altai and northwestern Tian Shan mountain ranges, which he became ever more enamored of and whose beauty and massive scale stunned him, was when he first caught sight of the Northern Pamirs:

27. *"A Poem Occurred to Me West of Where We Gazed on the Great Snowy Mountains"*

This towering brilliance made by the Shaper of Things cannot be
    named,
But it spreads out from east to west, as formed by Heaven.
In the south, a range of white jade, lying athwart, links peaks
    together,
While to the north, keeping back the golden sands, it rings the
    level desert.
Below, it cradles springs providing unlimited water;
Above, it connects to the Milky Way with purity to spare.
I have traveled ten thousand *li* and am always slow to speak,
But here, I chant wildly, overcome by my emotions.

This enchantment with the landscape brought him out of silent contemplation, into noisy communication with the world through his poetry. The hold of the natural world grew as he entered Samarkand, where a familiar pastoral landscape was used to produce unfamiliar products. Fields of melons, fruit laden trees, and grapevines marked this landscape in the same way that rice and barley marked the Central Plain. He was aware that he was becoming increasingly consumed by this new world. As he remarks in poem 30, "Two Poems Written on the Walls of the Old Palace" II, there was a distinct boundary being formed between the mental—the world as the mind of the Way—and the physical:

Traveling forever through endless mountains and rivers,
Moved from traces in the mind to achieve some merit,
I know too well that, in these six directions of countless worlds,
Without attaining spiritual comprehension, one will never escape.

And again in poem 31, "Roaming West of the Outskirts, I Write a Poem":

In the gardens all is quiet, no bird calls;
Although the vegetation is lush, there are no birds.
Wind and sun slowly warm, flowers beguile.
With like-minded friends for this short while, we take in the scene,
Then return, chanting loudly, to await a world at peace.

And finally, self-doubt takes over in these lush garden paradises:

33. "Two Poems to Show My Fellow Wanderers" II

Deep in the heart of foreign lands ancient ruins still crisscross the
    land.
Friends in the Way from the land of Great Han wish to see the
    whole wide world.
Towers and pavilions of days past are everywhere open to view;
Grass and flowers from years long gone renew themselves in their
    proper season.
If nature—wind's change and light's movement—fully understands
    that these travelers are transient and reluctant to depart,
How can the evening's rays bear to send people away?
I wonder, How will this world's transient beauty
Compare to taking in eternal spring in a realm beyond Heaven?

This is a one of Qiu's more complicated poems. From one point of view,
it is a simple statement: "If the natural world understands that we are
loath to leave its beauty, why is there ever a sunset to send us home?"
The poem's meaning deepens, however, when we look at the term he
chooses for nature—literally "wind and light"—and how it seals a bond
of shared consciousness between the perceiver and the perceived. Nature
is not something static to be observed but, like wind blowing and light
shifting, is a process always in flux. By assigning agency to this world of
wind and light and endowing it with an ability to understand and endure
the emotional distress the poem's ending causes, the poem creates a
unified field of consciousness from what at first look appears to be a subject contemplating its object of perception. At this deeper level, nature
appears as constant flux, a materialization of the same essential ground
of being (that is, the Daoist Way) that creates human consciousness and
emotions. This is not the simple assigning of human feeling to natural
objects, as in the pathetic fallacy, but rather a deep awareness of what is
shared by all existing things, an awareness of the mind/heart as the seat
of both emotion and intuition.[33] In the poet's eye, a passing moment in
a natural scene becomes the movement of Yin and Yang, of light and its
absence, of the two cosmic forces interacting to create all things.

   If we consider how the poem begins by setting linear time (marked by
human history) against this eternal flux of nature's death and renewal, we
are led to understand that human cultural progress is destined to be signi-
fied only by artifacts that also deteriorate over time in a world of constant
change. The ontological response to this seems to lie in understanding

---

33 Classical Chinese uses the same term *xin* 心 (heart) also for the organ that is simul-
    taneously the seat of cognition, awareness, intuition, and emotion.

the self as sharing the cycle of nature's renewal and dying. In the final two couplets, the fascination evoked by a sensate natural order allows a brief, though ill-fated immersion in a moment of this change. The end of the sixth line uses the term *duansong* 斷送, which means to send someone home, but also means to send one to one's death. The juxtaposition of a transient guest or wanderer (*ke* 客) enjoying the garden with an existential person (*ren* 人) being snuffed like the last rays of evening, engenders a sudden understanding that one's life is but another process of birth and decay. Finally, this leads to an act of subjective cognition and judgment, where "I" is introduced, pondering over and perhaps anxious about this short and transient scene of human existence and whether it will compare to returning to the cosmic Way as pure and unformed potential. Insight and cognition come full circle: there is no being or nonbeing, only a moment's differentiation in the eternal productive power of the Way, which is both timeless and unattached to the visible world of being. Though beauty is present as an object of appreciation, one must guard against its beguiling ability to "understand" and its sense of compassion, for these have the power to confuse the mind and ensnare one in a short and transient scene of beauty, removing one from harmony with the Way itself.

The remainder of Qiu's poems, except for his farewell ode, return to occasional verses for social interaction or religious pedagogy. Qiu is not a great poet, or even a uniformly skilled one, although the poems written in Samarkand and while traveling to Chinggis's camp rise to the level of very good verse. It is in these moments that we get a picture of a very human authorial subject, struggling to maintain his spiritual equilibrium when the lure of nature (the myriad things) contests with the notion of a transcendent and formless Way. His final couplets of these last several poems presented here demonstrate a purposive consciousness that one, in the end, must steel oneself to combat the lure of the natural wonders of this new world.

History of the text and translations

Daoist Master Changchun's Journey to the West, in two books, was incorporated into the collection of Daoist texts known as the Daoist Canon (*Daozang* 道藏), in an edition compiled at Pingyang, Shanxi, in ca. 1237–1244 (the one supposedly destroyed under Qubilai). The earliest extant edition of the canon is the *Daoist Canon of the Zhengtong Reign* (*Zhengtong Daozang* 正統道藏), printed in 1445 during the Ming dynasty.[34] It provides the base text used here and in all modern editions. *Changchun's Journey* apparently did not elicit much comment

34 On the history of editions of the *Daoist Canon*, see EOT 1315–1319.

from Chinese scholars until the late Qing, when the text piqued the interest of the eighteenth-century scholar Qian Daxin, who penned a postscript to it.[35] Ruan Yuan 阮元 (1764–1849) presented a copy to the imperial library, and thereafter the book attracted more scholarly interest as a hitherto misidentified historical work, deserving a place in the well-developed literature on historical geography.[36] Wang Guowei made this work widely available when he published it in a separate edition with annotations in 1926. Thereafter it has enjoyed numerous republications in Chinese.[37]

An 1848 reprint of *Changchun's Journey* served as the basis for the first translation into a European language, by the Archimandrite Palladius (Pyotr Ivanovich Kafarov, 1817–1878), head of the Russian Orthodox mission in Beijing and a student of the great Russian sinologist Nikita Yakovlevich Bichurin (monastic name Hyacinth), who spent many years in Beijing in the early nineteenth century.[38] The Russian version, as well as Sir Henry Yule's *Cathay and the Way Thither* (1866), spurred Emil Bretschneider, a Baltic German scientist and doctor serving in the Russian Legation (the Orthodox Mission) in Beijing from 1866 to 1883, to publish a less complete English rendition of *Changchun's Journey* in London in 1887, in his *Mediaeval Researches from Eastern Asiatic Sources*. European and Russian interest in early Central Asian travelogues accompanied the expansion of Western imperial and colonial exploration and exploitation of Qing territories in the nineteenth century. Many of the lands traversed by Qiu Chuji and his disciples were reincorporated into the Chinese empire by the Manchu Qing dynasty, which inherited much shrunken Ming borders and proceeded to restore the Mongol-Yuan imperial reach.

The better-known English translation of Arthur Waley (1889–1966), with the evocative title *Travels of an Alchemist*, appeared in 1931. Waley's knowledge of Chinese (and Japanese) was largely self-acquired during his career at the British Museum. His cataloging work with British collections of "Oriental findings" of explorers across Central Asia, Mongolia, and the inner Asian frontiers of China, turned him into an avid translator of Chinese and Japanese literature (one who never set foot in those lands, unlike Bretschneider).[39] His exclusion of nearly all of Qiu's poems can

---

35   For Ruan Yuan 阮元, see Appendix 14, Wang Guowei's preface to *Changchun's Journey*.
36   Ruan Yuan, byname Boyuan 伯元.
37   See QXYJ03 9–10 for a list of modern editions.
38   Bretschneider 2001, 36. Bichurin evidently coined the name "Eastern Turkestan" to replace "Chinese Turkestan" and pair with "Western Turkestan." See Kamalov 2007, 33–34.
39   See Simon 1967.

perhaps be explained by an inadequate understanding of Daoism and his apparent decision that since they did not measure up to the great Tang poets he admired ("Ch'ang-ch'un has no reputation as a poet, and judging from the specimens in the *Hsi Yu Chi* [Journey to the West], he deserves none"), they did not warrant the effort to "torture them into a semblance of poetry" in English translation.[40] Our translation seeks to rectify Waley's omissions. Qiu's poems are subjective but also cultural documents that often reflect on movements, scenes, or feelings described in the prose passages. Our hope is to place our translation in the historical, cultural, and literary contexts vastly enriched by the fruits of nearly a century of worldwide scholarship not available to earlier translators.

Conventions of translation and transcription

The extant Chinese text is divided into two books. While marking this division, our translation breaks up the account into more organic sections with section heads that follow the itinerary of the journey. It also provides, in the right margin of the translation, a running chronology of Western dates corresponding to Chinese dates in the text. The translation makes use of direct speech (in quotation marks) where indicated by certain grammatical forms and adopted into recent vernacular Chinese editions. Since Qiu Chuji's poems circulated with titles absent in this text, we have inserted them from his collected works (QCJJ), where they may be found on pp. 186–198.

Identifiable individuals in the text are footnoted and more detailed discussions of the person or matter at hand may be found, when appropriate, in the explanatory notes following each book division. In addition to the original nine documents appended to *Changchun's Journey* in the *Daozang*, short texts directly related to *Changchun's Journey* that the translators considered of relevant interest are reproduced in the appendices with translations. Throughout, most personal and place names are retained in their original form and romanized in *pinyin* rather than translated, except in the case of commonly known places like Samarkand. In the latter instance, the differing Chinese transcriptions are inserted in *pinyin* in parentheses after the name. In the case of Daoist religious names, a translation is provided in parentheses upon the first occurrence of the name. In the case of Mongol and other non-Chinese personal names, when well known, we use the recognized reconstruction (e.g., Bo'orchu, Kishliq Darqan); otherwise when possible, we offer a reconstruction in parentheses after the first mention of the name, and

40 Waley 1931, ix–x.

for the reader's ease continue to use it throughout, as transcriptions may vary over the course of the narrative.

The transcription of Turko-Mongol names and terms follows conventions used in recent scholarship, especially in Igor de Rachewiltz's English translation *The Secret History of the Mongols*, with a few exceptions and simplifications: *q* is used instead of *kh* in the imperial title (Mo. *qan* / Tk. *khan*); *sh* instead of *š*; *ch* instead of *č*; *j* instead of *ĵ*; *gh* instead of a gamma. *Kitan* is now preferred to *Khitan* (but Qara Khitai or "Black Khitai" remains the twelfth-century Central Asian successor to the Kitan Liao state). Place names often appear in maps and scholarship transcribed with either *q* or *kh* at the beginning or end (e.g., the river in Mongolia may appear either as *Qalqa* or *Khalkh*), reflecting changes over time in different sound values in Uyghur and Mongolian, and the Mongol language's indebtedness to Uyghur, a Turkic language that provided the first script for writing Mongolian in the early thirteenth century. Linguists still debate the relative proximity, age, and relationship of Turkic and Mongolic names. For the purposes of clarity in this translation, the differences are insignificant.

Daoist Master Changchun's Journey to the West

長春真人西遊記，二卷
《正統道藏》正一部

長春真人西遊記序

長春子蓋有道之士。中年以來，意此老人固已飛昇變化，侶雲將而友鴻濛者久矣，恨其不可得而見也。己卯之冬，流聞師在海上，被安車之徵。明年春，果次於燕，駐車玉虛觀，始得一識其面。尸居而柴立，雷動而風行，真異人也。與之言，又知博物洽聞，於書無所不讀。由是日益敬。聞其風而願執弟子禮者，不可勝計。自二、三遺老，且樂與之游，其餘可知也。

　　居無何，有龍陽之行。及使者再至，始啓途而西。將別，道衆請還期，語以三載。時辛巳夾鍾之月也。迨甲申孟諏，師至自西域。果如其旨。識者歎異之。自是月七日，入居燕京大天長觀，從疏請也。噫，今人將事行役，出門傍徨，有離別可憐之色。師之是行也，崎嶇數萬里之遠，際版圖之所不載、雨露之所弗濡；雖其所以禮遇之者不爲不厚，然勞憊亦甚矣。所至輒徜徉容與，以樂山水之勝。賦詩談笑，視死生若寒暑，於其胸中曾不蒂芥。非有道者能如是乎？

1　Cloud General (Yunjiang 雲將) and Primeval Murk (Hongmeng 鴻蒙) are two legendary beings introduced in the early Daoist work *Zhuangzi*. See Zhuangzi, Watson, trans., 1968, 120–123.

Preface

Master Changchun was an adept in possession of the Way. Since middle age, I have long thought that this aged man had risen in flight to the immortal realm and was there associating with Cloud General and keeping company with Primeval Murk, and I regretted that it was impossible to meet him.[1]

In the winter of the *jimao* year, I heard through the grapevine that the Master was on the coast in Shandong and had received an imperial invitation to journey in comfort to visit Chinggis Qan. In spring of the following year, he did in fact make a stopover in Yan and stayed at Yuxu Monastery, where I first met him in person.[i] He sat as still as a corpse and stood like an old tree, but he moved like lightning and walked like the wind; truly he was a different order of being. In our discussions, I came to understand that he was widely knowledgeable and profoundly informed. He had read everything. My esteem for him rose daily. Upon hearing of his reputation, those who wished to become disciples surpassed all counting. Judging from the fact that several retired officials of the former Jin court delighted in spending time with him, we can surmise others of the same caliber also did. Not long after, he proceeded on to Longyang Monastery.[ii] 1219.11.9–1220.02.05

Only after the envoy came a second time did he finally set out to travel westward. As he was about to leave, his Daoist followers asked him when he would return, and he told them, "In three years." It was then the *xinsi* year (1221), second month; in the first month of the *jiashen* year, the Master arrived back from the Western Regions, just as he had indicated. Those who knew of this prediction marveled at its accuracy. From the seventh day of that month, he lodged in Yanjing at the Great Tianchang Monastery, after acquiescing to petitions and requests.[iii] ~1224.01.22–02.20 1224.01.28

Today when men set out to travel for business or duty, they dawdle, reluctant to leave home. When the Master set out on a journey traversing thousands of treacherous miles over unrecorded territory and arid wastelands, though he was reverently received everywhere, the rigors of the road were inescapably exhausting. Yet wherever he found himself, he would wander about completely at ease, taking pleasure in the beauty of the landscape, composing poems, chatting, and laughing. To him life and death were like the passage of summer and winter, nothing to unsettle his heart in the slightest. Could anyone who has not grasped the Way achieve

　　門人李志常，從行者也。掇其所歷而爲之記。凡山川、道里之險易，水土、風氣之差殊，與夫衣服、飲食，百果、草木、禽蟲之別，粲然靡不畢載。目之曰《西遊》，而徵序於僕。夫以四海之大，萬物之廣，耳目未接，雖有大智，猶不能遍知而盡識也。況四海之外者乎？所可考者，傳記而已。僕謂是集之行，不特新好事者之聞見。又以知至人之出處，無可無不可，隨時之義云。戊子秋后二日，西溪居士孫錫序。

such a state? His disciple Li Zhichang traveled with him and, compiling their experiences, he made this record. Everything was noted down in detail: the dangers of passage through mountains and river valleys; the variability of the water and soil and local practices; the differences in clothing, food, drink, fruits, trees, plants, insects, and animals.

Having titled his book *A Journey to the West*, Li requested a preface from me. Now, so immense is the world within the four seas and so manifold the myriad things, that anything unexperienced by one's own eyes and ears cannot be completely understood or thoroughly remarked upon, even should one have an abundance of knowledge. Is this not even more so for places beyond the four seas? What one can consider, therefore, is this record alone. I would add that the dissemination of this compilation will not simply refresh those experiences open to the curious; but by this record, the reader can understand that the publication of this work will not only bring something new to the experiences of the curious but also show one that the motives of the Perfected, no matter what, were always determined by the moment. Written in the *wuzi* year, 1228.08.09 second day after "Establishing Autumn," by the Retired Scholar of the Western Stream, Sun Xi.[iv]

長春真人西遊記卷上
門人真常子李志常述

父師真人長春子，姓丘氏，名處機，字通密，登州棲霞人。未冠出家，師事重陽真人。既而住磻溪、龍門十有三年。真積力久，學道乃成。暮年還海上。戊寅歲之前，師在登州，河南屢欲遣使徵聘。事有齟齬，遂已。明年住萊州昊天觀。夏四月，河南提控邊鄙使至，邀師同往。師不可，使者攜所書詩頌歸。繼而復有使自大梁來，道聞山東爲宋人所據，乃還。其年八月，江南大帥李公、彭公來請，不赴。爾後，隨處往往邀請。萊之主者難其事，師乃言曰：我之行止，天也；非若輩所及知。當有留不住時去也。

居無何，成吉思皇帝遣侍臣劉仲祿縣虎頭金牌，其文曰：如朕親行，便宜行事，及蒙古人二十輩，傳旨敦請。師躊躇間，仲祿曰：師名重四海，皇帝特詔仲祿踰越山海，不限歲月，期必致之。師曰：

---

2   In premodern China, one is already one *sui* at birth; at the next New Year's one turns two *sui*. "Coming of age" marks twenty *sui* and is a rite of passage for males, "the capping year," when they ritually bind up their hair to wear a cap. At this time they are also given a formal byname 字.

3   One can assume, considering the continuous fighting that plagued Shandong at the end of the Jin, that Qiu had decided to distance himself from the Jin court.

4   Daliang, modern Kaifeng, was then the Southern Capital of the Jin.

Book I
Recorded by His Disciple Master Zhenchang, Li Zhichang

My eminent Master, Master Changchun the Perfected, of the Qiu family, adopted the personal name of Chuji and the byname of Tongmi. He hailed from Qixia County in Dengzhou in Shandong. Leaving home before coming of age, he set out on the Daoist path under his teacher, Wang Chongyang the Perfected.[2] After that, he took up residence at Panxi (1174–1180) and then in Longmen (1180–1186), for a total of thirteen years.[v] There he exerted himself for a long time until at last his study of the Way was completed. In his twilight years he returned to the coast to his ancestral home at Qixia, Shandong.[vi] Prior to the *wuyin* year (1218), while the Master was at Dengzhou, the Jin court in Henan repeatedly dispatched envoys with gifts and invitations to visit the court there. But there was some contention, so the visit never happened.[3]

[In Shandong]

The next year, he took up residence at Haotian Monastery in Laizhou (Mt. Daji, Shandong). In summer, the fourth month, the Henan Frontier Supervisor arrived to request that the Master accompany him to the Jin court. The Master demurred, but the envoy took some of Qiu's poems and odes back with him. Another envoy was then dispatched from the Jin capital, Daliang, but on the way heard that Shandong had been occupied by the Song and went back.[4] In the eighth month of that year, the Jiangnan generals, their Excellencies Li[vii] and Peng,[viii] arrived with an invitation, but the Master did not go with them either.

1219.05.15–06.13

1219.09.11–10.09

The governor of Laizhou was concerned about the stream of unsuccessful envoys, so the Master explained to him, "My movements are up to Heaven; they are not something that people like you would understand. When I know I can no longer stay, I will depart." Before long, the Emperor Chinggis sent his servant Liu Zhonglu, bearing a golden tiger tablet inscribed with the words, "Authorized to conduct affairs as I would do in person."[ix] With twenty Mongols in his party, he conveyed the Emperor's oral edict and earnestly invited the Master to return with him.

When the Master hesitated, Zhonglu said, "The Master's name is known throughout the land. His Imperial Majesty has especially delegated me, Zhonglu, to travel over mountains and seas, and to bring you back with me no matter how long it takes." The Master replied, "Since

兵革以來，彼疆此界。公冒險至此，可謂勞矣。仲祿曰：

欽奉君命，敢不竭力。仲祿今年五月在乃滿國兀里
朵得旨。六月至白登北威寧，得羽客常真諭。七月
至德興，以居庸路梗，燕京發士卒來迎。八月抵京
城。道眾皆曰：「師之有無，未可必也。」過中山，
歷真定，風聞師在東萊。又得益都府安撫司官吳燕、
蔣元，始得其詳。欲以兵五千迎師。燕等曰：「京東
之人，聞兩朝議和，眾心稍安。今忽提兵以入，必
皆據險自固，師亦將乘桴海上矣。誠欲事濟，不必
爾也。」從之，乃募自願者得二十騎以行。將抵益
都，使燕、元馳報其師張林。林以甲士萬郊迎。仲
祿笑曰：「所以過此者，為求訪長春真人，君何以甲
士為？」林於是散其卒，相與接轡以入。所歷皆以
此語之，人無駭謀。林復給以馹騎。次濰州，得尹
公。冬十有二月，同至東萊，傳皇帝所以宣召之旨。

師知不可辭，徐謂仲祿曰：「此中艱食，公等

---

5 An *ordo* is a palace-camp.
6 A reference to *Analects* 5.7: "The Master said, 'If the Way is not put into practice, I
   will set off upon the sea in a small raft.'" This is most often understood to mean that
   Confucius wanted to wash his hands of people "not implementing the Way." See the
   commentary in Confucius, Slingerland, trans., 2003, 41.
7 The foregoing is Zhonglu's long message, delivered orally to Qiu Chuji. For a translation of Chinggis's actual rescript, see Appendix 1.

war has broken out, the borders have been constantly shifting. It must be acknowledged as a real achievement that Your Excellency has endured such difficulty traveling to see me." Zhonglu then said,

Would I dare not to exert myself fully to obey the lord's command? I, Zhonglu, received the command on the first day of the fifth month of this year, while staying at the Imperial *Ordo* in the country of the Naimans.[5] In the sixth month I reached Weining, north of Baideng (Shanxi, Datong region), where I obtained instructions from a Daoist named Changzhen. In the seventh month I reached Dexing (Hebei). Since the road through Juyong Pass was blocked, Yanjing dispatched troops to meet us. In the eighth month I reached the capital. The Daoists there told me that it was not at all certain that the Master was still alive. Continuing through Zhongshan (Hebei, Dingzhou) and Zhending (Hebei), I heard that the Master was staying at Donglai. I then obtained confirmation from Wu Yan and Jiang Yuan, officials in the Control Office at Yidu Prefecture. I wanted to bring five thousand soldiers with me, but Yan and the others said, "The people of the Capital East Circuit with headquarters in Qingzhou, Shandong, have heard that the Song and Mongol courts are discussing peace and have only just started to settle down. If you suddenly go in with five thousand soldiers, they will fortify themselves in strategic places, and the Master too might 'sail out to sea on a raft.'[6] If you really want your mission to succeed, do not do that." Following this advice, I recruited twenty volunteers to ride with me.

When we approached Yidu, I sent Wu Yan and Jiang Yuan to ride ahead and inform their commander, Zhang Lin.[x] Lin welcomed us in the outskirts with ten thousand troops in full armor. I laughed and said, "I have come this way to visit the Perfected Changchun. What are you doing with armored troops?" Lin thereupon dismissed the troops, and we rode abreast into the city. Every place we passed through I explained our mission thusly, and no one became frightened or hostile. Furthermore, Lin provided me with post horses to proceed on to Weizhou, where I found His Excellency Yin 尹 (Zhiping 志平, 1169–1251)[xi] and, in winter, the twelfth month, we arrived together at Donglai, where I have now delivered the command issued by the Emperor."[7]

1219.06.14

1219.07.13–08.11

1220.01.08–02.05

[Departing Shandong]

The Master understood that he could not refuse this invitation and spoke to Zhonglu in a measured fashion. "Food is scarce here. You should

且往益都。俟我上元醮竟,當遣十五騎來,十八日即行。」

於是,宣使與衆西入益都。師預選門弟子十有九人以俟其來。如期騎至,與之俱行。由濰陽至青社,宣使已行矣。問之張林,言:「正月七日,有騎四百,軍于臨淄,青民大駭。宣使逆而止之,今未聞所在。」師尋過長山及鄒平。

二月初,屆濟陽,士庶奉香火迎拜於其邑南。羽客長吟前導,飯於養素庵。會衆僉曰:「先月十八日,有鶴十餘自西北來,飛鳴雲間,俱東南去。翌日辰巳間,又有數鶴來自西南,繼而千百焉,或頡或頏,獨一鶴拂庵,盤桓乃去。今乃知鶴見之日,即師啓行之辰也。」皆以手加額。留數日。

二月上旬,[i] 宣使遣騎來報,已駐軍將陵。艤舟以待,明日遂行。十三日,宣使以軍來迓。師曰:「來何暮?」對:「以道路榛梗,特往燕京會兵,東備信安,西備常山。仲祿親提軍取深州、下武邑以闢路、構橋於滹沱,括舟於將陵,是以遲。」師曰:「此事非公不克辦。」次日絕滹沱而北。

二十二日至瀘溝。京官、士庶、僧道郊迎。

8 The *jiao* 醮 sacrifices, normally a three-day ceremony, are a Daoist service usually performed on the first or fifteenth day of the month, that is, on either the day of the new or full moon in the lunar calendar. See EOT 539–544. The Three Primes 三元 are the First Prime (Shangyuan 上元), a yearly festival day starting on the fifteenth day of the first lunar month; the Middle Prime (Zhongyuan 中元), the fifteenth day of the seventh lunar month, also known as the Ghost Festival (*guijie* 鬼節); and the Last Prime (*xiayuan* 下元), the fifteenth day of the tenth lunar month.

return to Yidu and wait for me to finish carrying out the *jiao* sacrifices 1220.02.20
on the First Prime.[8] Then send fifteen mounted men to fetch me, and I
will immediately set out on the eighteenth of the first month." 1220.02.23
    The imperial envoys and their escort then returned west to Yidu. The
Master made an initial selection of nineteen disciples in preparation and
awaited someone to come fetch us. At the appointed time, the mounted
escort arrived, and we all proceeded on together. After departing from
Weiyang prefecture, we reached Qingshe (Qingzhou, that is, Yidu), but
the Imperial Envoy (Liu Zhonglu) had already departed. When we asked 1220.02.12
about this, Zhang Lin explained, "On the seventh day of the first month,
four hundred horsemen encamped in Linzi, terrifying the inhabitants of
Qingshe. The Imperial Envoy directly went there to stop them, and his
whereabouts are currently unknown." The Master quickly went ahead
through Changshan and reached Zouping.
    We arrived as expected at Jiyang on the first day of the second month. 1220.03.07
A crowd of scholars and common folk burned incense and greeted us with
great respect south of the city. Chanting a scripture melodiously, a Daoist
priest led us on and fed us a meal at the Yangsu (Nurturing Plainness)
Cloister. The assembled congregation all said, "On the eighteenth day of
the previous month, a dozen or more cranes came from the northwest, 1220.02.23
flying and crying amid the clouds, all heading southeast. The next day
several cranes came from the southwest, and then thousands more came,
soaring and dipping. Only one approached the monastery, circled, and
flew off. We now know that the day the cranes appeared was the very
day that the Master began his journey!" They raised their hands together
to their foreheads in a show of respect. We stayed there for several days.
    In the first third of the second month, the Imperial Envoy had sent 1220.03.07–16
a mounted messenger to report that he had already stationed troops at
Jiangling and was waiting with moored boats to cross the Qinghe River.
We thereupon set out the next day. On the thirteenth day, the envoy came 1220.03.19
to meet us with a troop of soldiers. "Why are you so late?" the Master
asked. The envoy responded, "The route was blocked, and I had to make
a special trip to Yanjing to raise troops and to set up precautionary guards
in the east at Xin'an and west at Changshan. I had to lead the army to take
Shenzhou and subdue Wuyi to clear the road and build a bridge across
the Hutuo River, and I had to round up boats at Jiangling. That is why
I am late." The Master replied, "Without you, none of this would have
been accomplished." The next day we crossed the river and headed north. 1220.03.20

[At Yanjing]

On the twenty-second day we reached the Lugou Bridge, where Yanjing 1220.03.28
officials, scholars and commoners, and Buddhist and Daoist monks all

是日，由麗澤門入，道士具威儀，長吟其前。行省石抹公
館師于玉虛觀。自爾求頌、乞名者日盈門。凡士馬所至，
奉道弟子以師與之名，往往脫欲兵之禍，師之道廕及人如
此。宣撫王巨川楫上詩，師答云：

旌旗獵獵馬蕭蕭，
北望燕山度石橋。
萬里欲行沙漠外，
三春遽別海山遙。
良朋出塞同歸鴈，
破帽經霜更續貂。
一自玄元西去後，
到今無似北庭招。

　　師聞行宮漸西，春秋已高，倦冒風沙，欲待駕回朝
謁。又，仲祿欲以選處女偕行。師難之曰：「齊人獻女
樂，孔子去魯。余雖山野，豈與處子同行哉？」仲祿乃令
曷剌馳奏，師亦遣人奉表。

9   Lugou Bridge is the famous stone bridge over the Yongding River, about 15 miles
      southwest of Yanjing, built between 1189 and 1192 under Jin Emperor Zhangzong. It
      is also called the Marco Polo Bridge because Polo was the first Westerner to see and
      describe it. See Polo, Cordier et al., eds., 1903, vol. 2, 5–8.
10   "Complete regalia": that is, they were assembled in formal order, with pennants and
      flags in front, musical instruments in the rear.
11   The sea and mountains of Shandong, where he was dwelling.
12   The term *liangpeng* 良朋 here means "well matched" rather than "good friends"; in
      this context it means "a fellowship of persons of the Daoist order," "friends of the Way."
13   There is a play here on a Chinese saying for two things or actions being incommensura-
      ble, or for a person being superfluous: *gouwei xu diao* 狗尾續貂 (a dog's tail continues
      the sable's fur). Here Qiu alludes to the saying as a sign of humility, meaning that he
      (a dog's tail) is not the equal of Laozi (the sable). Frost, of course, signals old age.
14   Beiting, the name of an area in modern Xinjiang, was occupied at this time mostly by
      Turkic tribes, including Uyghurs. The last line can also mean, "Until now, when this
      worthless one 無似 is summoned to Beiting." Given the "sable tail" line, this was surely
      meant at a secondary level. Laozi is the reputed author of the Daoist text *The Way and
      Its Power*. According to an early legend, he journeyed westward, where he converted

welcomed us outside the city walls.[9] We entered Yanjing the same day through the western Lize Gate. Daoist priests had prepared complete regalia, and they melodiously chanted as they led us to His Excellency Governor Shimo (Xiandebu, Sendeb),[xii] who lodged the Master and his party at Yuxu Monastery.[10] Thereafter, throngs at the temple gates begging for blessings or requesting religious names multiplied daily. Many former Jin officials came, who were thus able to avoid the disaster of war by becoming Daoist disciples or receiving a religious name from the Master. In this fashion the Master's charismatic mantle protected the people. The Pacification Commissioner Wang Juchuan (1180–1240) presented a poem to the Master, and the Master responded with his own:[xiii]

[1. "Responding to Pacification Commissioner Wang Juchuan"]

Pennants flap and flutter, horses snuffle and whinny
As we cross a stone bridge, gazing north to Yan Mountains.
About to travel thousands of miles out beyond the desert
We hastily take our leave at the end of spring as sea and mountains
    recede in the distance.[11]
A fellowship of the Way, we exit the passes with returning geese.[12]
My tattered hat, experiencing frost, is "added on to sable."[13]
From the time the Lord of the Mysterious Origin went west
Until now, nothing can match this summons to Beiting.[14]

The Master heard that Chinggis's *ordo* was gradually moving to the West, and given his advanced years, he wanted to await the Emperor's return to pay his respects rather than to wearily brave the wind-tossed sand.[15] Moreover, Zhonglu intended to gather some virgins to take along as a gift to the Qan. The Master objected, "When the people of Qi offered young female entertainers to distract the Duke of Lu from his duties, Confucius quickly departed Lu.[16] I may be a common rustic, but how can I travel with young virgins?" Thereupon Zhonglu dispatched Hela (Qara) to transmit a memorial to Chinggis by fast post; the Master also sent along a messenger to present a petition asking the Qan to allow him to wait until the Qan returned.[17]

foreigners to Daoism. In later versions of the legend, he even became the Buddha, which would conveniently make Daoism older than Buddhism. See EOT 492–494.

15 Qiu was 72 by Western reckoning and 73 *sui* by Chinese reckoning.

16 The reference is to *Analects* 18.4. See Confucius, Slingerland, trans., 2003, 215, for discussion.

17 On Hela and other Mongols assigned to escort the party, see the Additional Note. The full text of Qiu's petition is in Appendix 2.

一日，有人求跋閻立本《太上過關圖》，題：

蜀郡西遊日，
函關東別時。
群胡皆稽首，
大道復開基。

又以二偈示衆。其一云：

雜亂朝還暮，
輕狂古到今。
空華空寂念，
若有若無心。

其二云：

觸情常決烈，
非道莫參差。
忍辱調猿馬，
安閑度歲時。

四月上旬，會衆請望日醮於天長。師以行辭，衆請益力。曰：「今茲兵革未息，遺民有幸，得一覲真人，蒙道廕者多矣。獨死者冥冥長夜，未沐薦拔，遺恨不無耳。」師許之。

18   "The Most-High Lord" here refers to Laozi.
19   That is, one's daily activity.
20 (a) That is, historical consciousness.
20 (b) "An alternate possibility for these two lines would be "Thoughts of phenomena, thoughts of absolute stillness, / A mind that sees their existence, a mind that does not."

One day someone came to request an inscription for Yan Liben's "Painting of the Most-High Lord Leaving the Pass."[xiv] The Master complied:

[2. "Inscription for Yan Liben's 'Painting of the Most-High Lord Leaving the Pass'"][18]

On that day when he roamed west to Shu
By departing the east from Hangu Pass,
A horde of Hu barbarians all kowtowed reverently,
For the Great Way was to be inaugurated again.

He also provided two *gāthās* (hymns) for the crowd.

[The First Gāthā]

Distracted disorder morning and evening,[19]
Frivolous abandonment from past to present.[20a]
Be aware of illusory flowers and illusions of the void[20b]
Be mindful of what exists and what does not.[21]

[The Second Gāthā]

Feelings stirred to passion often lead to being at odds;
Only the Way can negate differences.[22]
Endure shame, harmonize the monkey-like mind and the horse-
     like will,[23]
And so pass the years and seasons in ease.

In the first part of the fourth month, the Daoist assembly requested [1220.05.18] a *jiao* sacrifice on the day of the full moon at Tianchang Monastery. Owing to his imminent departure, the Master declined, but his followers redoubled their efforts, pleading, "Nowadays warfare goes on and on. We refugees are lucky to have this chance to gaze upon the Perfected, and many of us have received the protection of the Way. Only the dead in the boundless void of perpetual night, receiving no prayers of release, remain full of eternal regret." So the Master agreed to do it.

---

21 Illusory flowers are phenomena; stillness is a mental state that voids all phenomena. A mind of stillness realizes that all things are illusory but still conceives of the world in binary terms: activity / no activity. One must move beyond this to the undifferentiated Way.

22 Thus, it is best not to engage with differences produced in the creation of matter, the myriad things, which conceal the one truth behind them.

23 Desire and ambition.

時方大旱。十有四日,既啓醮事,雨大降。衆且以行
禮爲憂。師於午後赴壇,將事,俄而開霽。衆喜而歎曰:
「一雨一晴,隨人所欲。非道高德厚者,感應若是乎?」
明日,師登寶玄堂傳戒。時有數鶴自西北來,人皆仰之。
焚簡之際,一簡飛空而滅。且有五鶴翔舞其上。士大夫咸
謂師之至誠動天地。南塘老人張天度子真作賦美其事,諸
公皆有詩。醮竟,宣使劉公從師北行。

　　道出居庸,夜遇群盜于其北,皆稽顙以退,且曰:
「無驚父師。」

　　五月,師至德興龍陽觀度夏。以詩寄燕京士大夫云:

登真何在泛靈楂,
南北東西自有嘉。
碧落雲峰天景致,
滄波海市雨生涯。
神游八極空雖遠,
道合三清路不差。

---

24 The Baoxuan Hall, located inside Tianchang Monastery, was the specified place to
   carry out the *jiao* and other ceremonies, as well as a highly significant place in the
   last years of Qiu's life.

25 That is, why must one go far away to seek instruction from a master? "Miraculous
   raft" is a term borrowed from Buddhism, where it means the conveyance that takes
   one "to the other side" of the river, that is, to enlightenment. Qiu's point here is that
   rejecting family and leaving home to find a teacher is only one possible path.

26 That is, the Way is everywhere.

At the time a great drought had afflicted the area, but on the fourteenth day, once the *jiao* sacrifice had begun, it began to rain heavily, and
everyone worried about the prospects of carrying out the ritual. In the   1220.05.17
afternoon, the Master mounted the altar and was about to commence
the ceremony when suddenly the rain stopped. The crowd rejoiced,
marveling, "The sun shines and rain falls in accordance with his desires.
Only one of superior spiritual and moral attainment could elicit such
a Heavenly response!" The next day as the Master ascended Baoxuan
(Precious Mystery) Hall to conduct rites of initiation, many cranes flew
by from the northwest.[24] Everyone gazed up at them. When prayer slips
were burned, one floated up into the sky and vanished, while five cranes
frolicked in the air above it. The scholars all agreed that the Master's
utter sincerity had moved Heaven and earth. The Elder of the Southern
Pond, Zhang Tiandu,[xv] byname Zizhen, wrote a verse of rhyme prose
(*fu* 賦) that extolled the event, and the gentlemen in attendance all wrote
poems. At the conclusion of the *jiao* ceremony, His Excellency Imperial
Envoy Liu Zhonglu accompanied the Master on his northward journey.

[Through Juyong Pass to Stay at Longyang Monastery]

The road led out of Juyong Pass, and at night we encountered bandits
north of the pass. But the bandits kowtowed and pleaded for mercy as
they withdrew, saying, "Let us not disturb the eminent Master." In the
fifth month, the Master reached Longyang Monastery at Dexing to pass   1220.06.03–07.01
the summer. The Master sent a poem to the literati at Yanjing:

[3. "Sent to Gentlemen of the Way in Yanjing"]

How can becoming a Perfected lie solely in floating away on the
    miraculous raft?[25]
Every direction possesses its own fineness.[26]
Peaks of clouds in the blue void are the epitome of Heaven's
    scenery;
Mirages on the oceans are at the boundary where rain begins.[27]
The void in which the spirit roams freely, though distant,
Is the right path to where the Way combines the Three Purities.[28]

---

27   That is, the maker of things produces all manner of phenomena.

28   That is, if you can perfect your spirit to roam outside of your body, you are on the
    right path to attaining the Way. In the Daoist cosmos, the Three Purities are the three
    realms of Jade Clarity, Upper Clarity, and Great Clarity, which exist just below the
    Great Canopy Heaven. Each realm is populated by transcendent and sacred beings
    that guard "scriptures and sacred instructions that they reveal on occasion for the
    sake of suffering humanity." See EOT 840.

弱水縱過三十萬，
騰身頃刻到仙家。

　　時京城吾道孫周楚卿、楊彪仲文、師諳才卿、李士謙
子進、劉中用之、陳時可秀玉、吳章德明、趙中立正卿、
王銳威卿、趙昉德輝、孫錫天錫，此數君子，師寓玉虛日
所與唱和者也。王覯逢辰、王直哉清甫，亦與其遊。

　　觀居禪房山之陽，其山多洞府，常有學道修真之士棲
焉。師因契衆以遊。初入峽門，有詩云：

入峽清遊分外嘉，
群峰列岫戟查牙。
蓬萊未到神仙境，
洞府先觀道士家。
松塔倒縣秋雨露，
石樓斜照晚雲霞。
郤思舊日終南地，
夢斷西山不見涯。

29 The mythical Weak River (*ruoshui* 弱水) surrounds the abode of the transcendents; it will not support even a feather. The meaning of this line is "No matter what dangers or impediments you face." This last couplet seems to emphasize to his admirers and hopeful adepts in Yanjing that the impediments they face in their quest to know the Way—homes, wives, concubines, children—can be surmounted by a single moment of intuition (a change to one's being, a leap), which can place them among the transcendents.

30 Penglai Isles is the name of a mythical paradise, reputedly located off the coast of Shandong, where transcendent sylphs live out eternity. Its invocation often also refers to Qiu Chuji's home on the Shandong coast (EOT 788–790).

31 This line refers to the founding of the Quanzhen sect by Wang Zhe in the Zhongnan mountains south of modern Xi'an.

No matter how many thousands of times you must cross the Weak
    River,[29]
A single leap of the body and you are immediately among the
    transcendents.

At that time, among our Daoist friends in the Way who were in the
capital were the gentlemen Sun Zhou (byname Chuqing),[xvi] Yang Biao
(byname Zhongwen), Shi Xu (byname Caiqing), Li Shiqian (byname
Zijin), Liu Zhong (byname Yongzhi),[xvii] Chen Shike (byname Xiuyu),
Wu Zhang (byname Deming),[xviii] Zhao Zhongli (byname Zhenqing),[xix]
Wang Rui (byname Weiqing),[xx] Zhao Fang (byname Dehui),[xxi] and Sun
Xi (byname Tianxi). While in residence at Yuxu Monastery, the Master
had exchanged verses with all of them. Wang Gou (byname Fengchen)
and Wang Zhizai (byname Qingfu) also joined him on his strolls. Longyang Monastery sits on the southern slope of Mt. Chanfang,[xxii] which
contains many grottoes where hermits cultivating the Way dwell. The
Master often took his friends along to visit them. Upon entering the
mountain gorge, he composed a poem:

[4. "Roaming Mt. Chanfang and First Entering Defile Pass"]

To enter a gorge and serenely roam is exquisitely lovely,
With caves arrayed across peaks like jagged teeth of halberds.
Having yet to reach Penglai and the domain of divine
    transcendents,[30]
In these grotto precincts we can first observe men of the Way.
Like upside-down pagodas, pinecones hang dripping autumn's
    dew;
In the sun's oblique rays, stone towers shine in the sunset aura of
    evening clouds.
I turn my thoughts back to the land of the Zhongnan Mountains in
    former days,[31]
My dream is broken by western hills; I cannot see to the horizon.[32]

---

32 "Western Hills": Xishan 西山 (translated as "western hills" in Qiu's poem but as
    "Western Mountains" for the mountains in Jiangxi.) is a Daoist paradise in Jiangxi,
    the twelfth of the thirty-six Grotto Heavens on the earth in which transcendents
    reside. The term also refers to the cave dwellings of those seeking enlightenment.
    The Western Mountains of Jiangxi are also called the Free and Easy Wandering Moun-
    tains, which harks back to the chapter in the early Daoist work *Zhuangzi* titled "Free
    and Easy Wandering." The sight of the caves takes Qiu back to the founding of the
    Quanzhen sect. The "horizon" he wants to see is the Zhongnan mountains.

其地爽塏，勢傾東南，一望三百餘里。觀之東數里，平地有湧泉，清冷可愛。師往來其間，有詩云：

午後迎風背日行，
遙山極目亂雲橫。
萬家酷暑熏腸熱，
一派寒泉入骨清。
北地往來時有信，
東皋遊戲俗無争（耕夫牧竪堤陰讓坐）。
溪邊浴罷林間坐，
散髮披襟暢道情。

中元日，本觀醮。午後傳符授戒，老、幼露坐，熱甚，悉苦之。須臾，有雲覆其上，狀如圓蓋，移時不散，衆皆喜躍讚歎。又，觀中井水可給百衆，至是踰千人，執事者謀他汲。前後三日，井泉忽溢，用之不竭，是皆善緣天助之也。醮後，題詩云：

太上弘慈救萬靈，
衆生薦福藉群經。

33 The notes in small italic type were probably added by an editorial hand after the poems were done, perhaps at the time they were gathered for inclusion in *Journey to the West*. The forms of address used in the notes indicate that they were not added by Qiu.

34 The Middle Prime fell on the fifteenth of the seventh month. On this date also begins the Buddhist day of the Ullambana (Yulanpen) Festival, which seeks salvation for those suffering in hell. Daoists also held ceremonies in honor of the Officer of the Earth 地官. See EOT 834. This ceremony is more familiar to Westerners as the Obon or Bon Festival of Japan.

The land was open and bright, sloping to the southeast; a single glance could cover three hundred *li*. Several *li* east of the monastery, there was an artesian spring, appreciated for its clear and cold water. Walking amid all of this, the Master wrote:

[5. "Inscribing the Artesian Spring at Longyang Monastery in Dexing"]

After noon, I stroll into the wind with the sun at my back;
Distant mountains as far as the eye can see, jumbled clouds along
    the horizon.
Ten thousand families suffer the steaming heat of summer,
But a single cold spring infuses freshness into the bones.
From the northern lands come occasional letters,
On the eastern side we frolic in amiable concord.
Plowmen and shepherd boys invited us to sit and share the shade of the embankment.[33]
Done bathing in the creek, we sit among the trees;
Unbinding our hair, loosening our robes, we chat about the
    meaning of the Way.

On the day of Middle Prime, Longyang Monastery held the *jiao* 1220.08.14 ceremonies.[34] In the afternoon, talismans and observances were passed and received.[35] Old and young alike sat out in the open, tolerating the unbearable heat. Then clouds appeared overhead, forming a round canopy slow to disperse—an event that caused everyone to exclaim in wonder and joy. Furthermore, the well in the monastery could usually provide water for only about a hundred people. With over a thousand people there, organizers had planned to draw water from other sources. But for three days, the well water suddenly overflowed and was never depleted by use. This was all due to the miraculous aid of Heaven. After the *jiao* ceremony, the Master composed a poem:

[6. "Written after the Jiao Ceremony at Longyang Monastery in Dexing"]

The embracing compassion of the Great Ultimate rescues all
    sentient things,
As living beings make offerings for blessings by enlisting the
    scriptures.

---

35 Talismans were written by Daoist priests as an act uniting Heaven and humans. The
    power lies in the act of writing, not the actual text itself. If the text was not done with
    reverence, it had no power.

三田保護精神氣，
萬象欽崇日月星。
自揣肉身潛有漏，
難逃科教入無形。
且遵北斗齋儀法（南斗北斗皆論齋醮），
漸陟南宮火煉庭。

　　八月初，應宣德州元帥移剌公請，遂居朝元觀。中秋夜，有《賀聖朝》二曲。其一云：

斷雲歸岫，
　長空凝翠，
　　寶鑑初圓。
大光明，
　弘照亘流沙，
　　外直過西天。

人間是處，
　夢魂沈醉，
　　歌舞華筵。
道家門，
　別是一般清，
　　暗 ii 開悟心田。

---

36 The so-called Cinnabar Fields (*dantian* 丹田), which house the three elements of being. The lower field, just behind and below the navel, houses "essence" (*jing* 精). The middle field, in the center of the chest in the heart, harbors "pneuma" or "vital breath" (*qi* 氣). And the upper field, in the head, is the seat of "spirit" (*shen* 神).

37 The brightest of the myriad things. "Myriad images" signifies all things in the cosmos.

The Three Fields protect essence, spirit, and vital
    breath;[36][xxiii]
The myriad images venerate sun, moon, and stars.[37]
Surmising that our corporeal bodies are secretly tainted,[xxiv]
We would find it hard to enter the formless by evading rules of
    sacrifice.
So we follow the rituals of sacrifice according to *The Northern*
    Dipper Rituals

The texts Southern Dipper *and* Northern Dipper *both discuss procedures for* zhai *and*
jiao *rituals.*

To ascend in stages to the Court of Refining Souls in the Southern
    Palace.[38]

At the beginning of the eighth month, at the invitation of His Ex-   1220.08.30–09.08
cellency Yila (Yelü Tuhua), regional military commander of Xuande
Prefecture,[xxv] we went to reside at Chaoyuan (Audience with the Three
Primes) Monastery. On the evening of Mid-Autumn, the Master com-   1220.09.13
posed matching lyrics to the following *ci* lyric pattern:[39]

[a. *"Celebrating the Sagely Dynasty" I]*

Tattered clouds return to their mountain caves,[40]
    and azure congeals in the long void
        when the precious mirror is first full.
A radiating brilliance
    spreads its glow along the shifting sands,[xxvi]
        reaching past the Great West.[41]

Here in the world where people live
    dreaming souls are sunk in drunkenness,
        singing and dancing at elaborate feasts.
The gate of the Daoist
    is a different and purer sort of clarity,
        opening to the field of an enlightened heart.

38 Where souls are refined by fire to enter the realm of long life. *Zhai* rituals are those
    of penitence and purification, and are a necessary preliminary step to entering that
    realm. The poem describes rituals that lead one along the path of release.
39 Each lyric comprises two stanzas, separated by extra vertical space. A period in a
    sentence indicates the end of a rhyme line.
40 Clouds were thought to be a product of high mountains. Accordingly, a poetic name
    for stones is "the roots of clouds" (*yungen* 雲根).
41 That is, India.

其二云：

洞天深處，
　良朋高會，
　　逸興無邊。
上丹霄，
　飛至廣寒宮，
　　悄擲下金錢。

靈虛晃耀，
　睡魔奔迸，
　　玉兔嬋娟。
坐忘機，
　觀透本來真，
　　任法界周旋。

　　是後天氣清肅，靜夜安閑。復作二絕云：

長河耿耿夜深深，
寂寞寒窗萬慮沈。
天下是非俱不到，
安閑一片道人心。

---

42 In Daoist geography, the sacred mountains of China contained hidden grottoes (most commonly ten or thirty-six). There resided "transcendent beings walking the earth," waiting to be chosen to enter the heavenly paradise. See EOT 857.

43 The Palace of Spreading Cold is a celestial palace in the north where transcendent beings dwell, but the term also refers to the Palace of Spreading Cold in the moon, inhabited by a hare that pounds out the elixir of immortality with a jade mortar and pestle.

44 On the spiritual level, radiance; on the natural level, the shedding of yellow leaves in autumn.

[b. "Celebrating the Sagely Dynasty" II]

In the deepest part of the Grotto Heavens[42]
   are exalted meetings of like-minded friends,
      whose unbridled interests are boundless.
Up to the glorious empyrean
   they fly to the Palace of Spreading Cold,[43]
      silently casting down golden coins.[44]

In the noumenal void, light radiates all around,[45]
   the demon of sleep flees,[46]
      and the jade hare is gorgeous.[47]
Sitting in meditation to forget one's self and its entanglements with
  the world,
   one can see through to one's original and true nature
      and move freely within all realms of being.

From that point on, the weather was clear yet severe, and one peaceful night he wrote two more quatrains:[48]

[7. "Two Quatrains Written at Chaoyuan Monastery in Zhangde" I]

The Milky Way glistens and glitters, deepening with the night;
Alone at the cold window, all my cares sink away.
No rights or wrongs of the human world can reach me,
For there is nothing here but the tranquil heart of a Daoist.

45 The noumenal void is full of potential, before essence, spirit, or vital breath (*qi*) are formed. It is the same state attained by perfecting oneself. On the natural level, the radiance is that of the harvest moon.
46 Sleep was anathema to the Quanzhen sect, since it was the source of desire created by the world of Yin. Qiu Chuji's disciple Yin Zhiping is said to have taught his own disciples, "The three desires of eating, sleeping, and sex are the weightiest harms to practices of cultivation. If you eat too much, then you sleep too much; if you sleep too much, that is the origin of emotion and desire." See QYW vol. 6, 189.483. On another level, the sleep demon's flight is the bright moonlight that keeps one awake at night.
47 In Chinese mythology, the moon is occupied by a white hare that pounds out the elixir of immortality in a mortar.
48 The term that is used to describe the weather has more profound connections to the Chinese premodern concept of autumn, a season associated with the west, with punishments, and with harm. Its righteous ether (*yiqi* 義氣) kills most living things. Part of this view is the concordant belief that "things past their prime should be slain" (*wu guo qi sheng dang sha* 物過其盛當殺), as Ouyang Xiu put it in his famous "Rhapsody on Autumn Sounds" (Qiusheng fu 秋聲賦). See West 2005, 73–99.

其二云：

清夜沈沈月向高，
山河大地絶纖毫。
唯餘道德渾淪性，
上下三天一萬遭。

　　朝元觀攄州之乾隅，功德主元帥移剌公因師欲北行，
創構堂殿，奉安尊像。前後雲房、洞室，皆一新之。十
月間，方繪祖師堂壁，畫史以其寒將止之。師不許，日：
「鄒律尚且迴春，況聖賢陰有所扶持邪？」是月，果天氣
溫和如春，絶無風沙，由是畫史得畢其功。有詩云：

季秋邊朔苦寒同，
走石吹沙振大風。
旅鴈翅垂南去急，
行人心倦北征窮。
我來十月霜猶薄，
人訝千山水尚通。
不是小春和氣暖，
天教成就畫堂功。

　　尋阿里鮮至自斡辰大王帳下，使來請師。繼而宣撫王
公巨川亦至，日：「承大王鈞旨：『如師西行，請過我。』」
師首肯之。

---

49 Three Heavens are the highest of the nine levels of Heaven, created by the Three
    Pneumas in the original realm of the Dao. See EOT 851–852.
50 That is, they are not yet frozen solid.
51 What English designates as an Indian summer.

[8. "Two Quatrains Written at Chaoyuan Monastery in Zhangde" II]

The clear night deepens, the moon rises high,
And from the mountains and rivers of this land comes not the
    slightest sound.
All that is left now is the undifferentiated nature of the Way,
Up and down, in and out of the Three Heavens we go a million
    times.[49]

Chaoyuan Monastery is situated to the northwest of the prefecture, and its patron, His Excellency Regional Military Commander Yila, upon hearing that the Master was traveling north, initiated construction in the main halls and installed statues of the venerated patriarchs. He completely renovated the warren of residences for practitioners. In the tenth month, as they were painting murals on the walls of the patriarch's hall, the painters were about to quit because of the cold. The Master disagreed, saying, "If Zou Yan's pitch pipes can bring back the spring warmth,[xxvii] do you doubt how much more the hidden power of the sages and the virtuous can do so?" Sure enough, that month the weather grew as warm and comfortable as spring, and there was absolutely no wind. So the painters were able to complete their work, in honor of which the Master dedicated the following poem: `1220.10.28–11.26`

[9. "Celebrating the Artists' Completion of Wall Paintings in the Lineage Hall of Chaoyuan Monastery"]

The last month of autumn and the northern frontier are both
    bitterly cold;
Pushing rocks and blowing sand, the great winds howl.
Wings drooping, migrating wild geese head south in haste;
Hearts worn out, travelers to the north cease.
We came in the tenth month, the frost yet light;
People marveled that those rivers, uniced, still flowed through the
    many mountains.[50]
It's not the mild weather and warmth of a "little spring";[51]
It's that Heaven has ordered the completion of the paintings in the
    hall.

Soon after, Alixian came from the *ordo* of Great Prince Otegin (Wochen, one of Chinggis's younger brothers), being sent to invite the Master.[xxviii] On his heels came His Excellency Pacification Commissioner Wang Juchuan, who reported, "By special command of the Great Prince, I relate, 'If the Master is traveling west, please come visit me.'" The Master nodded in acceptance. That month the Master

是月，北遊望山。曷剌進表迴，有詔曰：「成吉思皇帝
勅真人丘師。」又曰：「惟師道踰三子，德重多方。」其終曰：

雲軒既發於蓬萊，鶴馭可遊於天竺。達磨東邁，元
印法以傳心；老氏西行，或化胡而成道。顧川途之
雖闊，瞻几杖以非遙。爰答來章，可明朕意。秋暑，
師比平安好，指不多及。

其見重如此。又勅劉仲祿云：「無使真人飢且勞，可
扶持緩緩來。」
師與宣使議曰：「前去已寒，沙路綿遠，道衆所須未
備。可往龍陽，乘春起發。」宣使從之。
十八日，南往龍陽。道友送別，多泣下。師以詩
示衆云：

生前暫別猶然可，
死後長離更不堪。
天下是非心不定，
輪迴生死苦難甘。

52 A direct response to the statement Qiu made in his memorial, "It is only I, Chuji,
who have falsely attained a reputation." See Appendix 2 for Qiu's request.
53 The Penglai Isles are invoked here to refer to Qiu Chuji's home on the Shandong coast
(EOT 788–790).
54 Bodhidharma was an itinerant sixth-century Indian monk from south India, founder of
the Chan (Jp Zen) school of Buddhism in north China and subject of many legendary
stories and exploits. See Broughton 2004.

made a tour of Mt. Wang.[xxix] The emissary Qara then returned from presenting the memorials to Chinggis, with an edict that began "The August Emperor, Chinggis, commands Master Qiu the Perfected to consider." Further on, it read, "It is precisely because the Master's Way surpasses the other three masters[xxx] that your virtue is valued everywhere."[52] At the end it said,

> Now that your cloud carriage has departed Penglai, you, the "crane rider," can roam all the way to India.[53] Bodhidharma came east and relied on the Dharma Seal to transmit the Buddha's mind;[54] Laozi journeyed west, perhaps to transform the Hu barbarians and complete the Way. Though the rivers and roads appear far, look to your armrest and staff, and they will not seem so remote.[55]
>
> Now I have answered the writ that came, and this will serve to make my wishes clear. In the autumn heat, Master, I wish you peace and security. I have nothing else to say in this directive.[56]

Such was the Emperor's weighty concern! He also instructed Zhonglu, "Do not allow the Master to suffer hunger or exhaustion; keep him comfortable and travel at an easy pace."

The Master reasoned with the Imperial Envoy. "It is already too cold to go on ahead, and the sandy road is long and winding. The Daoists who will accompany me have yet to prepare what they will need. Let us go back to Longyang and set out in the spring." The Imperial Envoy agreed with his plan.

When we departed south to Longyang on the eighteenth day, our friends in the Way shed tears of farewell as they saw us off. The Master composed a poem to show them: 1220.11.14

[10. *"Written on the Southward Return to Longyang, to Show to My Companions in the Way"*]

A brief parting in our lives seems manageable,
But the long separation after death is harder to bear.
The rights and wrongs of this world may unsettle the heart,
But lives and deaths on the wheel of Karma are a bitterness never
    sweetened.

---

55 The armrest and staff were items for the elderly to ease their life: an armrest for sitting, and a staff for support while walking.
56 For the full text of this edict, see Appendix 3.

翌日，到龍陽觀過冬。

十一月十有四日，赴龍巖寺齋。以詩題殿西廡云：

杖藜欲訪山中客，
空山沉沉淡無色。
夜來飛雪滿巖阿，
今日山光映天白。
天高日下松風清，
神遊八極騰虛明。
欲寫山家本來面，
道人活計無能名。

十二月，以詩寄燕京道友云：

此行真不易，
此別話應長。
北蹈野狐嶺，
西窮天馬鄉。
陰山無海市，
白草有沙場。
自嘆非玄聖，
何如歷大荒。

57 This couplet gestures toward Su Shi's famous poem on Mt. Lu, "I do not recognize the true face of Mt. Lu / Because my body is within the mountain," as well as toward the opening line of *The Way and Its Power*, "The Way that can be spoken of is not the constant Way, / The name that can be assigned as a name is not a constant name."

58 Wild Fox Ridge (*Yehu ling*) lies northwest of present-day Zhangjiakou, a strategic mountain range separating the north China plain from the Mongolian plateau. Heavenly horses are horses introduced from Central Asia, prized for their speed and stamina.

The next day we arrived at Longyang Monastery for the winter. On the fourteenth day of the eleventh month, the Master visited Longyan Temple to preside over a ritual fast, and inscribed a poem on the western corridor of the main hall:

1220.12.10

[11. "Using a Poem to Inscribe the Western Corridor of a Hall at Longyan Temple"]

With staff in hand, I hope to visit lodgers in the mountains;
Though vast and deep, the empty mountains are bleak and
    colorless.
Coming in the night, flying snow fills crevices and crannies,
And today the mountains' radiance reflects the white of the sky.
Beneath a sun high in the heavens, the wind is fresh in the pines;
My spirit travels the eight directions, soaring through the empty
    brilliance.
I want to describe the true face of such mountain dwellers,
But as a Daoist I lack the resources to give it a name.[57]

In the twelfth month he wrote several poems and sent them to his friends in Yanjing. Two of them said,

1220.12.27–1221.01.24

[12. "Two Poems to Send to My Companions in the Way in Yanjing" I]

This journey is truly difficult,
So these parting words should be prolonged.
To the north, we will climb Wild Fox Ridge,
To the west, go to the very end of the land of heavenly horses.[58]
No sea markets in the Yinshan (Tian Shan) Range,
Only sandy fields amid white grasses.[59]
I sigh that I am not Laozi, the Sage of Mystery.
What will it be like for me, crossing the vast wastelands?

---

59 Sea markets are refracted images of human habitation on the ocean, mirages that Qiu could see from his former perch in Shandong. The mountain range now known as the Tian Shan is an 1800-mile-long composite of minor ranges that begins near Ürümqi in Xinjiang, runs through Kyrgyzstan and Kazakhstan, and finally ends near Tashkent in Uzbekistan. Texts from the Jin era, however, refer to the Yin Mountains (Yinshan) north of the Ordos region as Tian Shan, while the Tian Shan range in Xinjiang is confusingly called Yinshan. "Sandy fields" describes old battlefields; a contemporary reader would conjure up images of a sandy field littered with the white bones of the fallen.

又云：

京都若有餞行詩，
早寄龍陽出塞時。
昔有上牀鞋履別，
今無發軫夢魂思。

復寄燕京道友云：

十年兵火萬民愁，
千萬中無一二留。
去歲幸逢慈詔下，
今春須合冒寒遊。
不辭嶺北三千里 （皇帝舊兀里多），
仍念山東二百州。
窮急漏誅殘喘在，
早教身命得消憂。

辛巳之上元，醮於宣德州朝元觀。以頌示衆云：

生下一團腥臭物，
種成三界是非魔。
連枝帶葉無窮勢，
跨古騰今不奈何。

---

60 Chen Shidao 陳師道 (1053–1101) wrote a poem titled "Parting from Lector Bao" 別
寶講主: "In bed at night shoes and feet part, / When are you going to bind up your
legs for the long trip?" His notes read, "The aged monk said, 'Those who are great
practitioners of our religion quickly part from their sandals when they go to bed.' This
means you must put on your leggings for a long trip. One's life is but a few breaths,
so one should be encouraged early on to go out in the world and learn from others."
Here, both preparing for a long trip and expressing deep feelings about having to part
from friends are compared to shedding one's shoes. See Chen Shidao 1995, 215–216.

61 The heartland of China, the Central Plain.

[13. "Two Poems to Send to My Companions in the Way in Yanjing" II]

If there are poems written to send me off in the capital,
Send them quickly to Longyang Monastery, whence I leave
    through frontier passes.
In times of old there was "bidding sandals farewell when retiring
    to bed."[60]
So now as I start my long trip, will your dreaming souls think
    of me?

He sent another to his friends of the Way in Yanjing:

[14. "Another Poem Sent to Companions of the Way in Yanjing"]

The fires of war for ten long years, the sorrows of tens of
    thousands;
And from these countless numbers, scarcely one or two remain.
Last year I had the good fortune to receive a compassionate edict,
So this spring I must join the trip and brave the cold.
I will not shrink from those three thousand *li* north of the range,
(to the former ordo of the Emperor)
But will always recall the two hundred prefectures east of the
    mountains.[61]
While a single breath abides in those distressed or spared from
    death,
I will find a way for their lives to find some relief from worry.

On the fifteenth day of the first month of the *xinsi* year, the Master   1221.02.08
performed the *jiao* ceremony at Chaoyuan Monastery. He showed the
congregation a *gāthā*:

[The Third Gāthā*]*

Born a bundle of stinking rankness,
Just a karmic seed that will sprout demons of right and wrong
    throughout the Three Realms.[62]
Intertwining branches flush with leaves of unlimited power
Leap out of the past and into the present—there being nothing we
    can do.

---

62 On the Three Realms, a concept borrowed from Buddhism, see EOT 849–851, 1253–
    1254. Here, the seeds planted within a soul from past actions account for the trials
    that a being will endure in spiritual progress through various reincarnations.

以二月八日啓行。時天氣晴霽,道友餞行於西郊,遮馬首以泣曰:父師去萬里外,何時復獲瞻禮。師曰:但若輩道心堅固,會有日矣。衆復泣請:果何時邪?師曰:「行止非人所能爲也。兼遠涉異域,其道合與不合,未可必也。」衆曰:「師豈不知,願預告弟子等。」度不獲已,乃重言曰:「三載歸,三載歸。」

十日,宿翠帲口。明日,北度野狐嶺。登高南望,俯視太行諸山,晴嵐可愛。北顧但寒沙衰草,中原之風,自此隔絕矣。道人之心,無適不可。宋德方輩指戰場白骨曰:「我歸當薦以金籙。此亦余北行中一端因緣耳。」

北過撫州。十五日,東北過盖里泊,盡丘垤、醶鹵地,始見人煙二十餘家。南有鹽池,迤邐東北去。自此無河,多鑿沙井以汲。南北數千里,亦無大山。馬行五日,出明昌界。以詩紀實云:

坡陁折疊路彎環,
到處鹽場死水灣。
盡日不逢人過往,

---

63 These were presumably the bones of Jin and Mongol soldiers killed in the decisive Battle of Wild Fox Ridge in 1211. The Mongols annihilated the Jin army and went on to besiege the Jin capital at Zhongdu (Yanjing).

64 The Golden Tablet Retreat is a ceremony to lead people's souls from the realm of darkness to light and to enter their names into the Register of the Divine. See EOT 203–205, 510–511, 579–580.

[To the Camp of Great Prince Otegin at Hulun Buir]

When we set out on our travels on the eighth day of the second month, 1221.03.03 the skies were clear. Our friends in the Way escorted us in farewell to the western outskirts of the city. Crowds of people, impeding the riders' progress, asked as they wept, "Master, you are going so very far away; when will we be honored with another visit?" The Master replied, "If you remain firm in your faith in the Way, that day will come." The crowd again asked tearfully, "And when will that be?" The Master said, "People's movements are not under their control. Couple that with the unpredictability of a path to a distant and strange land, and nothing is for certain." The throng said, "How is it possible that the Master does not know? We beg you to tell your disciples now." Seeing that they had to have an answer, he repeated, "In three years I will return. In three years I will return."

On the tenth day we spent the night at the Cuiping Pass,[xxxi] and the 1221.03.05 next day we crossed over Wild Fox Ridge. Ascending the heights, we looked southward and had a bird's eye view of the various peaks of the Taihang Mountains (which mark the boundary of the east China plain). Under clear skies the mist-shrouded mountains looked particularly enchanting. Gazing north, we saw only cold sands and sere grass. Here marked the end of the sights and customs of the Central Plain. Yet the heart of a Daoist is at home anywhere. Song Defang[xxxii] and his group pointed to the white bones scattered on the field of battle.[63] Song said, "Upon our return we should offer the Golden Tablet Retreat for their souls, for fate may have so arranged our northward journey for this purpose as well."[64]

Proceeding north, we passed through Fuzhou. On the fifteenth day, 1221.03.10 traveling northeast, we passed Gailipo—a land composed entirely of small mounds and salt fields—where we saw twenty or so homes, our first sign of human habitation. Salt ponds on the south side gradually meandered off to the northeast. From here on there were no rivers, and one had to sink wells in the sand to reach water. For thousands of *li* to the north and south one encounters no mountains of any size either. After 1221.03.15 a five-day ride we passed the Mingchang era (1190–1195) border fortifications of the Jin. The Master composed a poem to record the event:

[15. "Using a Poem to Relate the Facts as We Pass the Mingchang Boundary"]

Rising and falling, twisting and turning, the road turns back on
    itself;
Everywhere are salt beds and stagnant lakes.
All day we encounter no one coming or going;

經年時有馬迴還。
地無木植唯荒草，
天產丘陵没大山。
五穀不成資乳酪，
皮裘氊帳亦開顏。

又行六七日，忽入大沙陁。其蹟有矮榆，大者合抱。東北行千里外，無沙處絶無樹木。

三月朔，出沙陁，至魚兒濼，始有人煙聚落。多以耕釣爲業。時已清明，春色渺然。凝冰未泮，有詩云：

北陸祁寒自古稱，
沙陁三月尚凝冰。
更尋若士爲黃鵠，
要識修鯤化大鵬。
蘇武北遷愁欲死，
李陵南望去無憑。
我今返學盧敖志，
六合窮觀最上乘。

---

65 The products of curdled milk: curd cheese, yogurt, butter, etc.
66 The trees are Siberian elms, *Ulmus pumila*.
67 During Qingming, the Clear and Bright Festival, on the 105th day from the winter solstice, the Chinese sweep their ancestor's graves, offer sacrificial food, and gather as families to feast.
68 *Him* (*ruoshi* 若士) refers to a person who possesses the Way, here more specifically, to one who will transform into a yellow swan that will fly off into the void. The story refers to a certain Lu Ao, whose name appears in the penultimate line of the poem. A diviner in the court of the First Emperor of Qin, he traveled far north into the steppe,

Occasionally through the years a horse may return.
Not a single tree on the ground, only wild grasses;
Heaven has produced mounds and hills, but no large mountains.
The five grains do not ripen, so they rely on curdled milk;[65]
In hide coats and felt tents, they still beam with happiness.

We traveled on for another six or seven days, and suddenly emerged into a great desert.[xxxiii] Dwarf elm trees grow in the gravel, some big enough to wrap your arms around.[66] As we travel to the northeast for a thousand *li*, if there is no sandy soil, it will be barren of trees.

On the first of the third month, leaving the desert we arrived at a lake called Yu'erpo[xxxiv] (Fish Lake) and encountered a community largely composed of farmers and fisherfolk. At the time it was already Qingming, yet spring seemed far away, as the ice had not yet started to melt.[67] The Master wrote a poem about all this:

1221.03.21–22

1221.03.26

1221.03.29

[16. *"A Poem on Passing Yu'erpo"*]

The frigid weather in the northern lands has long been noted;
In the third month the desert can still freeze water.
I again seek *him* to transform into a yellow swan,[68]
To recognize the Great Leviathan becoming the Giant Roc.[69]
Su Wu, taken northward, was sad enough to long for death;[70]
Li Ling, gazing south, had no possible way to leave.[71]
For my part, I will revert to studying the resolve of Lu Ao,
To observe everything in all directions, and so achieve the highest
    Way.

where he saw a strange man dancing on a mountain top. Seeing Lu Ao, the man hid behind a boulder. In talking with him, Lu discovered a man of a high spiritual nature and felt ashamed. The man then rose into the sky. Lu Ao felt as if his own distant travels amounted to nothing, "I am like a grub to his swan. I have traveled all day and not moved an inch, yet I think it distant. How sad!" See the translation in Liu An, Queen et al., trans., 2010, 471–472.

69 The story of an immense fish turning into the equally large bird appears at the beginning of *Zhuangzi*.

70 Su Wu was an envoy to the Xiongnu during the reign (141–87 BCE) of Emperor Wu of the Han. He was held captive in the far north for many years before being released to return home. After his death he was honored for his loyalty.

71 Li Ling, a general under Emperor Wu, surrendered to the Xiongnu after his army was surrounded and his supplies were exhausted. He remained with the Xiongnu, married, and since the Emperor punished his betrayal by killing his entire family, found neither support nor reason to go home.

三月五日，起之東北。四旁遠有人煙，皆黑車白帳，隨水草放牧。盡原隰之地，無復寸木。四望唯黃雲白草。行不改途，又二十餘日，方見一沙河，西北流入陸局河。水濡馬腹，傍多叢柳。渡河北行三日，入小沙陀。

四月朔，至幹辰大王帳下。冰始泮，草微萌矣。時有婚嫁之會，五百里內首領，皆載馬湩助之。皂車、氈帳，成列數千。七日，見大王，問以延生事。師謂：「須齋戒而後可聞。」約以望日授受。至日，雪大作，遂已。大王復曰：「上遣使萬里，請師問道，我曷敢先焉。」且諭阿里鮮：「見畢東還，須奉師過此。」十七日，大王以牛馬百數、車十乘送行。

馬首西北，二十二日抵陸局河。積水成海，周數百里。風浪漂出大魚，蒙古人各得數尾。並河南岸西行，時有野薤得食。

五月朔亭午，日有食之。既，眾星乃見，須臾復明。時在河南岸（蝕自西南，生自東北）。其地朝涼而暮熱。草多黃花，水流東北。兩岸多高柳，蒙古人取之以造廬帳。

行十有六日，河勢遠西北山去，不得窮其源。西南接魚兒濼驛路，蒙古人喜曰：「年前已聞父師來。」因獻黍米石有五斗。師以斗棗酬之，渠喜曰：「未嘗見此物。」因舞謝而去。

72 Otegin's soothsayers apparently interpreted the snowfall as an omen of his inappropriate presumption and persuaded him to cancel the meeting.
73 They did not comply with his wish, but instead returned straight to Yanjing.
74 *Allium mongolicum.*

On the fifth day of the third month, we began traveling in a north-   1221.03.30
easterly direction. All around us we saw human habitation, nothing but
black carts and white tents and herders following the grass and water to
pasture their animals. When we passed out of the marshy plains, there
was not even the smallest tree or shrub. Only yellow dust clouds and
white grasses were in sight. Our route never shifted direction and it was
more than twenty days before we saw a sandy river flowing northwesterly
into the Luju (Kerulen) River. Its water came up to a horse's belly, and
tamarisks grew in dense thickets on the banks. Crossing the river and
proceeding north for three more days, we entered a small desert.^{xxxv}

On the first day of the fourth month, we arrived at the camp of Prince   1221.04.24
Otegin. The ice had begun to melt, and grass was just beginning to sprout.
A wedding celebration was in progress, and all the chiefs from five hundred *li* around had brought mare's milk to contribute to the festivities.
Black carts and felt tents stood arrayed in rows by the thousands. On
the seventh day the Master had an audience with the Prince, who asked   1221.05.01
about how to prolong life. The Master said, "It is necessary to fast and
cleanse oneself before one can hear about such things." They agreed that
the Master would instruct the Prince on the fifteenth day. When that   1221.05.16
day came, a great snow fell, so the meeting was canceled. The Prince
declared, "The Emperor sent an envoy such a great distance to invite
the Master to provide instruction in the Way. How dare I come before
him?"⁷² He also instructed Alixian, "Once the visit with Chinggis is
completed and you return east, you must accompany the Master back
here."⁷³ On the seventeenth day, the Prince supplied us with several
hundred head of horses and cattle, and ten carts to see us off. With the
horses' heads pointed northwest, we arrived on the twenty-second day   1221.05.23
at the Luju River, where the water collects to form a lake (Hulun Nur),
several hundred *li* in circumference. Windblown waves had thrown up
some large fish on the banks, and the Mongols each took several of
them. Following the south bank of the river, we proceeded westward,
and occasionally found wild onions to eat.⁷⁴

[Across the Mongolian Plateau to the Qatun's *Ordo*]   1221.05.23

On the first day of the fifth month, at midday, there was a full eclipse
of the sun,^{xxxvi} and the stars became visible. Soon the sunlight returned. At the time we were on the south bank of the *river; the eclipse*
swallowed the sun from the southwest and retreated from it to the northeast.
The land is cool in the mornings and becomes hot by sunset; yellow flowers dot the grass and tall willows grow on both banks of the
northeasterly flowing river. The Mongols use these willows to make
their tents.^{xxxvii}

又行十日，夏至。量日影三尺六七寸。漸見大山峭
拔，從此以西，漸有山阜。人煙頗衆，亦皆以黑車、白帳
爲家。其俗牧且獵，衣以韋毳，食以肉酪。男子結髮垂兩
耳。婦人冠以樺皮，高二尺許，往往以皂褐籠之，富者以
紅綃，其末如鵝鴨，名曰「故故。」大忌人觸，出入盧帳
須低回。俗無文籍，或約之以言，或刻木爲契。遇食同
享，難則爭赴。有命則不辭，有言則不易。有上古之遺風
焉。以詩敍其實云：

極目山川無盡頭，
風煙不斷水長流。
如何造物開天地，
到此令人放馬牛。
飲血茹毛同上古，
峨冠結髮異中州。
聖賢不得垂文化，
歷代縱橫只自由。

75 Because they had deviated to the east to visit Prince Otegin, they had earlier left this
main post road.
76 The fruit of the *Ziziphus jujuba* (*hongzao* 紅棗), sometimes called dates. See the Table
of Weights and Measurements in the front matter.
77 By using an eight-foot perpendicular pole to generate a shadow at high noon and
measuring the shadow, one could determine one's exact location.
78 On these hats (*boghtaq*), see Jackson 2009, 88–89, and Nugteren and Wilkens 2019.
The ends of the red silk resembles, one supposes, the blunt taper at the tails of these
fowl.
79 See the Introduction, p. xlii.

We traveled on another sixteen days. The river continued looping   1221.06.08
around the mountain to the northwest. We could not trace it to its source,
but to the southwest we reconnected with the Yu'erpo post road.[75] The
Mongols there greeted us happily, saying, "We heard last year that the
Master was coming." So, they offered us one *dan* and five *dou* of grain
(about 100 liters altogether), for which the Master returned the favor
with one *dou* of jujubes.[76] They were happy and said, "We've never seen
such things." After some elaborate rituals of thanks, they left.

We traveled on another ten days, and on the summer solstice, the sun's   1221.06.18
shadow measured three feet and six or seven inches.[77] Gradually a great
mountain, seemingly drawn up from the plains, came into view. Further
west, we began to encounter hills and increasing numbers of settlements,
all similarly composed of families with black carts and white tents. They
herd and hunt, clothe themselves in soft hides and down, and eat meat
and fermented milk (koumiss). The men wear their hair in two braids in
front or behind their ears. Women wear a hat made of birch bark, some
two feet high, usually covered with a black coarse material. The wealthy
use thin red silk. Its ends are like the tail of a goose or duck.[78] They call
it *gugu*. It is taboo to touch it. When entering and leaving the tent, they
must lower their heads and bend at the waist. By custom they have no
writing or records, and they make agreements and appointments orally
or cut a piece of wood to make tallies. When they find something to eat,
they share it, and in hardship they hasten to help each other. When they
receive an order, they do not shrink from it, and if they make a promise,
they never betray it. There is an air about them of the purer customs of
high antiquity. The Master composed a poem to narrate the facts:

[*17. "Traveling Again Along the Yu'erpo Post Road for Ten Days,
Relating the Facts in a Poem"*]

Endless mountains and streams as far as the eye can see,
Wind and mist without break, streams formed unceasingly.
Why, when the Shaper of Things formed Heaven and earth
And reached this place, did it make these people herd horses and
    cattle?
They drink blood and eat meat with the fur on, just as in high
    antiquity,
And wear high hats and braid their hair differently from the
    Central Regions.
Here sages and worthies were unable to pass down the
    transformative power of culture,
So through the ages these people have been free to do exactly as
    they please.[79]

又四程，西北渡河，乃平野。其旁山川皆秀麗，水草且豐美。東西有故城，基址若新，街衢、巷陌可辨，制作類中州。歲月無碑刻可考，或云契丹所建。既而地中得古瓦，上有契丹字。蓋遼亡，士馬不降者西行所建城邑也。又言西南至尋思干城，萬里外回紇國最佳處，契丹都焉，歷七帝。

六月十三日，至長松嶺後宿。松括森森，干雲蔽日，多生山陰澗道間，山陽極少。

十四日，過山度淺河。天極寒，雖壯者不可當。是夕宿平地。

十五日曉起，環帳皆薄冰。

十七日，宿嶺西。時初伏矣，朝暮亦有冰，霜已三降，河水有澌，冷如嚴冬。土人云：「常年五六月有雪，今歲幸晴暖。」師易其名曰大寒嶺。凡遇雨多雹。

山路盤曲，西北且百餘里。既而復西北，始見平地。有石河，長五十餘里，岸深十餘丈。其水清冷可愛，聲如鳴玉。峭壁之間有大葱，高三四尺。澗上有松，皆十餘丈。西山連延，上有喬松鬱然。山行五六日，峰迴路轉，林巒秀茂，下有溪水注焉。平地皆松樺雜木，若有人煙狀。

80 The bunching onions were *Allium fistulosum*.

We traveled another four stages, crossed the Tula River to the north-west, and at last entered open country. The mountains around the grass-land were all luxuriant and lovely, and water and grass were abundant and beautiful. On the east and west banks, we saw an old city, the foundations of which appeared as if newly built. One could easily discern both major streets and narrow lanes. The layout resembled that of cities in the Central Plain. No stone inscriptions existed that might disclose dates for the city. Some locals say the Liao built it, and indeed on a few old tiles retrieved from the ground, we found Liao (Kitan) script writing. It was probably constructed by soldiers who had abandoned the Liao on their westward journey.^{xxxviii} They also explained that, upon reaching Samarkand (Xunsigan) in the southwest, ten thousand *li* away, the Kitan made their capital in the finest place in Uyghur country and ruled there for the reigns of seven Emperors.^{xxxix}

On the thirteenth day of the sixth month, we lodged for the night on the far side of the Changsong (Long Pine) Range,^{xl} where thick stands of pine and juniper reach to the clouds and hide the sun. The trees grew profusely in the ravines on the north side of the mountain but were sparse on the mountain's southern flanks. On the fourteenth we passed over the mountains and crossed a shallow river. The weather became so cold that even the hardier among us could not bear it. That night we camped in the open country. Arising at dawn on the fifteenth, we discovered a thin layer of ice all around the tents. On the seventeenth day we camped on the west side of the range. Although it was the first day of the hottest thirty days of the year, it froze every morning and evening. Frosts had already blanketed the earth three times, and the water in the river was as cold as during a hard winter. The local people said, "Often there is snow in the fifth and sixth months. Luckily, this is a mild, warm year." The Master renamed it "Frigid Ridges." Whenever it rained, there was usually hail. The mountain paths wound tortuously to the northwest for over a hundred *li*.

Continuing further to the northwest, we finally reached level ground. There we came upon a stony-banked river of fifty or more *li*, with banks more than a hundred feet deep and delightfully pure, cold water that purled like the sound of jade ornaments. On the steep sides of the ravine grew bunching onions some three or four feet high, and the pines by the ravine were all over a hundred feet tall.⁸⁰ To the west the mountains continued one after another, densely blanketed with soaring pines. We traveled among the mountains for five or six days, the road turning to follow the curve of the peaks. The forested peaks were lush and luxuriant, and below them streams funneled down. Mixed pine and birch trees carpeted the plain, and we thought we discerned signs of human

1221.07.04

1221.07.05

1221.07.06
1221.07.08

尋登高嶺，勢若長虹，壁立千仞，俯視海子，淵深恐人。

二十八日，泊窩里朵之東。宣使先往奏稟皇后，奉旨請師渡河。其水東北流，泝漫没軸，絶流以濟。入營，駐車南岸，車帳千百。日以醍醐、湩酪爲供。漢、夏公主皆送寒具等食。黍米斗白金十兩。滿五十兩可易麵八十斤。蓋麵出陰山之後二千餘里，西域賈胡以橐馳負至也。中伏帳房無蠅。窩里朵，漢語行宮也。其車輿、亭帳，望之儼然。古之大單于未有若此之盛也。

七月九日，同宣使西南行五六日。屢見山上有雪，山下往往有墳墓。及升高陵，又有祀神之跡。又三二日歷一山，高峰如削，松杉鬱茂。西有海子，南出大峽，則一水西流。雜木叢映於水之陽，韭茂如芳草，夾道連數十里。北有故城曰曷剌肖。西南過沙場二十里許，水草極少，始見回紇決渠灌麥。

81　From these high prices for a scarce new commodity and other references, one may glimpse the emerging consumer culture and new tastes of Mongolian elites (see Allsen 2019).

82　The Xiongnu were an early nomadic confederation that had built an empire to the north of the Han dynasty in China from the third century BCE to the first century CE.

83　Japanese cedars, *Cryptomeria japonica*.

habitation. Then we ascended a high ridge in the shape of a long rain-
bow, its steep walls rising a thousand fathoms, so that looking down at
the lake from above, with a bird's eye view, it seemed an abyss so deep
that it terrified us.

On the twenty-eighth day, as we approached the *ordo* from the east,   1221.07.19
the Imperial Envoy went ahead to report the Master's arrival to the
Empress (*qatun*) and returned with her invitation to cross the river to
visit her camp.[xli] Its waters flow to the northeast, and it fully covered the
axles of our carts. We forded straight across the current. Upon entering
the encampment, we halted the carts on the southern bank. We saw
thousands of tents and carts supplying clarified butter, fermented mare's
milk, and yogurt to the *ordo* daily. The Han (Jin) and Xia princesses
(*qatuns* living in this *ordo*)[xlii] both sent us supplies of fried breads and
other foodstuffs, one *dou* of millet and ten *liang* of white silver. It takes
a full fifty *liang* of silver to purchase eighty *jin* of flour, evidently because
the flour is brought on camels to these parts from over two thousand *li*
beyond the Yinshan (Tian Shan) Range, by foreign (Hu) merchants of
the Western Regions.[81] Though we were in the hot season, there were no
flies in the tents. The word "*ordo*" means what we would call a "traveling
palace" in Chinese. The ancient rulers of the Xiongnu never had anything
as magnificent as these carriages and tent-pavilions.[82]

[To the City of Chinqai and into the Yinshan (Tian Shan) Range]

On the ninth day of the seventh month, the Imperial Envoy led us to-   1221.07.29
ward the southwest for five or six days, and on the way we frequently
sighted snow on the mountaintops and grave sites in the foothills below. When we finally ascended a high mound, we saw more traces of
sacrificial offerings. After several days we passed another mountain, its
high peaks as though pared by a knife, its pine trees and cedars lushly
verdant,[xliii] and there was a lake to the west.[83] Emerging south from a
great gorge, we found a river flowing westward, with thickets of assort-
ed trees growing on the northern bank.[84] Bunching onions, growing as
thick as green grass, lined both sides of our path for several dozen *li*. To
the north were the remnants of an old walled city called Helaxiao.[xliv]
To the southwest, after crossing a sandy field of about twenty *li*, where
water and vegetation were extremely scarce, we had our first sight of
Uyghurs, who were breaching a ditch to irrigate a field of barley.

---

84   Here the travelers emerged from the Khangai Range into the so-called Great Lakes
    Basin of western Mongolia, before entering the Altai Mountains west of it. See Atwood
    2020.

又五六日，踰嶺而南，至蒙古營宿。拂旦行，迤邐南山，望之有雪。因以詩記其行：

當時悉達悟空晴，
發軔初來燕子城
（撫州是也）。
北至大河三月數（即陸局河也，四月盡到，約二千餘里），
西臨積雪半年程（即此地也。山常有雪。東至陸局河約五千里，七月盡到）。
不能隱地迴風坐（道法有迴風、隱地、攀斗藏天之術），
卻使彌天逐日行。
行到水窮山盡處，
斜陽依舊向西傾。

郵人告曰：「此雪山北，是田鎮海八剌喝孫也。八剌喝孫，漢語為城。中有倉廩，故又呼曰倉頭。」

七月二十五日，有漢民工匠絡繹來迎，悉皆歡呼歸禮，以彩幡、華蓋、香花前導。又有章宗二妃，曰徒單氏、曰夾谷氏，及漢公主母欽聖夫人袁氏，號泣相迎，顧謂師曰：「昔日稔聞道德高風，恨不一見，不意此地有緣也。」

---

85 That is, Buddha's teachings came from the West, and Daoist teachings will now come from the East.

In another five or six days, we had passed over the range and headed ~1221.08.05–09 south, arriving at a Mongol camp, where we spent the night. At daybreak we set out. We could see snow on top of the mountains, which wound their way south. To record this trek, the Master composed a poem:

[18. "Recording This Portion of the Trip with a Poem"]

Back then Siddhartha Buddha achieved enlightenment,
And now we have set out, arriving first at Yinzicheng.[85]
That is, Fuzhou.
Northward for three months, we reached the Great River;
The Luju River. We all arrived at the end of the fourth month, after traveling some two thousand or more li.
To the west we looked down upon accumulated snows, a half-year's journey.
That is, to this place, where the mountains are frequently snow-covered. East to the Luju River is about five thousand li. We reached here at the end of the seventh month.
We cannot travel by sitting and practicing "Hiding in the Earth" or "Swirling Wind";
Daoist methods for spirit travel include the techniques of "Swirling Wind," "Hiding in the Earth," "Climbing on the Northern Dipper," and "Storing Away Heaven."[86]
But rather, day after day, we moved over Heaven's expanse.
Going to a place where rivers end and mountains cease,
While the setting sun, as always, tilted toward the west.

A courier reported to us, "North of this snowy mountain is the *Balahesun* of Tian Zhenhai (Chinqai's Balaghasun)."[xlv] *Balahesun* translates into Chinese as "city." Because it houses granaries, it is also called "Head Granary."

On the twenty-fifth day of the seventh month, a steady stream of 1221.08.14 Chinese artisans came to greet us, all happily calling out to us and giving us gifts. Wielding colored pennants, canopies, incense, and flowers, they led us into the city. There we also found two consorts of Jin Emperor Zhangzong (r. 1190–1208), Lady Tudan and Lady Jiagu, as well as Lady Qinsheng, Madame Yuan,[xlvi] mother of the Han (that is, Jin) Princess (whom we met previously). Madame Yuan wept loudly as they greeted us, then turned and said to the Master, "In the old days we were accustomed to hearing of your principled Daoist manner and regretted we never had any chance to meet you. Who could have guessed we were destined to see you here?"

---

86 All these being Daoist Inner Alchemy techniques for freeing the *hun* soul to wander outside of the body. See EOT 762–766, and EOT 766–772.

翌日，阿不罕山北鎮海來謁，師與之語曰：「吾壽已高，以皇帝二詔丁寧，不免遠行數千里方臨治下。沙漠中多不以耕耘爲務，喜見此間秋稼已成。余欲於此過冬，以待鑾輿之迴，何如。」宣使曰：「父師既有法旨，仲祿不敢可否。惟鎮海相公度之。」公曰：「近有勑：『諸處官員如遇真人經過，無得稽其程。』蓋欲速見之也。父師若需於此，則罪在鎮海矣。願親從行，凡師之所用，敢不備？」

師曰：「因緣如此，當卜日行。」

公曰：「前有大山高峻，廣澤沮陷，非車行地。宜減車從，輕騎以進。」用其言，留門弟子宋道安輩九人，選地爲觀。人不召而至，壯者効其力，匠者効其技，富者施其財。聖堂方丈，東廚西廡，左右雲房（無瓦，皆土木），不一月落成，榜曰棲霞觀。

時稷黍在地。八月初，霜降，居人促收麥，霜故也。大風傍北山西來，黃沙蔽天，不相物色。師以詩自嘆云：

丘也東西南北人，
從來失道走風塵。

The next day, from north of the Abuhan Mountains,^{xlvii} Chinqai arrived to pay respects to the Master. The Master told him, "In spite of my advanced age, the Emperor has sent me two edicts insisting on my presence. So I had perforce to travel over several thousand *li* to reach your domain. There are very few people farming in the desert, so it gladdens me to see the autumn crops ready for harvest here. I would like to pass the winter at this spot and wait for the imperial carriage to return. Would that be possible?"

The Imperial Envoy said, "Once the revered Master has received an imperial directive, I, Zhonglu, dare not make the decision of what is or is not permissible. Only Minister Chinqai can make that decision." His Excellency Chinqai then explained, "Recently there came an imperial command with the instruction 'Officials in all places through which the Perfected is passing must not in any way delay his journey.' The Emperor wishes to meet with you at the earliest opportunity, and if you insist upon stopping here, then I will bear the blame. Rest assured that I am ready and willing to accompany you in person from now on and dare not shirk from providing for all your needs and wants."

The Master replied, "Since it is thus fated, we should augur a propitious day to start our journey." His Excellency responded, "Ahead lie great mountain ranges with high peaks and expansive marshes in which it is easy to get bogged down; it is not a route fit for carts or carriages. It would be best to reduce the number of the carts in the retinue and proceed ahead on lightly loaded mounts." Following this advice, the Master left behind his disciples Song Dao'an and eight others to select a site to build a monastery.^{xlviii} People volunteered their help; sturdy laborers exerted their strength, artisans exhausted their skills, and the wealthy donated their riches. The sages' hall and abbot's chamber, a kitchen on the east and veranda on the west, and cells for monks *(not tiled, all made of mud and wood)* on either side, were all completed in under a month. The inscribed tablet over the front entrance read "Qixia Monastery."^{xlix}

At that time the millet crop was still in the ground.^l Frost fell at the beginning of the eighth month, and the inhabitants hastened to harvest the barley because of the frost. A fierce wind blew out of the west, skirting the northern mountains, and yellow sand blocked out the sky; one could not make out the shape of objects. The Master penned a poem to lament his own state:

[19. "Sighing over My Life"]

I, Qiu, am a person who has gone in every direction,
And having lost the way, I am now running through the wind and
    dust.[87]

不堪白髮垂垂老，
又踏黃沙遠遠巡。
未死且令觀世界，
殘生無分樂天真。
四山五嶽都遊遍，
八表飛騰後入神。

八日，攜門人虛靜先生趙九古輩十人，從以二車、蒙古驛騎二十餘，傍大山西行。宣使劉公、鎮海相公又百騎。李家奴，鎮海從者也，因曰：「前此山下精截我腦後髮，我甚恐。」鎮海亦云：「乃滿國王亦曾在此爲山精所惑，食以佳饌。」師默而不答。

西南約行三日，復東南過大山，經大峽。中秋日，抵金山東北。少駐，復南行。其山高大，深谷長坂，車不可行。三太子出軍，始闢其路。乃命百騎挽繩縣轅以上，縛輪以下。約行四程，連度三嶺。南出山前，臨河止泊。從官連幕爲營。因水草便，以待鋪牛、驛騎，數日乃行。有詩三絕云：

八月涼風爽氣清，
那堪日暮碧天晴。
欲吟勝槩無才思，
空對金山皓月明。

---

88 Originally the four mountains of Buddhist lore: The Mountain of Aging, the Mountain of Illness, the Mountain of Death, and the Mountain of Senility; that is, all the stages of human decline. The Five Marchmounts are the sacred mountains of China. Here Qiu remarks that he has thought about his old age and traveled to the spiritual sites in China, but a true spiritual state lies beyond the mortal realm.

89 Li Jianu's name literally means Li the house servant.

I cannot bear being so old that my white hair hangs down,
Yet I still must tread across yellow sands to journey afar.
Before I die, let me briefly observe time and space,
Since in my last years I am not fated to enjoy the harmony of
   Heaven.
I have explored all the Four Mountains and the Five
   Marchmounts,[88]
But only after I fly beyond the world itself will I enter a spiritual state.

On the eighth day of the eighth month, taking along the disciple Zhao   1221.08.26
Jiugu[li] and ten others, we skirted the mountains to the west, traveling
with two carts in tow and more than twenty Mongol mounted couriers.
Imperial Envoy Liu, Minister Chinqai, and a hundred riders all accompanied us. Li Jianu, who was in Chinqai's service, subsequently related to
us, "Once, a wight at the base of this mountain cut the hair off the back
of my head, terrifying me."[89] Chinqai also said, "The king of the Naiman
country was once beguiled by mountain wights here, and he fed them
the finest food that he had." The Master fell silent and did not respond.

We traveled about three days to the southwest, and then heading
southeast we crossed a great mountain and passed a large gorge. On
the day of Mid-Autumn (the fifteenth of the eighth lunar month), we   1221.09.02
reached the northeast side of the Jinshan (Altai) Mountains and stopped
for a while before going on southward. These mountains are high and
massive, with deep valleys and long slopes that make them impassable for
carts. The army of the Third Prince (Chinggis Qan's third son, Ögödei)
first opened these passes when he went west. Our mounted escorts were
ordered to attach ropes to the shafts of the carts to pull them up the
slopes and tie the wheels tightly when letting them down. We traveled
for about four stages and crossed three ranges in succession, emerging
finally from south of the mountain and stopping on the banks of a river.[lii]
The retinue attendants set up tents in a continuous row to form a camp.
Because water and grass were right at hand, we waited several days to
take proper care of the oxen and post-station mounts before leaving. After
several days we set out, and the Master composed three short poems:

[20. "Three Quatrains" I]

Autumn winds in the eighth month are brisk and fresh,
But are no match for the clarity of the azure void at night.
I want to chant about this beautiful realm, but lacking the talent
   and inspiration,
I simply face the pure white moonlight on the Jinshan (Altai) Range.

其二云：

金山南面大河流，
河曲盤桓賞素秋。
秋水暮天山月上，
清吟獨嘯夜光毯。

其三云：

金山雖大不孤高，
四面長拖拽腳牢。
橫截大山心腹樹，
干雲蔽日競呼號。

　　渡河而南，前經小山，石雜五色。其旁草木不生，首
尾七十里。復有二紅山當路。又三十里，醎鹵地，中有
一小沙井，因駐程挹水爲食。傍有青草，多爲羊馬踐履。
宣使與鎮海議曰：「此地最難行處，相公如何則可？」公
曰：「此地我知之久矣。」同往謁師，公曰：「前至白骨
甸，地皆黑石。約行二百餘里，達沙陁。北邊頗有水草。
更涉大沙陁百餘里，東西廣袤，不知其幾千里。及回紇
城方得水草。」師曰：「何謂白骨甸？」公曰：「古之戰
場。凡疲兵至此，十無一還，死地也。頃者乃滿大勢亦敗
于是。遇天晴晝行，人馬往往困斃，唯暮起夜度，可過
其半。明日向午得及水草矣。少憩，俟晡時即行。當度
沙嶺百餘，若舟行巨浪然。又明日辰巳間，得達彼城矣。

90 In the cardinal direction alignment of the Five Phases, autumn is associated with the
west, metal, death's onset, and the color white.
91 QXYJ05 71, n. 18, sees the last two lines as a personification of the trees, which "howl"
in distress at their deaths (that is, make the sounds large trees make as they are felled
to make bridges). But the text does not mention trees being felled, so "howl in the
wind" could refer just to the sound of strong winds blowing through the forest.
92 This was probably the Gurbantünggüt Desert north of Qitai, in Xinjiang.
93 A military term for being trapped in a place from which there is no escape.
94 This happened in 1204.

[21. "Three Quatrains" II]

A great river flows from the southern face of the Jinshan (Altai)
    Mountains,
And I linger by the river's bends to enjoy the white autumn.[90]
A mountain moon rises above autumnal waters into dusking skies:
A lone whistle, solitary chanting, a shining orb in the night.

[22. "Three Quatrains" III]

The Jinshan (Altai) peaks are massive, not just lofty;
They stretch out on four sides to pull the foothills tight.
Trees cut across the belly and heart of the great mountains,
Jutting into the clouds and blocking the sun as they howl in the
    wind.[91]

We forded the river and went south, crossing over a hill with varie-
gated rocks. For seventy *li* or so, neither grass nor shrubs grew.[liii] Then
two reddish mountains stood in our path.[liv] Another thirty *li* on, in a
salty wasteland we came upon a small well in the sand, so we stopped
to draw water and prepare a meal. Nearby was a stretch of green grass
that had been well trampled by sheep and horses.

The Imperial Envoy deliberated with Chinqai, saying, "This place is
the most difficult part of the journey. What does the Minister advise?"
His Excellency Chinqai replied, "I have long been familiar with this land."
When they went to consult with the Master, His Excellency explained,
"Ahead we will come to the Plain of White Bones, where the earth is all
black stone. After another two hundred *li* we will arrive at the northern
edge of the desert, which has plenty of water and grass.[92] Still further on
we will cross about one hundred *li* of a large desert, so wide from east
to west that no one knows how many thousand *li* it is. Then, only upon
reaching a Uyghur city will we find grass and water." The Master asked,
"Why is it called the Plain of White Bones?" Minister Chinqai replied,
"It is an ancient battlefield. When the exhausted soldiers reached it, not
even one in ten could make it back home. It is a site of death.[93] Not long
ago, Chinggis's army defeated the main forces of the Naiman here.[94]
Should a crossing be attempted by day in clear weather, men and horses
often end up dying. Only by setting out after sundown and crossing at
night will we be able to make it more than halfway. Toward noon the
next day, we will reach water and grass. Let us rest for a bit, and we will
set out immediately after our evening meal. We will be crossing over
more than a hundred sand dunes, which will be just like a boat plowing
through billowing waves. And the next morning before noon, we will

夜行良便，但恐天氣黯黑，魑魅魍魎爲祟，我輩常塗血馬首以厭之。」

師乃笑曰：「邪精妖鬼，逢正人遠避。書傳所載，其孰不知？道人家何憂此事？」日暮遂行。牛乏，皆道弃之，馭以六馬，自爾不復用牛矣。

初在沙陁北，南望天際若銀霞。問之左右，皆未詳。師曰：「多是陰山。」翌日，過沙陁，遇郊者，再問之，皆曰：「然。」於是途中作詩云：

高如雲氣白如沙，
遠望那知是眼花。
漸見山頭堆玉屑，
遠觀日腳射銀霞。
橫空一字長千里，
照地連城及萬家。
從古至今常不壞，
吟詩寫向直南誇。

八月二十七日，抵陰山後。回紇郊迎，至小城北，酋長設蒲萄酒及名果、大餅、渾葱。裂波斯布，人一尺。乃言曰：「此陰山前三百里和州也。其地大熱，蒲萄至夥。」

翌日，沿川西行。

---

95 The flatbreads, which we know as naan bread (in Chinese, *nang* 饢), are still a staple of Uyghur cuisine.

arrive at the town. Traveling at night is convenient all around, but I fear that wights and sprites will attempt to bring disaster upon us. Our practice normally is to smear blood on our horses' heads to subdue them."

At that the Master laughed and replied, "Evil spirits and demonic ghosts will keep away when they come upon an upright person. This is recorded in books, and everyone knows it. Why should a man of the Way be anxious about such things?"

At sundown we set out. The oxen were exhausted, so we abandoned them on the road and made do with a team of six horses. From here on out we did not use oxen again. Looking south as we entered the desert from the north, the horizon appeared as a silvery sunset glow. I inquired about this from those around us, but none were clear about it. The Master then said, "It is probably the Yinshan (Tian Shan) Range."[lv] The next day after crossing the desert, we encountered inhabitants on the town's outskirts and asked again. They all said, "That's correct." The Master wrote a poem about it en route:

[23. "Written on the Road While Passing Through a Desert"]

High like cloudy vapors, white like sand,
As we gazed from afar, it seemed that our vision was blurred.
Gradually we saw the mountaintops, piled with chips of jade.
From afar we observed sunbeams shooting through the silvery
    clouds.
Cutting a thousand *li* across the sky in a straight line,
The mountains shine on the ground and link together cities and
    ten thousand homes.
For time immemorial they have never known harm.
I composed a poem, then, to sketch their wonders for southerners
    back home.

[Through the Yinshan (Tian Shan) Range to Samarkand and the Imperial Camp]

On the twenty-seventh day of the eighth month, we arrived at the Yinshan (Tian Shan) Range, and residents in the outskirts of the Uyghur city there came to greet us. When we got to the north side of the small city,[lvi] the local chief laid out grape wine and fine fruits, large flatbreads, and Uyghur onions, as well as a foot-long piece of Persian cloth for each person in our party.[95] People told us, "Three hundred *li* from this point in the Yinshan (Tian Shan) Range lies the town of Hezhou (Qocho, Gaochang).[lvii] The land there is very hot, and grapes are exceedingly abundant." The next day we proceeded west following a plain and passed

1221.09.14

歷二小城，皆有居人。時禾麥初熟，皆賴泉水澆灌得有，秋少雨故也。西即鼈思馬大城，王官、士庶、僧道數百，具威儀遠迎。僧皆赭衣，道士衣冠與中國特異。泊于城西蒲萄園之上閣。時回紇王部族勸蒲萄酒，供以異花、雜果、名香。且列侏儒伎樂，皆中州人。

士庶日益敬。侍坐者有僧、道、儒。因問風俗，乃曰：「此大唐時北庭端府。景龍三年，楊公何爲大都護，有德政，諸夷心服，惠及後人，于今賴之。有龍興西寺二石刻在，功德煥然可觀。寺有佛書一藏。唐之邊城往往尚存。其東數百里有府曰西凉。其西三百餘里有縣曰輪臺。」

師問曰：「更幾程得至行在？」皆曰：「西南更行萬餘里即是。」

其夜風雨作，園外有大樹，復出一篇示衆云：

夜宿陰山下，
陰山夜寂寥。
長空雲黯黯，
大樹葉蕭蕭。
萬里途程遠，
三冬氣候韶。
全身都放下，
一任斷蓬飄。

96 The king, or Idiqut, was himself away campaigning with the Mongols in Central Asia.

two small towns, both inhabited. The grain crops were just ripening. Everything relied upon spring-water irrigation because there is so little rainfall in autumn.

West of these two cities was the large town of Besh-Baliq.^lviii People by the hundreds—king's officials, scholars, commoners, Buddhists, and Daoists—came far out of the city to greet us in a most solemn and impressive manner. The Buddhists all wore dark reddish-brown robes, while the garb of the Daoists differed markedly from that worn in the Central Lands. We stayed on the upper floor of a pavilion in a vineyard west of town, where the Uyghur king's family refreshed us with grape wine and offered rare flowers, various fruits, and choice incense.^96 We were also entertained by actors, dwarfs, and female dancers, all from the Central Lands.

The local inhabitants grew more solicitous each day, and among those in attendance were Buddhists, Daoists, and classical scholars, so we asked them about the local customs. They told us, "This was the Tang-period Beiting Protectorate. In the third year of the Jinglong era [709], His Excellency Yang He^lix was the protector general. His governance was just, and all the barbarians willingly submitted. The legacy of his benevolence has carried on for generations, and it serves us even to this day. In the Longxing West Monastery there are two early inscribed stelae still extant that verify the transformative nature of his virtuous accomplishments. The temple also houses a set of Buddhist scriptures. Many frontier towns of the Tang period remain. Several hundred *li* east of here is a prefecture called Xiliang. Some three hundred *li* west of here is a county called Luntai."^lx

The Master asked, "How many more stages lie between here and the imperial camp?" They all replied, "It's another ten thousand or more *li* to the southwest."

That evening a wind whipped up, and it rained. Beyond the vineyard stood a large tree, prompting the Master to compose another verse to share with his followers:

[24. "A Rainstorm at Night, a Large Tree outside the Garden: Another Piece for the Group"]

We overnighted at the Yinshan (Tian Shan) Range,
Where the nights are desolate and silent.
Clouds in the vast emptiness are dun and dark;
Leaves on the great trees sough and murmur.
A journey of ten thousand *li* is so far
That the wintertime climate here feels like the warmth of spring,
All notion of perfecting the self is abandoned;
Let it drift like a rootless tumbleweed.

九月二日西行，四日宿輪臺之東。迭屑頭目來迎。南
望陰山，三峰突兀倚天。因述詩贈書生李伯祥，生相人。
詩云：

三峰並起插雲寒，
四壁橫陳遶澗盤。
雪嶺界天人不到，
冰池耀日俗難觀（人云，向此冰池之間觀看則魂識昏昧）。
巖深可避刀兵害（其巖險固，逢亂世堅守，則得免其難），
水衆能滋稼穡軋（下有泉源，可以灌溉田禾，每歲秋成）。
名鎮北方為第一，
無人寫向畫圖看。

又歷二城，重九日，至回紇昌八剌城。其王畏午兒與
鎮海有舊，率諸部族及回紇僧皆遠迎。既入，齋于臺上。
洎其夫人勸蒲萄酒，且獻西瓜。其重及秤，甘瓜如枕許，
其香味蓋中國未有也。園蔬同中區。有僧來侍坐正使譯者
問：「看何經典？」僧云：「剃度受戒，禮佛為師。」蓋此
以東昔屬唐故。西去無僧道，回紇但禮西方耳。

97   These three Bogda peaks make up the western portion of the Tian Shan.
98   The image is that of a basin that collects rivulets of snowmelt from the mountain
     peaks.
99   The vocabulary of this last couplet suggests that the mountain has a prominence that
     merits it a place of honor. The couplet draws a subtle comparison with paintings in
     the Lingyan Gallery of twenty-four famous men who helped the founding emperor
     of the Tang establish his state. What we have translated above as "surpasses" literally
     means "to squash down" or "suppress."
100 The author seems to read the transliteration *weiwu'er* 維吾爾 as a name here, rather
     than as a variant transcription for Uyghur (usually transcribed in the text as *huihe*
     回紇).
101 The melons described here may refer to a cultivar originally from the Xinjiang region
     called the Hami melon (similar to cantaloupe).

On the second day of the ninth month we traveled on to the west,
finally lodging four days later east of Luntai. The head of the Tarsa (Christians)[lxi] came out to greet us. Looking south at the Yinshan (Tian Shan)
mountains, one could see three peaks towering loftily against the sky.[lxii]
The Master took this opportunity to write a poem to give to the scholar
Li Boxiang, who was from Xiangzhou, Henan. The poem reads,

[25. "For the Student Li Boxiang"]

Three alps rise and in a line pierce the cloudy cold;[97]
Four scarps, faces unbroken, coil around a basin of rivulets.[98]
Snowy ranges delimit a Heaven no man can reach;
Glaciers of ice shine in the sun and are hard to look at.
> *People say, "If you stare at these glaciers, then your soul and consciousness will be befud-
> dled and blinded."*

The cliffs are so deep that they offer escape of injury from knife or
sword;
> *The cliffs are so impenetrable that they can be clung to in times of chaos to escape difficulty.*

The streams are bountiful, irrigating the dry land that people can
sow and reap.
> *There are artesian sources, so it is possible to irrigate fields and crops, giving a full harvest
> every year.*

Its fame surpasses all in the Northern regions, and it is clearly first
among all,
But no one has depicted its likeness in a painting or sketch.[99]

We passed two other towns, and on the day of the Double Ninth
we reached the Uyghur city of Changbala (Jambaliq).[lxiii] The ruler,
Weiwu'er, and Chinqai are old acquaintances; he led the various tribes
people and all the Uyghur monks far out of the city to greet us.[100] After we entered the town, they prepared a banquet for us on the upper
floor of a pavilion. His wife encouraged us to drink wine and offered us
muskmelons, sweet, too heavy for the scale, and as big as pillows, with a
fragrance and flavor unknown in the Central Lands.[101] The garden vegetables, however, do resemble those in the Central Lands. A monk came to
sit in attendance upon us, and we had the translator ask, "What dharma
scriptures have you read?" The monk responded, "I have received the
tonsure and taken precepts, and I revere Buddha as my teacher." This
must be because this and areas to its east were once under Tang rule.
West of here there are no Buddhists or Daoists, and the Uyghurs pray
only to the West.[102]

102   That is, toward Mecca as followers of Islam.

翌日，並陰山而西。約十程，又度沙場。其沙細，遇風則流，狀如驚濤，乍聚乍散，寸草不萌。車陷馬滯，一晝夜方出。蓋白骨甸大沙分流也。

南際陰山之麓。踰沙，又五日，宿陰山北。詰朝，南行長坂七八十里，抵暮乃宿。天甚寒，且無水。晨起，西南行約二十里，忽有大池，方圓幾二百里。雪峰環之，倒影池中。師名之曰天池。

泑池正南下，左右峰巒峭拔，松樺陰森，高踰百尺。自巔及麓，何啻萬株。眾流入峽，奔騰洶湧，曲折灣環，可六、七十里。

二太子扈從西征，始鑿石理道，刊木爲四十八橋，橋可並車。薄暮宿峽中。翌日方出，入東西大川。水草豐秀，天氣似春，稍有桑棗。

次及一程。

九月二十七日至阿里馬城。鋪速滿國王暨蒙古荅剌忽只領諸部人來迎。宿於西果園。土人呼果爲阿里馬，蓋多果實，以是名其城。其地出帛，目曰「禿鹿麻」，蓋俗所謂種羊毛織成者。時得七束，爲禦寒衣。其毛類中國柳花，鮮潔細軟，可爲線、爲繩、爲帛、爲綿。農者亦決渠灌田，土人唯以瓶取水，戴而歸。及見中原汲器，喜曰：「桃花石諸事皆巧。」「桃花石」，謂漢人也。

---

103 The great majority of these bridges endured up to the Qing dynasty (QXYJ03 128, n. C7), and as suggested on the return journey, "the forty-eight-bridge section" seems to have become an informal designation of this familiar geographical zone.

104 The ruler of Almaliq, Siqnaq Tegin, was out campaigning with Chinggis Qan, so this person would probably have been his heir or some other relative. See Juvaynī 1997, 82.

105 The transcription *tuluma* most likely refers to cotton (*tolima*). See the discussion in Pelliot 1959, 514–515.

The next morning, we headed west following the Yinshan (Tian Shan) Range and traveled for ten stages, crossing another desert.[lxiv] The sand was fine and drifted with the wind like frightening waves, quickly gathering and just as quickly dispersing, and not a single blade of grass sprouted in it. The carts sank into it and the horses were brought to a standstill. It was one whole day and night before we got out of the sand. This must be a branch of the great desert by the Plain of White Bones, stretching all the way to the foot of the Yinshan (Tian Shan) in the south. It was another five days of desert before we camped overnight north of the Yinshan (Tian Shan). On the following morning we marched south down a long mountain slope for seventy or eighty *li*, making camp only as night began to fall. The weather was extremely cold, and there was no water. Arising at daybreak, we traveled southwest for about twenty *li*, suddenly coming upon a great lake about two hundred *li* in circumference.[lxv] It was surrounded by snowy peaks, which reflected in the lake's water. The Master named it "Heavenly Lake." Following the lake, we proceeded due south downhill. All around us towered steep tors and peaks, and a dense dark forest of innumerable pine and birch trees over a hundred feet tall ran from the mountains to the foothills. Countless streams tumbled into gorges, rushing in surging turbulence, bending and twisting, winding and turning back on themselves for sixty or more *li*.

The Second Imperial Prince (Chaghadai, Chinggis's second son), who accompanied the campaign to the west, was the first to gouge out a path through the rocks, felling trees to make forty-eight bridges, wide enough to permit two carts to cross side by side.[103] At dusk we camped in a gorge, and just as we were emerging from it the next day, we entered a great river valley stretching east to west, with abundant grass and water. The weather was spring-like, and we spotted a few mulberry and jujube trees. We stopped to put things in order, then went on a stage further.

On the twenty-seventh day of the ninth month, we arrived at the town of Almaliq.[lxvi] The Muslim prince and Mongol imperial agent (*darughachi*) led all sorts of people out to meet us.[104] They lodged us in an orchard on the west side of town. The local word for the crab apple is *alma*,[lxvii] from which the town acquired its name, owing to the abundance of this fruit. Silk is produced here; the kind called *turma* is probably woven from what is popularly called "sheep wool planted in the earth."[105] We acquired seven bundles to make warm clothing. The hairs are pure, fine, and soft, resembling the willow catkins of the Central Lands, and they can be spun into thread or ropes, or woven into cloth or padding. The farmers also dig canals to irrigate their fields, but local inhabitants only use pitchers to scoop water and carry it back on their heads. When they saw our water-drawing implements from the Central Plain, they all exclaimed, "The Tabgach are so clever in all they do!" *Tabgach* is a term that refers to Han people.[lxviii]

1221.10.06

1221.10.14

師自金山至此，以詩記其行云：

金山東畔陰山西，
千巖萬壑攢深溪。
溪邊亂石當道臥，
古今不許通輪蹄。
前年軍興二太子，
修道架橋徹溪水（三太子修金山，二太子修陰山）。
今年吾道欲西行，
車馬喧闐復經此。

銀山鐵壁千萬重，
爭頭競角誇清雄。
日出下觀滄海近，
月明上與天河通。

參天松如筆管直，
森森動有百餘尺。
萬株相倚鬱蒼蒼，
一鳥不鳴空寂寂。

羊腸孟門壓太行，
比斯大略猶尋常。
雙車上下苦敦攦，
百騎前後多驚惶。
天池海在山頭上，
百里鏡空含萬象。
縣車束馬西下山，
四十八橋低萬丈。

106 Vertical spacing within the poem signals units grouped by different rhymes.

Having arrived from the Jinshan (Altai) Mountains to this spot, the Master composed a verse to record the journey:

[26. "A Poem to Record the Journey from the Jinshan (Altai) Mountains to the City of Almaliq"][106]

East of the Jinshan (Altai) Mountains and west of the Yinshan
   (Tian Shan),
A thousand cliffs and ten thousand valleys collect deep streams.
Jumbles of rocks on the stream banks block the road,
Hindering wheel and hoof from time immemorial.
Two years ago, as the campaign began, the two Princes[107]
Improved the roads and built bridges over the streams.
The Third Prince worked on the Jinshan (Altai); the Second Prince on Yinshan (Tian
   Shan).
This year, our Way was to venture to the West,
And the clamor of cart and horse once again came through.

Countless silver mountains and iron cliffs in layers,
Head-to-head and horn-to-horn, showed off their pure power.
As the sun appeared, we gazed down and an azure sea seemed near,
The moon grew brighter as above it merged into the Milky Way.

Pines that reached to the heavens were as straight as brushes,[108]
Thick and luxuriant, all a hundred feet tall or more.
Ten thousand trees leaned against each other, overwhelmingly green,
Not a single bird called in the empty silent stillness.

Sheep's Entrails and Meng Gate dominate the Taihang,[109]
Yet seem ordinary compared to here.
Paired carts going up or down risk toppling and
Often alarm the hundred horsemen in front and back.
The Heavenly Lake sits on top of the mountains,
A hundred-*li* mirror of emptiness, holding the myriad images.
Carts were suspended and horses were hobbled as they descended
   to the west;
Forty-eight bridges spanned drops of a hundred thousand feet.

---

107 Chaghadai and Ögödei.

108 Chinese writing brushes were made of a long shaft with a small amount of rabbit hair at the end.

109 Sheep's Entrails: a mountain that twists and turns like the entrails of a sheep, located in Shanxi. Meng Gate: a pass across the Taihang Mountains, whose location is a matter of debate.

河南海北山無窮，
千變萬化規模同。
未若茲山太奇絶，
磊落峭拔加神功。

我來時當八九月，
半山已上皆爲雪。
山前草木暖如春，
山後衣衾冷如鐵。

連日所供勝前。又西行四日，至荅剌速没輦（没輦，河也）。水勢深闊，抵西北，流從東來，截斷陰山。河南復是雪山。

十月二日，乘舟以濟。南下至一大山，北有一小城。又西行五日，宣使以師奉詔來，去行在漸邇，先往馳奏。獨鎮海公從師。西行七日，度西南一山。逢東夏使迴，禮師於帳前，因問來自何時。使者曰：「自七月十二日辭朝。帝將兵追筭端汗至印度。」

明日遇大雪，至回紇小城。雪盈尺，日出即消。

十有六日，西南遇板橋渡河。晚至南山下，即大石林牙（大石，學士林牙小名）。其國王遼後也。自金師破遼，大石林牙領眾數千走西北，移徙十餘年，方至此地。其風土、氣候與金山以北不同。平地頗多，以農桑爲務，釀薄蒲萄爲酒，果實與中國同。

---

110 Over the Chu River, where the Qara Khitai capital of Balasaghun lay, founded by Yelü Dashi, the "realm of Dashi Linya."

Endless mountains run from south of the Yellow River to the
    steppes in the north,
But their transformations follow the same pattern.
They are no match for the extraordinary singularity of this
    range—
Stacked in a jumble, drawn up high, seemingly the result of divine
    labor.

I came here in the eighth and ninth month,
And snow covered more than halfway down their peaks.
In front of the mountains, shrubs and trees were as warm as spring,
But behind them, our clothes and comforters were as cold as iron.

For several days we were supplied far better than before, and again we proceeded westward for another four days and arrived at Talas *monian (monian means river).*[lxix] The water is deep and wide; it flows on toward the northwest, coming from the east, cutting through the Yinshan (Tian Shan) Range. There are more snow-capped mountains south of the river. On the second day of the tenth month, we crossed the river by boat and then proceeded southward to a large mountain, on the north side of which was a small city. We proceeded on another five days. Because the Master had received an edict, and since we were getting ever closer to the Temporary Palace, Imperial Envoy Liu raced ahead to make a formal report. Only Chinqai remained to escort the Master. We traveled seven more days toward the west, crossing a mountain to the southwest, where we encountered an envoy from Eastern Xia returning from an audience with the Emperor.[lxx] He paid homage at the Master's tent. Asked when he had begun his return journey, the envoy replied, "I left the court on the twelfth day of the seventh month, just as the Emperor was about to pursue the Sultan-qan (of Khwarazm) to India."[lxxi]

    The next day a great snow fell, and we came to a small Uyghur town. The snow was a foot deep, but it melted as soon as the sun came out. On the sixteenth day, traveling southwest we crossed over a river on a wooden plank bridge.[110] Toward evening we arrived at the foot of the Nanshan. This is the realm of Dashi Linya *(Dashi means scholar; Linya was his personal name).*[lxxii] The rulers of the country were descendants of the Liao royal family. When the Jin destroyed Liao, Dashi Linya led thousands of troops to the northwest and finally reached this spot after more than a decade. The terrain and climate here are different from that north of the Jinshan (Altai). Level plains abound, sericulture and farming are regular occupations, grapes are fermented to make wine, and the fruits and nuts are the same as in the Central Lands.

1221.10.18

1221.10.23

1221.10.30

1221.08.01

1221.11.01

惟經夏秋無雨，皆疏河灌溉，百穀用成。東北西南，左山右川，延袤萬里，傳國幾百年。

乃滿失國，依大石士馬復振，盜據其土，繼而篝端西削其地。天兵至，乃滿尋滅，篝端亦亡。

又聞前路多阻，適壞一車，遂留之。

十有八日，沿山而西。七、八日，山忽南去，一石城當途。石色盡赤，有駐軍古跡。西有大塚，若斗星相聯。又渡石橋，並西山行五程，至塞藍城，有小塔。回紇王來迎入館。

十一月初，連日雨大作。四日，土人以爲年，旁午相賀。是日，虛靜先生趙九古語尹公曰：「我隨師在宣德時，覺有長徃之兆，頗倦行役。嘗蒙師訓『道人不以死生動心，不以苦樂介懷，所適無不可。』今歸期將至，公等善事父師。」數日示疾而逝，蓋十一月五日也。

師命門弟子葬九古于郭東原上。

111　Perhaps the Akyrtas site near Taraz, Kazakhstan. The walls, now in ruins, were built with large blocks of dark red stone. See Lin Meicun 2016, 47.

112　Sairam City: a city east of present-day Shymkent, Kazakhstan. In Perso-Arabic, the name, also written as "Sayram," means "white water." See YS 63.1571. The pagoda was more likely a minaret. The traveler Liu Yu wrote in 1259 that all "Uyghurs" (Huihe) worshiped there. See Chen Dezhi 2015, 86. A tenth-century brick minaret still stands in Sairam.

113　This ruler and his subjects were probably Muslim Turks (Qangli, Qipchak), also allied with the Mongols. *Journey to the West* generally refers to all Central Asians as Uyghurs.

Since there is no rain in summer or fall, they channel river water for irrigation to ripen their crops. Their land is surrounded by mountains to the east and river valleys to the west, and encompasses more than ten thousand *li*. Their dynasty lasted several hundred years.

When the Naimans lost their state to the Mongols, they relied upon Dashi to rebuild their army; they then seized and occupied the lands of Dashi (Qara Khitai).[lxxiii] Later on, the Sultan (Khwarazm-shah) nibbled away their territory on the west. When the Heavenly (Mongol) Army arrived, the Naimans were extinguished, and the kingdom of the Sultan was also destroyed.

We heard that the road ahead had many obstacles. It so happened that one of our carts was ruined, so we left it behind. On the eighteenth day we followed the mountains westward. In seven or eight days the mountains abruptly turned south, and we encountered a walled city built entirely of red stone that held control of the road, and there were signs of an old military garrison.[111] Large tomb mounds on the western side were linked together in the shape of the Big Dipper. We crossed a bridge also of stone and followed the mountains southwest for five stages, arriving at Sairam City, where there is a small pagoda.[112] The Uyghur ruler invited us to lodge there.[113]

In the beginning of the eleventh month, it rained hard for days on end. On the fourth day the locals marked the New Year and celebrated with each other around noon.[114] That day, Master Xujing, Zhao Jiugu, said to Yin Zhiping, "When I reached Xuande as part of the Master's company, I became aware of the portents of my final 'long journey.' I am worn out by this mission. But I have received the Master's instruction that men of the Way are unmoved by life or death and are indifferent to bitterness or joy—they abide regardless. Now the time of my death is near. All of you must continue to serve our Father-Master well." Symptoms began to reveal themselves in several days, and he died. That was the fifth day of the eleventh month. The Master instructed us, his disciples, to bury Jiugu on the plain east of town. We then immediately set out again.

1221.11.03

1221.11.19

1221.11.20

114 The author mistakes the end-of-Ramadan celebrations with those typical of the Chinese New Year. According to the Hajri calendar, the date in the text would have been two days after the thirtieth and final day of Ramadan for the year 618 AH (1221.11.17). Islamic New Year began at the advent of the first month, Muharram (1222.02.15). The celebrations mentioned here probably refer to the holy day Eid al-Fitr, "breaking fast," held when the first lunar crescent of the next month is visible.

即行西南。復三日，至一城。其王亦回紇，年已耄矣。備迎送禮，供以湯餅。明日又歷一城。復行二日，有河，是爲霍闡没輦。由浮橋渡，泊於西岸。河橋官獻魚於田相公，巨口無鱗。其河源出東南二大雪山間，色渾而流急，深數丈，勢傾西北，不知其幾千里。河之西南，絶無水草者二百餘里，即夜行。復南望大雪山，而西山形與邪米干之南山相首尾。復有詩云：

造物崢嶸不可名，
東西羅列自天成。
南橫玉嶠連峰峻，
北壓金沙帶野平。
下枕泉源無極潤，
上通霄漢有餘清。
我行萬里慵開口，
到此狂吟不勝情。

又至一城，得接水草。復經一城，回紇頭目遠迎，飯于城南。獻蒲萄酒，且使小兒爲緣竿舞刀之戲。再經二城，山行半日，入南北平川，宿大桑樹下。其樹可蔭百人。前至一城，臨道一井，深踰百尺，有回紇叟驅一牛挽轆轤汲水以飲渴者。初，帝之西征也，見而異之，命蠲其賦役。

---

115 Near present-day Tashkent, Uzbekistan.
116 Now known as Syr Darya, flowing out of the Tian Shan, through Uzbekistan, Kyrgyzstan, and Kazakhstan, before emptying into the Aral Sea.

Heading southwest another three days, we arrived at a city.[115] Its king ~1221.11.24, 26 was also a Uyghur in his eighties or nineties, and he had prepared a lavish reception for us, sending gifts and providing us noodles in soup. The next day we passed another town and after two more days came to a river, the Khojand-müren.[116] We crossed a pontoon bridge and rested on the west bank. The bridge master presented Minister Chinqai with a fish having a huge mouth and no scales.[lxxiv] This river flows out between two large snow-capped mountains on the southeast. Its waters are muddy and turbulent, and its deep flow bends to the northwest for unknown thousands of *li*. Southwest of the river there is absolutely no water or grass for over two hundred *li*.[lxxv] So we traveled at night to where we could see the Great Snowy Mountains that turned west in the distance.[lxxvi] These mountains join with the mountains south of Samarkand (Xiemisigan) to enclose the city.[lxxvii] The Master put this into poetry:

[27. "A Poem Occurred to Me West of Where We Gazed on the Great Snowy Mountains"]

This towering brilliance made by the Shaper of Things cannot be
    named,
But it spreads out from east to west, as formed by Heaven.
In the south, a range of white jade, lying athwart, links peaks
    together,
While to the north, keeping back the golden sands, it rings the
    level desert.
Below, it cradles springs providing unlimited water;
Above, it connects to the Milky Way with purity to spare.
I have traveled ten thousand *li* and am always slow to speak,
But here, I chant wildly, overcome by my emotions.

We reached another city, where we finally found water and grass. Passing another town, we were greeted by the Uyghur elders, who came far out of the city to welcome us and feed and give us wine in the city's south. They also had children entertain us with pole climbing and sword dances. We passed two other cities and traveled on through the mountains for half a day until we descended into a north-to-south river valley. We camped there, under a large mulberry tree, one with enough shade to shelter a hundred people. Farther on, we approached a town and went by a well that was more than a hundred feet deep. An old Uyghur man was driving an ox that turned a pulley to draw up water for drinking and cooking. When Emperor Chinggis first passed here on his way into battle, he marveled at the contraption and ordered the man exempt from tax and labor duties.

仲冬十有八日，過大河，至邪米思干大城之北。太師
移剌國公及蒙古、回紇帥首載酒郊迎。大設帷幄，因駐車
焉。宣使劉公以路梗留坐中，白師曰：「頃知千里外有大
河，以舟梁渡，土寇壞之。況復已及深冬，父師似宜來春
朝見。」師從之。少焉，由東北門入。

其城因溝岸爲之。秋夏常無雨。國人疏二河入城，分
遶巷陌，比屋得用。方筭端氏之未敗也，城中常十萬餘
户。國破而來，存者四之一。其中大率多回紇人，田園自
不能主，須附漢人及契丹、河西等。其官長亦以諸色人爲
之。漢人工匠雜處城中。有岡高十餘丈，筭端氏之新宮據
焉。太師先居之。以回紇艱食，盜賊多有，恐其變出，居
于水北。師乃住宮，嘆曰：「道人任運逍遙，以度歲月。
白刃臨頭，猶不畏懼。況盜賊未至，復預憂乎？且善惡兩
途，必不相害。」從者安之。

太師作齋，獻金段十，師辭不受。遂月奉米、麵、
鹽、油、果、菜等物，日益尊敬。公見師飲少，請以蒲萄
百斤新作釀。師曰：「何必酒邪？但如其數得之待賓客足
矣。」其蒲萄經冬不壞。

又見孔雀、大象，皆東南數千里印度國物。師因暇日
出詩一篇云：

---

117 That is, Uyghurs along with other Turkic- and Iranian-speaking (Tajik) Muslim
   inhabitants of Samarkand. The military commanders in the city, however, almost
   certainly were Uyghurs in Mongol service, for the Khwarazm-shah's local Turkic
   Qangli and Tajik guards had been annihilated in the conquest (Juvaynī 1997, 115–122).

In the second month of winter, on the eighteenth day, we crossed a large river and reached north of the city of Samarkand (Xiemisigan).[lxxviii] The Grand Preceptor and Duke of State and Governor Yila (Yelü Ahai) as well as Mongol and Uyghur commanders carried wine outside the city, where they set up a large tent to greet us. So we halted our carts there. Imperial Envoy Liu had remained among them because the road to Chinggis's headquarters was blocked. He explained this to the Master saying, "I have just learned that a thousand *li* ahead there is a large river (the Amu Darya) crossed by a pontoon bridge that has been destroyed by bandits. Moreover, deep winter will soon be upon us, so it would be advisable for the revered Master to await spring to visit the Court." The Master agreed, and after a bit we entered the city by the northeast gate.

The city walls were erected along canal banks. Since it does not usually rain in summer and autumn, the inhabitants of the city channeled two rivers into the city and divided them among the streets and lanes to provide water for every household to use. Before the Sultan was defeated, there were more than a hundred thousand households in the city. Since the fall of the city, only one in four remains, most of them Uyghurs.[117] Since Uyghurs cannot claim the fields as their own, they must entrust them to the Chinese, Kitans, and Tanguts who had been relocated here. A variety of people fill official posts. Chinese artisans live dispersed throughout the city. In the center is a ridge more than a hundred feet high, upon which the Sultan's new palace had been built. Governor Yila lived there at first, but the Uyghurs were plagued by food shortages and bandits. Fearing an incident, he moved north of the river. The Master was thus lodged in the palace, and said with a sigh, "A man of the Way passes his years and months by letting his fate drift as it will. Feeling no terror as a naked blade comes near his head, how much less does he worry about bandits and robbers who have yet to appear? In any case, the good and the evil follow separate paths and are unlikely to harm each other." His disciples found reassurance in this remark.

The Grand Preceptor Yila had a vegetarian banquet prepared for us, and he also offered us ten measures of gold. The Master refused it, so the Governor, with ever increasing solicitude, presented a monthly provision of supplies such as rice, flour, salt, oil, fruits, and vegetables. Observing that the Master ate very little, he proposed to make some new wine from one hundred catties of grapes. But the Master replied, "Why must we make wine? If we had that many grapes, it would be enough for us to entertain our guests." Those grapes lasted all winter without spoiling.

We also saw elephants and peafowl, which come from the distant land of India to the southeast. Enjoying a day of leisure, the Master composed a poem.

二月經行十月終，
西臨回紇大城墉。
塔高不見十三級（以甎刻鏤玲瓏，外無層級，內可通行），
山厚已過千萬重。
秋日在郊猶放象，
夏雲無雨不從龍。
嘉蔬麥飯蒲萄酒，
飽食安眠養素慵。

師既住冬，宣使泊相公鎮海遣曷剌等同一行使臣領甲兵數百前路偵伺。

漢人往往來歸依。時有籌曆者在旁，師因問五月朔日食事。其人云：「此中辰時食，至六分止。」師曰：「前在陸局河時，午刻見其食既。又西南至金山，人言巳時食至七分。此三處所見各不同。按孔穎達《春秋疏》曰：『體映日則日食。』以今料之，蓋當其下，即見其食；既在旁者，則千里漸殊耳。正如以扇翳燈，扇影所及，無復光明。其旁漸遠，則燈光漸多矣。」

師一日故宮中，遂書《鳳棲梧》詞二首于壁。其一云：

一點靈明潛啓悟。
天上人間，
　不見行藏處。
四海八荒唯獨步。

118　It was a Muslim minaret, interpreted by Qiu as a Buddhist pagoda.
119　In traditional Chinese symbolic lore, dragons were thought to govern lakes, rivers, and rainfall, and would rise concealed in the clouds.
120　Qiu alludes to *Analects* 7.11: "The Master remarked to Yan Yuan, 'It is said, "When employed, one exercises (what one has been taught); when set aside, one holds himself in reserve (for the proper time)." Surely this applies only to you and me?'" That is, one should judge the proper time to utilize what one has been taught. Here a slight twist in meaning suggests that there is a state above this duality where the teaching does not pertain.

[28. "A Poem upon Reaching Samarkand (Xiemisigan)"]

Setting out in the second month, finishing only ten months later,
Heading toward the west we approached the grand walls of this
    Uyghur city.
Its pagoda is tall, its thirteen levels impossible to see;
It is made of bricks carved as openwork to admit light, with no visible levels on the outside.
    The inside, however, is open all the way up.[118]
The mountains were deep, with folds for ten thousand *li*.
Elephants are pastured in the outskirts during autumn days,
But there is no rain, no dragon arising in the summer clouds.[119]
Fine vegetables, wheat as a staple, and wine made from grapes—
We eat our fill, sleep securely, and nourish our ordinary lethargy.

In such fashion the Master passed the winter, while the Imperial Envoy
and Minister Chinqai dispatched Qara and the other Mongol attendants
to lead several hundred armored soldiers to scout out the road ahead.

As Chinese frequently sought initiation from the Master, we had
a calendrical and astrological expert on hand, so the Master asked
him about the eclipse on the first of the fifth month of that year. The
man said, "In the morning hours, the eclipse covered six-tenths of the
sun and then stopped." The Master said, "Before, when we were at
the Kerulen River, we saw a total eclipse around noon. Then again at
the Jinshan (Altai) Mountains to the southwest, someone said, 'In the
mid-morning hours, the eclipse reached seven-tenths.' These three
instances were all different. According to the *Supplemental Commentary on the Chunqiu* of Kong Yingda,[lxxix] 'when the moon hides the
sun, there is an eclipse.' Calculating for this instance, it appears that
if you are directly under the moon, you will see a total eclipse. But as
you move away laterally, the difference will become gradually greater
over a thousand *li*. Just like a fan covering a light, no light escapes the
fan's shadow. The farther one gets to the side of the fan's shadow, the
more light will emerge."

One day the Master made a trip to the Sultan's old palace, and while
there wrote two songs on the wall, in the following lyric pattern:

[c. "The Phoenix Perches on the Parasol Tree" I]

A drop of pure intelligence conceals the beginning of
    enlightenment;
Neither in Heaven nor in the world
    do we see a place to act or withdraw in anticipation.[120]
In the world bound within the four seas and the wilds beyond, one
    simply walks alone;

不空不有誰能覰。[121]

瞬目揚眉全體露。[122]
混混茫茫，
　法界超然去。
萬劫輪迴遭一遇。
九玄齊上三清路。

　其二云：

日月循環無定止。
春去秋來，
　多少榮枯事。
五帝三皇千百祀。
一興一廢長如此。

死去生來生復死。
生死輪迴，
　變化何時已。
不到無心休歇地。
不能清淨超於彼。

　又詩二首。其一云：

東海西秦數十年，
精思道德究重玄。
日中一食那求飽，
夜半三更強不眠。
實跡未諧霄漢舉，

121　Above both emptiness and nameable form, in a realm where this dichotomy does
　　not exist, one without consciousness.
122　Whole form: the essence of all reality.

Neither empty nor possessing form, how could one be seen?[121]

But in the wink of an eye or the arch of an eyebrow, the whole
    form is revealed.[122]
Unclear and undefined, vast and limitless—
    it transcends this experiential realm.
In the infinite time of transmigration, we experience a single
    chance encounter;
Through the Nine Heavens, we rise together on the path to the
    Three Clarities.[123]

[d. "The Phoenix Perches on the Parasol Tree" II]

Sun and moon revolve in endless cycles with no set stopping
    point.
Spring comes and autumn goes,
    flourishing and withering innumerable times.
Thousands of sacrifices to the Five Emperors and Three
    Sovereigns;
One rises, another falls, and so it always is.[124]

One dies, then is born, born then dies again.
Boundless change never stops
    on the wheel of transmigration.
Never reaching the resting place of no-mind,
Unable to cleanly transcend the "that."

He also wrote two poems:

[29. "Two Poems Written on the Walls of the Old Palace" I]

For decades, along the eastern seacoast or in western Qin
    (Shaanxi),
I concentrated on the Way and its virtue, probing the doubly
    mysterious.
Eating once at noon, never seeking to eat my fill,
At the third watch at midnight, I forced myself to stay awake.[125]
Though my actual deeds diverged from the Way, nevertheless I was
    raised to the Milky Way,

123 To become transcendent.
124 Referring here to the sequence of historical dynasties.
125 See Book I, n. 46.

虛名空播朔方傳。
直教大國垂明詔，
萬里風沙走極邊。

　　其二云：

弱冠尋真傍海濤，
中年遁跡隴山高。
河南一別升黃鵠，
塞北重宣釣巨鼇。
無極山川行不盡，
有爲心跡動成勞。
也知六合三千界，
不得神通未可逃。

　　是年閏十二月將終，偵騎迴，同宣使來白父師言：二
太子發軍，復整舟梁，土寇已滅。曷剌等詣營謁太子，言
師欲朝帝所。復承命云：「上駐蹕大雪山之東南。今則雪
積山門百餘里，深不可行，此正其路。爾爲我請師來此，
聽候良便。來時當就彼城中遣蒙古軍護送。」師謂宣差
曰：「聞河以南千里絕無種養。吾食須米麵蔬菜，可迴報
太子帳下。」

　　壬午之春正月，把欖始華。類小桃，俟秋採其實，食
之，味加胡桃。

126　Chinggis Qan's empire.
127　His home in Shandong.
128　His teacher, Wang Chongyang, died.
129　That is, they called, summoning him.

My false reputation uselessly spread and was transmitted to the
   north.
Just let the Great State send down its enlightened edict,[126]
And through endless miles of wind and sand, I will race to the
   farthest border.

[30. "Two Poems Written on the Walls of the Old Palace" II]

In my twentieth year I sought the Truth by the billowing sea,[127]
In my middle years I hid my traces in the heights of the Longshan
   range.
At his last parting in Henan, my master "ascended on a yellow
   crane,"[128]
North of the passes again they summoned me, "fishing out a
   leviathan."[129]
Traveling forever through endless mountains and rivers,
Moved from traces in the mind to achieve some merit,
I know too well that, in these six directions of countless worlds,
Without attaining spiritual comprehension, one will never escape.

That year, toward the end of the intercalary twelfth month, the scouts 1222.02.12
returned with the Imperial Envoy to explain to the revered Master that
the Second Prince Chaghadai had restored the pontoon bridge and
annihilated the bandits. Qara and his men paid a visit to the Prince's
camp and reported that the Master wished to present himself to the
Emperor. They also relayed the Prince's order, saying, "The Emperor
has temporarily halted southeast of the Great Snowy Mountains (here,
the Hindu Kush). Now deep snow covers the hundred *li* of the passes,
making it impossible to travel along this route. Please invite the Master
to come to my camp here and wait until it is convenient to travel. Upon
arrival he should lodge within the walls of the town, and Mongol troops
will be dispatched to escort him on his way." The Master addressed the
envoy, saying, "I have heard that for a thousand *li* south of the Amu
River there is no cultivated land at all. For sustenance I require grain,
flour, and vegetables; please return and inform the Prince's camp."[130]

In the first month of spring of the *renwu* year, the almond trees 1222.02.12–03.14
began to flower.[131] This tree is like the "small peach," and you must
wait until autumn to pick the fruit to eat it.[132] It tastes like the walnut.

130 Qiu tactfully declines Chaghadai's invitation in favor of remaining in Samarkand,
      where the cuisine would be more to his liking than that available in a Mongol camp.
131 Almonds are referred to by their common Eurasian name of *badam*, which in Chinese
      is rendered *balan* 巴欖.
132 A "small peach": an early ripening peach that has little flesh on it.

　　二月二日春分，杏花已落。司天臺判李公輩請師遊郭西，宣使洎諸官載蒲萄酒以從。是日，天氣晴霽，花木鮮明，隨處有臺池樓閣，間以蔬圃。憩則藉草，人皆樂之。談玄論道，時復引觴。日昃方歸。作詩云：

陰山西下五千里，
大石東過二十程。
雨霽雪山遙慘淡，
春分河府近清明（邪米思干大城，大石有國時名爲河中府）。
園林寂寂鳥無語（花木雖茂，並無飛禽），
風日遲遲花有情。
同志暫來閑睥睨，
高吟歸去待昇平。

　　望日乃一百五旦，太上真元節也。時僚屬請師復遊郭西。園林相接百餘里，雖中原莫能過，但寂無鳥聲耳。遂成二篇，以示同遊。其一云：

二月中分百五期，
玄元下降日遲遲。
正當月白風清夜，
更好雲收雨霽時。

133　These are probably the Pamir Mountains, east-southeast of Samarkand.

On the second day of the second month, the spring equinox,^{lxxx} when the almond blossoms had already dropped, His Excellency Bureau of Astronomy Supervisor Li and others invited the Master to go sightseeing west of the city wall. The Imperial Envoy and other officials came along, bringing wine. That day the rain had stopped, and the weather was clear; the trees and flowers were fresh and bright. Everywhere we went there were towers, pools, and pavilions interspersed with vegetable gardens. We sat on the grass to rest, and everyone found it delightful. We discussed the Way and passed wine cups from time to time. Only as the sun began to set did we return to town. The Master composed a poem on the occasion:

[31. *"Roaming West of the Outskirts, I Write a Poem"*]

From the Yinshan (Tian Shan), we descended westward five
   thousand *li*,
East of Qara Khitai through twenty stages.
Rain clears, the snowy mountains in the far distance are bleak;[133]
At the Spring equinox, Hezhongfu draws near the Clear and Bright
   Festival;
The great city of Samarkand (Xiemisigan), during the time of the Dashi state, was called
   Hezhongfu.
In the gardens all is quiet, no bird calls;
Although the vegetation is lush, there are no birds.
Wind and sun slowly warm, flowers beguile.
With like-minded friends for this short while, we take in the scene,
Then return, chanting loudly, to await a world at peace.

The full moon of the second month marked the morning of the one hundred and fifty years of Laozi's life, as well as the festival for celebrating the Supreme Realized One's birthday. On that day that same entourage again invited the Master to stroll west of the city wall in the gardens and parks that spread out for over a hundred *li*. They are equal to the best gardens in the Central Plain, although silent and empty of birdsong. The Master composed two verses to share with his fellow ramblers:

[32. *"Two Poems to Show to My Fellow Wanderers" I*]

The second month divides in the middle, a celebration of Laozi's
   birth;
The Mysterious Origin descends, the days grow warmer.
With a gentle night breeze and bright moon,
It is even better now that clouds are gone and the rain has stopped.

匝地園林行不盡，
照天花木坐觀奇。
未能絕粒成嘉遁，
且向無爲樂有爲。

　　其二云：

深蕃古跡尚橫陳，
大漢良朋欲遍巡。
舊日亭臺隨處列，
向年花卉逐時新。
風光甚解留連客，
夕照那堪斷送人。
竊念世間酬短景，
何如天外飲長春。

　　三月上旬，阿里鮮至自行宮。傳旨云：「真人來自日出之地，跋涉山川，勤勞至矣。今朕已迴，亟欲聞道，無倦迎我。」次諭宣使仲祿曰：「尔持詔徵聘，能副朕心。佗日當置汝善地。」復諭鎮海曰：「汝護送真人來，甚勤。余惟汝嘉。」仍敕萬戶播魯只以甲士千人衛過鐵門。師問阿里鮮以途程事。對曰：「春正月十有三日自此初發。馳三日，東南過鐵門。又五日，過大河。二月初吉，東南過大雪山，積雪甚高，馬上舉鞭測之，猶未及其半。下所踏者，復五尺許。南行三日，至行宮矣。且師至，次第奏訖。上說，留數日方迴。」

We stroll around the garden, unable to traverse it all;
Sky, trees, and flowers—we sit contemplating the wondrous sight.
Still unable to give up food and escape the world as a transcendent,
I will use Nonaction and, happily, make things better for all.

[*33. "Two Poems to Show to My Fellow Wanderers" II*]

Deep in the heart of foreign lands ancient ruins still crisscross the
   land;
Friends in the Way from the land of Great Han wish to see the
   whole wide world.
Towers and pavilions of days past are everywhere open to view;
Grass and flowers from years long gone renew themselves in their
   proper season.
If nature—wind's change and light's movement—fully understands
   that these travelers are transient and reluctant to depart,
How can the evening's rays bear to send people away?
I wonder—how will this world's transient beauty
Compare to taking in eternal spring in a realm beyond Heaven?

In the first part of the third month, Alixian arrived from the Emperor's 1222.04.14–23
traveling palace and conveyed a decree: "The Perfected has come from
where the sun rises, traversed mountains and river valleys, and exhausted himself to reach this place. I am also returning and eager to hear him
expound on the Way. Pray do not be too weary to come and meet me."
The Emperor further sent a message to Imperial Envoy Zhonglu, saying,
"In upholding my edict to bring the guest here, you accomplished what I
wished. Someday I will reward you with an excellent position." Again, to
Chinqai he said, "You have been very diligent in escorting the Perfected
here, for which I am grateful." He further ordered the Myriarch Bo'orchu to
take a thousand armored soldiers and defend the Master's passage through
the Iron Gate.[lxxxi] The Master questioned Alixian about the journey ahead,
and the latter replied, "I set out from here on the thirteenth day of the first 1222.02.25
month of spring and rode for three days, passed through the Iron Gate to
the southeast, and then after another five days crossed the Amu Darya. On
the first day of the second month, I crossed the Great Snowy Mountains
to the southeast. The snow was so deep that if I stuck my whip in from 1222.03.15
horseback to measure it, it went in halfway without reaching bottom.
Even the snow that had been trampled underfoot was about five feet deep. 1222.03.18
Proceeding south for three days I reached the Imperial Camp. I reported
the specifics of the Master's arrival, which gladdened the Emperor, and
after several days, I set out on the return journey."

師遂留門人尹公志平輩三人于館。以侍行五六人同宣使輩，三月十有五日，啓行。

四日過碣石城。預傳聖旨，令萬户播魯只領蒙古回紇軍一千，護送過鐵門。東南度山，山勢高大，亂石縱橫。衆軍挽車，兩日方至山前。沿流南行，軍即北入大山破賊。

五日至小河，亦船渡。兩岸林木茂盛。

七日，舟濟大河，即阿毋没輦也。乃東南行，晚泊古渠上。渠邊蘆葦滿地，不類中原所有。其大者經冬葉青而不凋。因取以爲杖，夜橫轅下，轅覆不折。其小者葉枯春換。少南，山中有大實心竹，士卒以爲戈戟。又見蜴蜥，皆長三尺許，色青黑。時三月二十九日也。因作詩云：

志道既無成，
天魔深有懼。
東辭海上來，
西望日邊去。
雞犬不聞聲，
馬牛更遞鋪。
千山及萬水，
不知是何處。

134　Modern Shahri-sabz, about 80 kilometers south of Samarkand in southern Uzbekistan.

135　Probably the tributary Sherabad (Shirabad), which flows out of the mountains west of Dushanbe in Tajikistan and south into the Amu Darya.

Thereupon the Master decided to leave Yin Zhiping and three other disciples at the guesthouse, and to take along five or six of his remaining disciples to assist him on the journey. His group, along with the Imperial Envoy, set out on the fifteenth day of the third month. Four days later   1222.04.28
we passed Kesh.[134] There we met up with Myriarch Bo'orchu, who had   1222.05.02
obeyed the earlier imperial command to assemble a thousand Mongol and Uyghur troops and escort us through the Iron Gate. Proceeding south, we crossed steep mountains, strewn with rocks. With the help of the army, after two days we finally got our carts to the other side. We   1222.05.04
marched south along a river and then our armed escort turned north to reenter the mountains and engage with bandits. On day five we came to a small river, which we crossed by boat.[135] Dense forests grew on both banks of the river. On the seventh day we crossed the great river on boats—this was the Amu *müren*—and proceeded southeast. Toward evening we stopped by an old canal, with banks overgrown by reeds of a kind not seen in the Central Plain.[lxxxii] The leaves on the largest reeds stay green all winter and do not fall off, so we used them to make staves to raise the shafts of our carts, and the shafts did not fall or break. As for the smaller reeds, their leaves dry up in winter but bud again in spring. A bit farther south, in the mountains we saw a kind of large bamboo with a solid stem; soldiers use it to make pole arms. We also saw greenish-black lizards over three feet long.[136] It was the twenty-ninth day of the third   1222.05.12
month, and the Master composed a poem:

[34. "Composed on the Twenty-ninth Day of the Third Month"]

As my resolve to cultivate the Way remains unfulfilled,
I deeply dread the Demon King's temptations.
Leaving the east and coming from the ocean,
I head west and go to the edge of the horizon.
I hear no sounds of chickens or dogs,[137]
And exchange horses and oxen at the courier stations.
A thousand peaks, countless rivers,
Who knows where we are?

---

136 Probably the desert monitor lizard *Varanus griseus*.
137 The sound of chickens and dogs: evidence of human habitation. The phrase echoes section 80 of *The Way and Its Power* describing the idyllic self-sufficiency of ancient society, in which people might hear the chickens and dogs in neighboring villages, yet never leave their own community or mingle with outsiders. See Laozi, Roberts, trans., 2019, 154–155.

又四日，得達行在。上遣大臣喝剌播得來迎，時四月五日也。館舍定，即入見。上勞之曰：「佗國徵聘皆不應，今遠踰萬里而來，朕甚嘉焉。」對曰：「山野詔而赴者，天也。」上悅，賜坐。食次，問：「真人遠來，有何長生之藥以資朕乎？」師曰：「有衛生之道，而無長生之藥。」上嘉其誠實，設二帳於御幄之東以居焉。譯者問曰：「人呼師為騰吃利蒙古孔（譯語謂天人也），自謂之邪？人稱之邪？」師曰：「山野非自稱，人呼之耳。」譯者再至曰：「舊奚呼？」奏以「山野四人事重陽師學道，三子羽化矣。唯山野處世，人呼以先生。」上問鎮海曰：「真人當何號？」鎮海奏曰：「有人尊之曰師父者、真人者，曰神仙者。」上曰：「自今以往，可呼神仙。」

時適炎熱，從車駕廬於雪山避暑。

上約四月十四日問道。外使田鎮海、劉仲祿、阿里鮮記之；內使近侍三人記之。將及期，有報回紇山賊指斥者，上欲親征。因改卜十月吉。師乞還舊館。上曰：「再來不亦勞乎？」師曰：「兩旬可矣。」上又曰：「無護送者？」師曰：「有宣差楊阿狗。」

---

138   Near modern Taliqan, Afghanistan.

139   When Daoist masters die, their noncorporeal selves were thought to turn into feathered beings, usually cranes, and fly up to the heavens.

140   "Uyghur" here most likely refers to Muslim-Turk partisans of the Khwarazm-shah, whom Chinggis was determined to exterminate. That summer Chinggis gave chase to Jalal ad-Din and captured his Qangli ally, Malik Qan. Chinggis then sent Bala after Jalal ad-Din and returned to his camp at Taliqan, where he met with Qiu Chuji when the latter returned in the late fall. See YS 1.22.

141   *Agou* literally means "Doggy." It may have been a name given because he was born in the year of the Dog.

[With the Qan in Afghanistan, Samarkand, and Central Asia]

In another four days we arrived at the Imperial Camp.[138] The Emperor sent his high official Qara Böde to greet us.[lxxxiii] It was the fifth day of the fourth month. After getting settled in our lodgings, we were ushered at once into the imperial presence. The Emperor said, "You did not respond to the summons of other rulers, yet today you have come here from a great distance, which gratifies me no end." The Master replied, "It is Heaven's will that this mountain rustic should obey your edict and make the journey." His Majesty was pleased and asked him to take a seat. Refreshments and drinks were served, and then the Emperor asked, "Now that you have come all this way, what secret elixir for long life can you provide me?" The Master replied, "There is the Way of good health, but no elixir for long life." His Majesty appreciated the Master's candor and ordered two tents to be erected to the east of his residence in which we would stay. The translator then inquired, "People call the Master *Tengri möngke kün*, 'Heavenly Eternal Being.' Is that what you call yourself, or what others call you?" The Master said, "This mountain rustic does not call himself that; it is merely what others call him." The translator again asked, "What then would you permit us to call you?" The Master humbly explained, "Three other disciples and I served Wang Chongyang in the study of the Way. Now the others have transformed into feathered beings, and only I remain in the world, so people usually address me as teacher."[139] His Majesty inquired of Chinqai, "How should the Perfected be addressed?" Chinqai dutifully responded, "Those who respect him call him 'Revered Master,' or 'Perfected,' or 'Divine Transcendent.'" His Majesty replied, "From today on, he shall be called Divine Transcendent." It was approaching the hot season, and we followed the Imperial Carriage into the Snowy Mountains to escape the summer heat.

1222.05.17

The Emperor appointed the fourteenth day of the fourth month as the time to inquire into the Way, with the outer officials Chinqai, Liu Zhonglu, and Alixian recording the event, along with three personal servants from among the inner officials. As the day approached, a report came that Uyghur mountain bandits had instigated attacks, and the Emperor wanted to lead the campaign in person.[140] Therefore, it was divined that the tenth month would be auspicious. The Master petitioned to return to his old lodging (in Samarkand) during the interim. The Emperor said, "Will you be too exhausted to come back?" The Master replied that he could make the trip in twenty days. The Emperor then said, "But there is no one to escort you." The Master replied, "There is the imperial envoy Yang Agou."[141]

2022.05.26

又三日，命阿狗督回紇酋長以千餘騎從行，由佗路
迴。遂歷大山，山有石門，望如削蠟。有巨石橫其上若橋
焉。其下流甚急。騎士策其驢以涉，驢遂溺死，水邊尚多
橫屍。此地蓋關口，新爲兵所破。出峽，復有詩二篇。其
一云：

水北鐵門猶自可，
水南石峽太堪驚。
兩崖絕壁攙天聳，
一澗寒波滾地傾。
夾道橫屍人掩鼻，
溺溪長耳我傷情。
十年萬里干戈動，
早晚迴軍復太平。

其二云：

雪嶺皚皚上倚天，
晨光燦燦下臨川。
仰觀峭壁人橫度，
俯視危崖栢倒縣。
五月嚴風吹面冷，
三膲熱病當時痊。
我來演道空回首，
更卜良辰待下元。

始師來觀，三月竟。草木繁盛，羊馬皆肥。及奉詔而
回，四月終矣。百草悉枯。又作詩云：

Three days later, Agou was ordered to oversee a Uyghur chief who gathered a thousand mounted soldiers to accompany us on the return journey. We returned by a different route, following a great mountain through a stone gap that looked like sliced wax, with huge stone slabs laid across the top to form a bridge. Below it ran a torrential current. As the riders whipped the supply donkeys to cross the river, many animals drowned. Human corpses still lay scattered along the banks. Apparently, this was a strategic pass through the mountains, which had recently been conquered by our army. Emerging from the ravine, the Master composed two poems:

[35. "Two More Poems on Coming Out of the Defile" I]

The Iron Gate route seemed passable north of the river,
But the stony gorge on the south was unbearably alarming.
On both sides precipices held up the towering sky,
And the chilly surge of a mountain stream debouched and roiled
  o'er the ground.
People covered their noses because of corpses strewn about the
  narrow path,
But it was the long-eared asses drowned in the stream that
  sickened my heart.
War has raged for ten years and over huge distances,
But in the end, armies will go back and peace will be restored.

[36. "Two More Poems on Coming Out of the Defile" II]

Above, snow-capped mountains lean against the heavens,
Below, the glare of the sun's early rays falls on river valleys.
Looking up to survey the precipices, we cross the mountains;
Looking down from the steep cliffs, we see cypresses suspended
  upside down.
In the fifth month a cruel wind freezes the face,
And a fever in the vital organs at once abates.
I came to spread the Way, so why look back?
Having augured a propitious time to return, I must now wait for
  the *Xiayuan* festival.[142]

When the Master first presented himself at the Emperor's camp after the third month had passed, the grass was verdant, the vegetation lush, and the horses and sheep fattened up. By the end of the fourth month when the Emperor approved of his return, the grass had withered, and all the vegetation had disappeared. So he composed another poem:

外國深蕃事莫窮，

陰陽氣候特無從。

纔經四月陰魔盡（春冬霖雨，四月純陽，絕無雨），

郤早彌天旱魃凶。

浸潤百川當九夏（以水溉田），

摧殘萬草若三冬。

我行往復三千里（三月去，五月回），

不見行人帶雨容。

　　路逢征西人回，多獲珊瑚。有從官以白金二 易之，近五十株，高者尺餘。以其得之馬上，不能完也。繼日乘涼宵征。五六日達邪米思干（大石名河中府）。諸官迎師入館，即重午日也。

143　The *yin-* and *yang qi* of these foreign lands defies the normal rhythms of the cosmos as Chinese understood it. The abnormalities of the foreign here find cosmological expression, but also implicitly challenge notions of the normal. Periods of unstable or changing climate were omens of the cosmos out of joint.

[37. "Another Poem on Returning to Samarkand (Xiemisigan) after
Being Summoned by Rescript"]

Deep in the heart of foreign lands, there is no shortage of
    surprises;
Even the seasons and climate fluctuate erratically.[143]
The fourth month just passed, and the *yin* demons have ceased;
Spring was cold with continuous rain; the fourth month saw unabated sunshine and
    no rain at all.[144]
The fierce gods of drought have already filled the sky.
A hundred streams saturate the land to endure the ninety days of
    summer,
River water is used to irrigate fields.
But all the plants have died as though it were the last three months
    of winter.
I have traveled back and forth three thousand *li*,[145]
Going in the third month, returning in the fifth.
Yet have never met a single traveler bearing traces of rain.

Along our route we encountered people returning from the western
campaign, and many had taken coral as loot. Some of our subordinate
officers exchanged two *yi* of silver for fifty branches of coral, the tallest
over a foot in length.[146] But when loaded onto horseback, it proved
difficult to keep it from breaking. Taking advantage of the evening cool
to travel at night, we reached Samarkand (Xiemisigan) after five or six
days. *(The Qara Khitai called it Hezhongfu.)* All the officials came out to escort
us to our lodging; it was the fifth day of the fifth month.   1222.06.15

---

144 According to the Chinese calendar, set in the heartland of the Central States, cessa-
    tion of rains marks the advent of true *yang*, which should occur in the sixth month.
145 Between Samarkand and the Qan's camp in Afghanistan.
146 See the Table of Weights and Measures in the front matter. On the Mongols' love
    of coral and its sources, see Allsen 2019, 126–128.

長春真人西遊記卷下
門人真常子李志常述

宣差李公東邁，以詩寄東方道衆云：

當時發軔海邊城，
海上干戈尚未平。
道德欲興千里外，
風塵不憚九夷行。
初從西北登高領（即野狐嶺），
漸轉東南指上京（陸局河東畔東南望上京也）。
迤邐直西南下去（西南四千里到兀里朵，又西南二千里到陰
山），
陰山之外不知名（陰山西南一重大山，一重小水，數千里到邪
米思干大城，即館於故宮）。

師既還館。館據北崖，俯清溪十餘丈。溪水自雪山
來，甚寒。仲夏炎熱，就北軒風臥，夜則寢屋顛之臺。

六月極暑，浴池中。師之在絕域，自適如此。

河中壤地宜百穀，唯無蕎麥、大豆。四月中麥熟。土
俗收之，亂堆於地，遇用即碾，六月始畢。太師府提控李
公獻瓜田五畝，味極甘香，中國所無。

---

1   The former Liao Supreme Capital.

Book II

Recorded by His Disciple Master Zhenchang,
Li Zhichang

Envoy Li left us to travel back east, taking with him a poem from the
Master for his congregation of the Way there:

*[38. "His Excellency Imperial Envoy Li Goes Eastward, and I Send a
Poem to Friends of the Way in the East"]*

When I departed from the city by the sea,
The fighting along the coast had not yet calmed.
We wished to spread the Way and its power beyond a
thousand *li*,
Unafraid of wind and dust, we traveled among barbarian peoples.
At first ascending the high mountains from the northwest,
That is, Wild Fox Ridge.
We gradually turned to the Supreme Capital in the southeast.[1]
Along the east bank of the Kerulen River, southeast toward the Supreme Capital.
We wound our way down to the southwest,
*Two thousand li southwest to the Ordo, then another two thousand li to the Yinshan
(Tian Shan) Range.*
Beyond the Yinshan (Tian Shan), not knowing names for places.
*There is a large mountain and a small river southwest of the Yinshan (Tian Shan). The
large city of Samarkand (Xiemisigan) is several thousand li beyond; the Master
stayed in the old palace there.*

The Master returned to his lodging, which abutted a cliff on the north
and looked down on a fresh, icy rivulet about a hundred feet below, flowing out of the snow-capped mountains. It was the hot part of midsummer,
and so the Master would lie by the north end of his chamber to catch the
breeze from the open corridor, while at night he slept on the terrace on
the roof. The sixth month was so unbearably hot that he bathed in pools.   1222.07.11–08.08
Thus did the Master acclimatize himself to this distant land.
    The land around Hezhong (Samarkand) is suitable for growing the
various grains, except for buckwheat and soybeans. In the fourth month
the grain ripens. When the residents reap the grain, they pile it randomly
over the land, and whenever they want some, they winnow a bit. By
the beginning of the sixth month the harvest is completed. Supervisor
Li in the Governor's yamen[i] presented the Master with a melon field of
five *mu* (approx. 0.7 acres), with melons so very sweet, unlike any in

間有大如斗者。六月間，二太子迴。劉仲祿乞瓜獻之，十枚可重一擔。果、菜其贍，所欠者芋、栗耳。茄實若麤指而色紫黑。

男女皆編髮。男冠則或如遠山帽，飾以雜綵，刺以雲物，絡之以纓。自酋長以下，在位者冠之。庶人則以白麼斯（布屬）六尺許盤於其首。酋豪之婦纏頭以羅，或皂或紫，或繡花卉織物象，長可五六尺。髮皆垂，有袋之以緜者，或素或雜色，或以布帛爲之者。不梳髻，以布帛蒙之，若比丘尼狀，庶人婦女之首飾也。衣則或用白氎，縫如注袋，窄上寬下，綴以袖，謂之襯衣，男女通用。車舟農器制度頗異中原。國人皆以鍮石銅爲器皿，間以磁，有若中原定磁者。酒器則純用琉璃，兵器則以鑌。市用金錢，無輪孔，兩面鑿回紇字。其人物多魁梧有膂力，能負戴重物，不以擔。婦人出嫁，夫貧則再嫁。遠行踰三月，則亦聽他適。異者或有鬚髯。

國中有稱大石馬者，識其國字，專掌簿籍。遇季冬，設齋一月。比暮，其長自刲羊爲食，與席者同享，自夜及旦。餘月則設六齋。

2   If a muskmelon, this may refer to the Hami melon. If a watermelon, that would account
    for the weight. On the introduction of "western melons" (西瓜, watermelons) to the
    Chinese heartland, see Laufer 1919, 438–445.

3   *Yushitong* is chalcopyrite, a form of copper iron sulfide found whole naturally; that is,
    it does not need to be extracted from other ores. Ding ware is a style of white ceramic
    ware, mostly porcelain, produced at the kilns of Dingzhou, Hebei.

4   The script could be either Arabic or Persian.

5   Persian for "learned scholar." In Chinese, transcribed as *dashiman*.

6   The "end of winter" is the twelfth month in the Chinese lunar calendar. There is some
    confusion here. The Ramadan celebrations in the years the group was there occurred
    primarily in the month of November. As we have seen above (Book I, n. 114), the
    author assumed that this was a celebration of the beginning of a lunar new year, as

the Central Plain, and some as large as a *dou* (approx. 6.7 liters).[2] In the middle of the sixth month, when the Second Imperial Prince (Chaghadai) had returned, Liu Zhonglu (who had accompanied Chaghadai) sent the Master melons, ten melons weighing one *dan* (76 kilograms). Fruits and vegetables are very abundant; they lack only taro and chestnuts. Eggplants are the size of coarse fingers and are dark purple.

1222.07.21–30

Men and women both braid their hair. The men's caps look like a distant mountain, and are embroidered with clouds and other patterns, then covered by gems and pearls linked with tassels into a net. From the chiefs on down, those with rank wear such hats, while commoners wrap a piece of white cotton muslin about six feet long around their heads. The wives of wealthy and prominent men wrap their heads with silk gauze five or six feet in length, some black or purple, some embroidered with flowers or plants, others with woven images. Wives and daughters of commoners wear their hair down, stuffed into a pouch of silk floss netting, either plain or multicolored, or one of silk cloth. They do not comb their hair into a bun but conceal it with silk so that it resembles a Buddhist nun's cowl. Their garb consists of a white cotton garment, sewn like a mesh bag, tight above and loose below, and with sleeves attached. It is called a "lining robe" and is worn by both men and women.

Their boats, carts, and farming implements, and their manner of using them, are all different from such of the Central Plain. Locals all use "copper" to cast implements, and occasionally also make porcelain resembling Ding ware.[3] They make drinking vessels from colored glass, while military implements are fashioned of wrought iron or steel. In the markets they use gold coins with no hole in the middle and Uyghur script on both sides.[4] Physically, the people are tall and muscular, capable of carrying great loads without a shoulder pole. After a woman marries, if her husband becomes impoverished, the woman may remarry, and if her husband has traveled for more than three months without returning, she may take someone else in marriage. Some of the women are unusual in having facial hair.

Among the people, the *danishmand* are literate in their country's script and responsible for keeping records.[5] At the end of winter, people fast for a month, and at sunset on the last day of the fast period, the elders slaughter a lamb for food to share at a feast that lasts until dawn.[6] During

in China, on the day of the second or third new moon after the winter solstice. This generalized statement here should probably be understood more as meaning "toward the end of the year," rather than as meaning the specific "last month of the lunar year."

又於危舍上跳出大木如飛簷，長闊丈餘，上搆虛亭，四垂
纓絡。每朝夕，其長登之，禮西方，謂之告天。不奉佛，
不奉道。大呼吟於其上。丁男女聞之，皆趍拜其下。舉國
皆然，不爾則弃市。衣與國人同，其首則盤以細麼斯，長
三丈二尺，骨以竹。

師異其俗，作詩以記其實云：

回紇丘墟萬里疆，
河中城大最爲強。
滿城銅器如金器，
一市戎裝似道裝。
剪鏃黃金爲貨賂，
裁縫白氎作衣裳。
靈瓜素椹非凡物，
赤縣何人搆得嘗。

當暑，雪山甚寒，烟雲慘淡。師乃作絕句云：

東山日夜氣濛鴻，
曉色彌天萬丈紅。
明月夜來飛出海，
金光射透碧霄空。

師在館，賓客甚少，以經書遊戲。復有絕句云：

北出陰山萬里餘，
西過大石半年居。

7   Just as the Buddhists do, notes QXYJ03 188, n. C9. This work concludes that, like the
    Chinese, these Muslims must have had six fasts in addition as well. Besides Ramadan,
    however, there are only two other major holy days, each of ten days. One celebrates
    the end of Ramadan (Eid al-Fitr), and the other celebrates Abraham's sacrifice of his
    son, Ismail (Eid al-Adha).
8   That is, a minaret. This structure is hard to identify. Qiu here may be describing the
    great mosque of Samarkand, evidently a masterpiece of Seljuk architecture, destroyed
    by Chinggis Qan. Or, given his description, he may be looking at a wooden mosque,
    also common at the time.
9   Referring here to the Alai Mountains in southwest Kyrgyzstan, which run from the
    Tian Shan westward and are the northernmost range in the Pamirs.

the remaining months of the year, they observe six other fasts.⁷ On their
tall buildings, a large timber, some ten by ten *zhang* (approx. 9 meters)
square, juts above like upraised roof corners (in China), upon which is
constructed a hollow tower.⁸ Strands of gems hang from each of its four
corners. Every sunrise and sunset, an elder (muezzin) ascends the tower
and bows toward the west; this is called "petitioning Heaven." He chants
out from the tower, but does not worship the Buddha or the Dao. As soon
as adults below hear the chant, they all hasten to prostrate themselves
in worship. This is the case across the country, and if someone does
not pray, they are executed in the marketplace. The *danishmand* dress
the same as everyone else, except that their turbans are wrapped with
a piece of muslin twelve feet long, which is strengthened with bamboo.

The Master considered their customs quite odd and composed a verse
to record the occasion:

[39. *"Writing a Poem on Passing Hezhong to Record Its Facts"*]

In the far distant Uyghur country of hills and ruins,
The great city of Hezhong is the largest and strongest.
A city full of brass implements that resemble gold,
And military attire everywhere that looks like Daoist garb.
They mint gold coins to use for trade,
And tailors make clothing of white cotton cloth.
The marvelous melons and white mulberries are out of the ordinary.
Who back home in the heartland could get to taste such things?

It was the height of summer at the time, and yet the Snowy Mountains
were very cold, covered in pale mist and clouds. Thereupon the Master
created two poems of four lines:

[40. *"Two Quatrains"* I]

Day and night the eastern mountains are in a murky haze,⁹
The color of dawn filling the boundless sky with far-reaching red.
Bright moons come at night, flying out of an ocean of sand,
And golden rays of the sun shoot through the emptiness of blue skies.

As the Master was at home and very few guests dropped in, he found
pleasure in reading the scriptures. His other quatrain read,

[41. *"Two Quatrains"* II]

North, we came out of the Yinshan (Tian Shan), more than ten
    thousand *li*,
West, we passed through the Dashi country, staying for half a year.

遐荒鄙俗難論道，

靜室幽巖且看書。

七月載生魄，遣阿里鮮奉表詣行宮，稟論道日期。

八月七日，得上所批荅，八日即行。太師相送數十里，師乃曰：回紇城東新叛者二千户，夜夜火光照城，人心不安，太師可迴安撫。太師曰：「在路萬一有不虞奈何？」師曰：「豈關太師事？」乃迴。

十有二日，過碣石城。

十有三日，得護送步卒千人，甲騎三百。入大山中行，即鐵門外別路也。涉紅水澗，有峻峰高數里。谷東南行，山根有鹽泉流出，見日即爲白鹽。因收二斗，隨行日用。又東南上分水嶺，西望高澗若冰，乃鹽耳。山上有紅鹽如石，親嘗見之。東方唯下地生鹽，此方山間亦出鹽。回紇多餅食，且嗜鹽，渴則飲水。冬寒，貧者尚負餅售之。

十有四日，至鐵門西南之麓。將出山，其山門瞰峻，左崖崩下，澗水伏流一里許。

中秋抵河上。其勢若黃河，流西北。乘舟以濟，宿其南岸。西有山寨，名團八剌。山勢險固。三太子之醫官鄭公途中相見，以詩贈云：

自古中秋月最明，

---

10 QXYJ03 192–193, n. C1, observes that the increased number of troops sent to escort the Daoist visitors this second time through the Iron Gate indicates a continued state of unrest among the conquered population there.

11 Evidently the same item now sold as pink Himalayan rock salt.

12 When there is no snow melt to create the streams.

13 Probably the Amu Darya; the comparison with the Yellow River indicates a strong flow of turbid water.

14 Location uncertain, but probably east or southeast of Balkh. See QXYJ03 195, n. C3. Variously identified as Talqun or Kerduan, but not Taliqan, which was farther east.

A desolate place with vulgar customs, it is difficult to discuss the Way.
Here in my quiet room by a hidden cliff, I am content to read.

On the night of the new moon, the sixteenth of the seventh month, the 1222.08.24
Master dispatched Alixian to the Emperor's traveling palace with a petition
concerning the approaching date for the Master's discussion of the Way.
On the seventh day of the eighth month, we received His Majes- 1222.09.13
ty's response, and the next day we set out. The governor accompanied
us for several dozen *li*, until the Master said, "East of the Uyghur city
(Samarkand) are several thousand households that have just rebelled,
and every night fires light up the city. The people are anxious; you, sir,
may return and tend to them." The governor responded, "But what if
something untoward should occur along your way?" The Master replied,
"How could that be your fault?" Whereupon the Governor returned.
On the twelfth day we passed the town of Kesh. On the thirteenth 1222.09.18, 19
day about a thousand infantry and three hundred armored riders arrived
to escort us onward.[10] Entering the gap between great mountains, we
followed a different route beyond the Iron Gate. We forded a creek of
red water between lofty peaks several *li* high. The ravine turned to the
southeast, where a salt spring flows from the foot of the mountain; when
exposed to sunlight, it immediately turns into white salt. We gathered
two pecks and used it daily while traveling. Continuing southeast, we
went up the range that divides two river systems. Looking west, we
saw a high ravine that seemed full of ice, which turned out to be salt.
On top of the peak were rocks of red salt, which we tasted.[11] Back east,
only the lowlands produce salt, whereas here one also finds salt in the
mountains. The Uyghurs eat lots of flatbreads, preferably with salt, and
the resulting thirst induces them to drink water. Even during the cold
winter, the poor carry around pitchers of water for sale.[12]
On the fourteenth day, we reached a slope southwest of the Iron Gate.
We were coming out of the mountains, where the pass was quite precip- 1222.09.20
itous. The cliff side to our left had collapsed in a landslide, and the water
there flowed underneath and around the rubble for about a *li*. On the day
of the Mid-Autumn Festival, we reached the river, which flows northwest 1222.09.21
with a current like that of the Yellow River.[13] We crossed by boat and
camped on the southern bank. To the west is a mountain fortress called
Tuanbaliq, located in an unassailable fastness.[14] On the road we met His
Excellency Zheng Shizhen,[ii] the personal physician of Ögödei, the Third
Imperial Prince. The Master commemorated the encounter in a poem:

[42. "At Mid-Autumn I Offer a Poem to the Medical Officer of the
Third Prince"]

The moon is always brightest at Mid-Autumn,

凉風屆候夜彌清。
一天氣象沉銀漢，
四海魚龍耀水精。
吳越樓臺歌吹滿，
燕秦部曲酒肴盈。
我之帝所臨河上，
欲罷干戈致太平。

　　沂河東南行三十里乃無水，即夜行。過班里城，甚
大。其衆新叛，去尚聞犬吠。黎明飯畢，東行數十里。有
水北流，馬僅能渡，東岸憩宿。

　　二十二日，田鎮海來迎及行宮。上遣復鎮海問曰：
「便欲見邪，且少憩邪。」師曰：「入見是望。且道人從
來見帝，無跪拜禮，入帳折身叉手而已。」既見，賜渾
酪，竟乃辭。上因問：「所居城內，支供足乎。」師對：
「從來蒙古、回紇、太師支給。迩者食用稍難，太師獨
辦。」翌日，又遣近侍官合住傳旨曰：「真人每日來就食，
可乎？」師曰：「山野修道之人，唯好靜處。」上令從便。

　　二十七日，車駕北迴。在路屢賜蒲萄酒、瓜、茶食。

　　九月朔，渡航橋而北。師奏：「話期將至，可召太師
阿海。」其月望，上設幄齋莊，退侍女左右，

---

15 Autumn.
16 The poet criticizes Chinese regimes in both the north and south by comparing Jin
    to the preimperial warring states of Yan and Qin and comparing the Southern Song
    to the battling southern states of Wu and Yue. His point, perhaps, is that squabbling
    about land to be lost or won among Chinese states distracts them from mounting an
    effective defense against the Mongol onslaught.
17 "Disappeared" is a euphemism for the slaughter of inhabitants (QXYJo5 130, n. 3).
    Chinggis first took the city in 1221 and the people surrendered; then they revolted,
    so he returned in the fall of 1222 to retake it, and he massacred the inhabitants. See
    QXYJo2 B.4b–5a for historical sources.

And in that season of cool breezes, the night sky is completely
 clear.[15]
All phenomena of the night sky disappear into the Milky Way,
And fish and dragons in the four seas glisten in the water's brilliance.
The towers and daises of Wu and Yue ring forth with songs and
 flutes,
The armies of Yan and Qin feast on food and wine.[16]
I go to the Emperor's camp beside the river,
Seeking to end the wars and restore great peace.

We went thirty *li* to the southwest against the current until the river ended and immediately continued traveling through the night. We passed by
Balkh, a very large city. The populace had recently rebelled and had been
disappeared, but we could still hear the barking of abandoned dogs.[17]
At the break of day, after finishing breakfast, we traveled east for several
dozen *li* and came to a north-flowing stream that the horses could just
barely ford. We made camp on the eastern bank to rest.

On the twenty-second day, Chinqai came to greet us. When we
arrived back at the Imperial Camp at Taliqan, His Majesty again sent
Chinqai to inquire of the Master, "Are you ready to be presented now,
or would you like to rest first?" The Master answered, "I would like to
go now. But when followers of the Way have an audience with an emperor, they do not kneel or bow. When we enter the tent, we will bend
at the waist and salute with clasped hands, but no more." Once they had
been presented to the Emperor, they finished the ceremonial offering of
koumiss, of which the Master did not partake. The Emperor inquired,
"Were you sufficiently supplied in the city (of Samarkand)?" The Master
responded, "Before, we were always provisioned by the Mongols, the
Uyghurs, and the Governor. Only recently has it been hard to find the
right food for us, but the Governor managed it." The following day His
Majesty sent a personal servant, Qaju,[iii] to convey a message: "Would
the Perfected like to come here daily to dine?" The Master replied, "A
peasant cultivating the Way desires only a quiet place." His Majesty ordered that he be allowed to do as he wished.

On the twenty-seventh day, the Imperial Carriage began its return
journey northward, and along the way the imperial party frequently sent
us wine, melons, tea, and other foodstuffs. At the beginning of the ninth
month, after crossing the Amu on a pontoon bridge and proceeding
north, the Master humbly addressed a message to His Majesty, "The
date for our discussion is upon us. Could you please inform Governor
Ahai?" At the full moon of this month, His Majesty commanded that a
dignified tent be erected, ordered his female servants and attendants to

1222.09.28

1222.10.03

1222.10.07–16

1222.10.21

燈燭煒煌，唯闍利必鎮海、宣差仲祿侍於外。師與太師阿海、阿里鮮入帳坐。奏曰：「仲祿萬里周旋，鎮海數千里遠送，亦可入帳預聞道話。」於是召二人入。師有所說，即令太師阿海以蒙古語譯奏，頗愜聖懷。

十有九日，清夜，再召師論道，上大悅。

二十有三日，又宣師入幄，禮如初。上溫顏以聽，令左右錄之。仍勅誌以漢字，意示不忘。謂左右曰：「神仙三說養生之道，我甚入心，使勿泄於外。」

自爾扈從而東，時敷奏道化。

又數日，至邪米思干大城西南三十里。

十月朔，奏告先還舊居。從之。上駐蹕于城之東二十里。

是月六日，暨太師阿海入見。上曰：「左右不去，如何？」師曰：「不妨。」遂令太師阿海奏曰：「山野學道有年矣，常樂靜處。行坐御帳前，軍馬雜遝，精神不爽。自此或在先，或在後，任意而行，山野受賜多矣。」上從之，既出，帝使人追問曰：「要禿鹿馬否？」師曰：「無用。」

于時，微雨始作，青草復生。

仲冬過半，則雨雪漸多，地脉方透。自師之至斯城也，有餘糧則惠飢民。又時時設粥，活者甚眾。

18 *Cherbi*, chamberlain (later equivalent to minister, Ch. *zaixiang* 宰相). In the Mongol imperial household, the *cherbi* had the duty "to supervise the domestic staff of the Qan's establishment" (de Rachewiltz 2004, 445).

19 Other sources, especially Yelü Chucai's anti-Daoist account, suggest that Li Zhichang here loyally embellished the impact and reception of Qiu Chuji's words. See the Introduction, n. 27. "For a transcript of a later lecture by Qiu, dated to November 20, 1222, see Appendix 12."

withdraw, and set the lights blazing. Outside, only the *cherbi*, Chinqai, and the Imperial Envoy Zhonglu waited.[18] The Master entered the tent with Governor Ahai and Alixian and when they sat down, the Master humbly addressed His Majesty, "Zhonglu has been our constant companion over a great distance, and Chinqai has performed many errands on our behalf. Could they be allowed to enter the tent and listen to our discourse on the Way?" Thereupon these two men were summoned into the tent. His Majesty ordered Governor Ahai to translate the Master's discourse into Mongolian. The Emperor was quite pleased with the Master's sage words.

On the nineteenth day, the night was bright and calm. The Emperor summoned the Master a second time to lecture on the Way, and again was greatly pleased. The Master was once more summoned into the Emperor's tent on the twenty-third day, and the rituals of the discussion were the same. The Emperor listened with a relaxed expression. He ordered those around him to record the Master's words (translated into Mongolian), and to transcribe the sermon into Chinese to ensure remembrance of the event. To his attendants the Emperor remarked, "The Divine Transcendent has spoken three times on the Way of nourishing life; his words have penetrated my heart. Do not let them be divulged outside of this company." From then on, we followed as part of the imperial entourage on its journey east, and from time to time the Master spoke to the Emperor on the art of transforming oneself through the Way.[19]

After several days, we reached thirty *li* southwest of Samarkand. On the first day of the tenth month, the Master requested to return to his old lodging in the Sultan's former palace, and His Majesty allowed it. The Emperor, meanwhile, set up camp some twenty *li* east of the city. On the sixth day of that month, Governor Ahai showed the Master in for an audience, and the Emperor said, "Might the attendants remain this time?" The Master agreed that it would do no harm and then asked Governor Ahai to petition the Emperor, "I have studied the Way for many years and find constant pleasure in serenity. The area in front of the Emperor's traveling palace is bustling with carts and horses, and my spirits are perturbed. Perhaps from now on, if I could travel a bit ahead of or behind the imperial entourage, I would be grateful." The Emperor approved his request. After His Majesty had departed, he sent someone to ask, "Do you require any *tuluma* (cotton cloth)?" The master replied, "I have no use for it."

Around this time there were occasional drizzles, and green grass began to spring up. In midwinter, the eleventh lunar month, the rain and snow gradually increased, and water reached the veins of the earth. From the time the Master arrived in the city, he distributed his extra food to the starving, and on occasion he had set up gruel stations. Large numbers of people thereby survived.

1222.10.25

1222.10.29

1222.11.05

1222.11.10

1222.12.05–1223.01.03

二十有六日，即行。

十二月二十三日，雪，寒。在路牛馬多凍死者。

又三日，東過霍闡没輦（大河也）。至行在，聞其航橋中夜斷散，蓋二十八日也。

帝問以震雷事，對曰：「山野聞國人夏不浴於河，不浣衣，不造氈，野有菌，則禁其採者，畏天威也。此非奉天之道也。常聞三千之罪，莫大於不孝者，天故以是警之。今聞國俗多不孝父母，帝乘威德，可戒其衆。」

上悅曰：「神仙是言，正合朕心。」勅左右紀以回紇字。師請徧諭國人，上從之。又集太子諸王大臣曰：「漢人尊重神仙，猶汝等敬天。我今愈信真天人也。」乃以師前後奏對語諭之，且云：「天俾神仙爲朕言此，汝輩各銘諸心。」師辭退。

逮正旦，將帥醫卜等官賀師。

十有一日，馬首遂東，西望邪米思干千餘里，駐大果園中。

十有九日，父師誕日，衆官灶香爲壽。

二十八日，太師府提控李公別去，師謂曰：「再相見也無？」李公曰：「三月相見。」師曰：「汝不知天理，二三月決東歸矣。」

20 The Syr Darya.
21 Chinggis Qan had evidently proceeded on ahead, allowing Qiu Chuji's party to travel in the rear.
22 From the context, it appears that Qiu Chuji met with Chinggis Qan in person on this occasion. The Mongols' fear of thunder and lightning is noted in many Chinese and European travel accounts of the era.
23 Juvaynī 1997, 140, records that the Qan met with his sons near the Syr Darya in the winter of 1222–1223.
24 As indicated above, these teachings were originally kept secret, known only to those who participated in the discussions.
25 The 28th day in the text is clearly a scribal mistake for the 18th.

Our journey recommenced on the twenty-sixth day of the eleventh 1222.12.30
month. On the twenty-third day of the twelfth month, the snow and 1223.01.26
cold were so severe that many of our animals froze to death on the
road. Three days later, we crossed the Khojand-müren. (*This is a large* 1223.02.01
river.[20]) When we reached the Imperial Camp, we heard that the river's
pontoon bridge had been torn apart and scattered in the middle of the
night, probably on the night of the twenty-eighth day.[21]

The Emperor inquired if we were frightened by the thunder and 1223.01.30
lightning, and the Master replied, "I have heard that in summer the
Mongol people do not bathe in rivers, do not wash their clothing, do not
make felt, and are forbidden from gathering mushrooms in the fields—
all out of fear of Heaven's power. That is not the way to serve Heaven.
I have heard that of the three thousand crimes, none is greater than a
lack of filial piety. Thunder is what Heaven uses to warn us. It is known
that Mongol customs by and large do not enjoin showing reverence to
parents. Your Majesty can take advantage of your daunting charisma to
admonish Your multitude."[22]

Delighted, the Emperor said, "These words of the Divine Transcendent accord exactly with my own thoughts." He ordered his attendants to
make a record in the Uyghur (Mongolian) script. The Master petitioned
to proclaim the matter widely to people, and His Majesty concurred. He
also assembled the Imperial Princes, the princes of the extended clan,
and the great officials, to announce, "The Chinese revere the Divine
Transcendent just as all of you pay homage to Heaven. I am now even
more convinced that he is a celestial being!"[23] Then he instructed the
men about what the Master had conveyed in his conversations.[24] He
also said, "Heaven has sent the Divine Transcendent to reveal this for
my sake; each of you, etch this upon your hearts." The Master took his
leave and withdrew.

On the first of the new year *guiwei*, generals, doctors, diviners, and 1223.02.02
other officials came to congratulate the Master. On the eleventh day, our 1223.02.12
horses set out eastward. Samarkand (Xiemisigan) now lay a thousand *li*
to our west. We halted to rest in a large fruit orchard.

On the nineteenth day we celebrated the Master's birthday, and the 1223.02.20
officials all burned incense to wish him a long life. On the eighteenth
day, His Excellency Li, supervisor of the Governor's yamen (in Samarkand), had come along with us this far to bid a proper farewell and was
about to go back when the Master asked him, "Will we see each other
again?"[25] Li responded, "We will meet again in the third month." The
Master replied, "You do not understand Heaven's intent. I will have
returned to the east by the second or third month."

二十一日，[iii]東遷一程，至一大川。東北去賽藍約三程。水草豐茂，可飽牛馬，因盤桓焉。

二月上七日，師入見。奏曰：「山野離海上，約三年迴。今兹三年，復得歸山固所願也。」上曰：「朕已東矣，同途可乎？」對曰：「得先行便。來時，漢人問山野以還期，嘗荅云『三歲』。今上所諮訪敷奏訖。因復固辭。」上曰：「少俟三五日，太子來。前來道話，所有未解者，朕悟即行。」

八日，上獵東山下，射一大豕。馬蹄失馭，豕傍立，不敢前。左右進馬，遂罷獵，還行宮。師聞之，入諫曰：「天道好生。今聖壽已高，宜少出獵。墜馬，天戒也。豕不敢前，天護之也。」上曰：「朕已深省，神仙勸我良是。我蒙古人，騎射少所習，未能遽已。雖然神仙之言在衷焉。」上顧謂吉息利荅剌汗曰：「但神仙勸我語，以後都依也。」自後兩月不出獵。

二十有四日，再辭朝。上曰：「神仙將去，當與何物？朕將思之，更少待幾日。」師知不可遽辭，徊翔以待。

三月七日，又辭。上賜牛馬等物，師皆不受。曰：「秪得馴騎足矣。」上問通事阿里鮮曰：「漢地神仙弟子多少？」對曰：「甚衆。

26 The Chirchik River, a tributary of the Syr Darya in Uzbekistan.
27 See Book I. 1, n. 112.

Traveling east one stage, on the twenty-first day we reached a large 1223.02.22
river.[26] Three stages northeast brought us to Sayram, where plentiful
pasture allowed the horses and cattle to eat their fill, so we lingered 1223.03.10
there for a while.[27] On the seventh day of the second month, the Master
had an audience with the Emperor and humbly requested, "I left the
coast with the intent to return in three years. Now that those three years
have nearly passed, it is time to go back. That is my resolute desire." His
Majesty responded, "I too am traveling east. Why not travel with me?"
To which the Master replied, "It would be convenient if I could go on
ahead. When I first came out, the Han people asked me when I would
return. My answer was 'in three years.' All that His Majesty desired to
consult me about, I have explained." He again insisted on taking his
leave. The Emperor said, "Wait a few days, please. When the Imperial
Princes came last time to discuss certain matters, I still had questions
about your earlier discourse on the Way. Once I am fully enlightened
you may depart."

On the eighth day, the Emperor went hunting in the foothills of the 1223.03.11
eastern mountains and shot at a large boar. His horse tripped, and he
lost control. The boar stood nearby, not daring to advance. His entourage rushed in with another horse. The hunt was called off, and the
Emperor returned to his traveling palace. When the Master heard about
the incident, he went to remonstrate with the Emperor, saying, "It is a
principle of Heaven to love life. Now Your Majesty is advanced in years,
and it would be better if you hunted less. Your falling from your horse
is a caution from Heaven. The boar not advancing is Heaven protecting you." The Emperor responded, "I have already come to this deep
realization. It is right that the Divine Transcendent should exhort me,
but we Mongols practice riding and hunting from a young age, and it
cannot be suddenly stopped. Nevertheless, I have taken your words to
heart." Turning to Kishliq Darqan,[iv] he said, "From now on, the Divine
Transcendent's words of exhortation shall guide all my actions." And
for two months thereafter he did not go out to hunt.

On the twenty-fourth day, the Master again went to bid farewell to 1223.03.27
the Emperor. His Majesty said, "The Divine Transcendent is about to
depart. What should I give you? While I think about it, please wait at
least a few more days." The Master understood that he could not just
take his leave and would have to wait for permission. On the seventh 1223.04.09
day of the third month, he again went to bid farewell, and the Emperor
made gifts of horses, cattle, and provisions, but the Master declined them
all, saying, "Horses from the post station are all that we require." His
Majesty asked the interpreter Alixian, "Does the Divine Transcendent
have many disciples in the Han lands?" "Yes, many," came the reply,

神仙來時，德興府龍陽觀中，常見官司催督差發。」上謂
曰：「應于 [iv] 門下人，悉令蠲免。」仍賜聖旨文字一通，
且用御寶。因命阿里鮮（河西也）爲宣差，以蒙古帶、
喝剌八海副之，護師東還。

十日辭朝行。自苔剌汗已下，皆攜蒲萄酒、琮果，相
送數十里。臨別，衆皆揮涕。

三日至賽藍大城之東南。山有蛇兩頭，長二尺許，土
人徃徃見之。

望日，門人出郊，致奠于虛靜先生趙公之墓。衆議欲
負其骨歸。師曰：

四大假軀，
終爲弃物。
一靈真性，
自在無拘。

衆議乃息，師明日遂行。

二十有三日，宣差阿狗追餞師於吹没輦之南岸。

又十日，至阿里馬城西百餘里，濟大河。

四月五日，至阿里馬城之東園。二太子之太匠張公
固請曰：「弟于所居營三壇，四百餘人晨參暮禮，未嘗懈
怠。且預接數日，伏願仙慈渡河，俾壇衆得以請教，幸
甚。」

師辭曰：「南方因緣已近，不能遷路以行。」復堅請，
師曰：「若無佗事，即當往焉。」

28　Alixian's observation seems very opportunistic, yet there exists a stele engraving of the
　　1223 edict granting such to the Quanzhen sect (see Appendix 4 for the text of this edict).

29　On these names, see the Additional Note.

30　The disciple who died here on 1221.11.20 on the Daoists' outbound journey.

31　Here Qiu seems to adopt a learned phrase or idiom from Buddhism. The lines do
　　not rhyme but have a rhythmic tonal antithesis that makes for something like blank
　　verse in English.

32　The Four Greats appear in *The Way and Its Power* as the Way, heaven, earth, and hu-
　　mans, but here more likely refer to the Four Greats of Buddhism—earth (hardness),
　　water (moisture), fire (warmth), and wind (activity), properties thought to make up
　　the human body.

"On the Divine Transcendent's outbound journey, I saw officials come to Longyang Monastery in Dexing Prefecture demanding payment of taxes." The Emperor said, "There should be a decree exempting all of his disciples from taxes." His Majesty thereupon presented the Master a written imperial edict with words to that effect and affixed the royal seal to it.[28] Further, he commanded Alixian (*a Tangut from Hexi*) to serve as imperial envoy, with Menggudai and Hela Bahai as his deputies, and to escort the Master back east, before returning to the Qan.[29]

[Return to the East]

On the tenth day the Master bade farewell to the Emperor, and we set out. From the *darqans* on down, everyone brought wine and precious fruits to present to us and traveled with us several dozen *li* to send us on our way. When we parted, they brushed away tears. Three days later, we reached the mountain southeast of the large city of Sayram where there was a two-headed snake more than two feet long, a common sight to the locals.

On the day of the full moon, the disciples went out to the eastern outskirts to offer a sacrifice to the dead at the grave site of Sir Zhao, Master Xujing.[30] The group deliberated about the desire to bear his bones home. The Master said:[31]

The "Four Greats" borrowed to make our corporeal body[32]
Are in the end only phenomenal objects to be discarded.
The one noumenal spirit that is true nature
Is something unfettered and free.

After this, the group's deliberations ceased. The next day the Master set out.

On the twenty-third day, Imperial Envoy Agou, bearing farewell gifts of food and wine, caught up with the Master on the southern bank of the Chu River. After another ten days, we came within a hundred *li* of Almaliq and crossed a large river (the Ili). On the fifth day of the fourth month, we reached the gardens east of Almaliq. His Excellency Zhang Rong,[v] chief carpenter of the Second Imperial Prince (Chaghadai), told us, "I, your disciple, have built three altars at my home, and over four hundred people worship there morning and evening without fail. Moreover, these last few days we have been preparing to welcome the Master, and earnestly entreat him to cross the river and instruct the believers at these altars. It would be a great blessing!"

The Master, however, demurred, "My destiny draws me southward; it is not possible to change my route." Zhang continued to beg him until the Master relented, "If nothing detains me unexpectedly, then I will go."

Margin dates: 1223.04.12 · 1223.04.15 · 1223.04.17 · 1223.04.25 · 1223.05.05 · 1223.05.06

翌日，師所乘馬突東北去，從者不能挽。於是張公等悲泣而言曰：我輩無緣，天不許其行矣。晚，抵陰山前宿。

又明日，復度四十八橋。緣溪上五十里，至天池海。東北過陰山後，行二日，方接元歷金山南大河驛路。復經金山東南，北並山行。

四月二十八日，大雨雪。翌日，滿山皆白。

又東北，並山行三日，至阿不罕山前。門人宋道安輩九人，同長春玉華會眾、宣差郭德全輩遠迎。入棲霞觀。歸依者日眾。師下車時，雨再降，人相賀曰：「從來此地經夏少雨，縱有雷雨，多於南北兩山之間。今日霑足，皆我師道廕所致也。」

居人常歲疏河灌田圃。至八月，禾麥始熟，終不及天雨。秋成則地鼠為害，鼠多白者。此地寒多，物晚結實。五月，河岸土深尺餘，其下堅冰亦尺許。齋後，日使人取之。

南望高嶺積雪，盛暑不消。多有異事，少西海子傍有風塚，其上土白堊，多粉裂其上。二三月中，即風起南山，崒穴先鳴，蓋先驅也。風自塚間出，初旋動如羊角者百千數。

33　That is, bolted either with Qiu Chuji in the saddle or in a cart pulled by the horse.

34　The "great river" is the Ulungur/Öröngö. See Book I, n. lii.

35　Site of the city of Chinqai. See Book I, n. xlv.

36　At least on this occasion, Qiu Chuji rode in a cart, not on horseback.

37　"Saturated" has the double meaning of being drenched both by the rain and by the Master's virtue.

38　Calcium carbonate, $CaCO_3$: found naturally in limestone, chalk, calcite, and marble. The residue on the mound that flakes off and is reduced to powder suggests chalk. The city of Chinqai having been located by archaeology, we can see in the writer's account of the surrounding topography an accurate description of the Sharga River valley. The lake to the west is the Shargiin Tsagaan Nuur. The mountains to the southwest and south align with topographical features of the basin.

39　Reflecting an ancient Chinese belief that the wind and clouds were produced by fissures and holes in the mountains.

But the next day the Master's horse bolted to the northeast, and those of our group who chased it could not stop it.[33] At this turn of events, His Excellency Zhang and the others lamented, "Destiny is not with us, for Heaven does not permit the Master to pay a visit!" By evening we had reached the Yinshan (Tian Shan) Range and stayed overnight in its foothills. On the next day, we again crossed the forty-eight bridges and followed the stream fifty *li* to its source, where it flowed from Heaven Lake (Lake Sayram). We went northeast, and two days later we passed   1223.05.09 the Yinshan (Tian Shan) and were able to reconnect to the original Great River Post Road along the southern side of the Jinshan (Altai) Range.[34] We once more passed to the southeast of the Jinshan, the mountains flanking us as we went north.

On the twentieth-eighth day of the fourth month, it snowed heavily.   1223.05.29 The mountains were white the next day. We went on toward the northeast, traveling parallel to the mountains until we reached the Abuhan Mountains.[35] There, Song Dao'an and the other eight disciples whom we had left behind, the Changchun and Yuhua congregations,[vi] and Imperial Envoy Guo Dequan all came from a distance to meet us and take us to Qixia Monastery. Day by day new adherents had flocked to the Way, swelling their ranks. When the Master descended from the cart, the rain started up again.[36] People rejoiced among themselves and said, "Before, there was little rain in the summer here, even though we have more thunderstorms than the area between the northern and southern mountain ranges. Today we are saturated owing to the protection of your Way, Master."[37]

In normal years the inhabitants dredge canals to irrigate their fields and gardens, and by the eighth month, when the barley and millet begin to ripen, there is never any rain. When the fall harvest matures, the voles become a menace. These rodents are mostly white. The land is so cold that everything bears fruit late. In the fifth month the soil on the canal banks is more than a foot deep, and below that is hard ice for another foot or so. Every day, after the main meal, the Master sent someone to measure it.

Far off to the south are high ranges with a snowpack that never melts, even at the height of summer. So numerous are the strange phenomena in these parts! Beside a lake that lies somewhat to the west are burial-like mounds shaped by the wind and covered in calcium carbonate from the cliffs that the wind distributes as powder over their tops.[38] In the second and third months, the wind whips up in the Southern Mountains—a phenomenon heralded by a whistling noise that issues from the holes in the cliffs.[39] When the wind blows out from the mounds, it creates whirlwinds like thousands of rams' horns. Quickly everything

少焉,合爲一風,飛沙走石,發屋拔木,勢震百川,息于巽隅。又,東南澗後,有水磨三四,至平地,則水漸微而絕。

山出石炭。又東有二泉,三冬暴漲如江湖,復潛行地中,俄而突出,魚鰕隨之。或漂没居民,仲春漸消。地乃陷。

西北千餘里,儉儉州,出良鐵,多青鼠。亦收禾 iv 麥。漢匠千百人居之,織綾羅錦綺。

道院西南望金山,其山多雨雹。五六月間,或有大雪,深丈餘。此地間有沙陀,出肉蓯蓉,國人呼曰唆眼。水曰兀速,草曰愛不速。

深入山陰,松皆十丈許。會衆白師曰:「此地深蕃,太古以來,不聞正教,唯山精鬼魅惑人。自師立觀,疊設醮筵,旦望作會,人多以殺生爲戒,若非道化,何以得然?」

先是壬午年,道衆爲不善人妬害,衆不安。宋公道安晝寢方丈,忽於天窗中見虛靜先生趙公曰:有書至。道安問:「從何來?」曰:「天上來。」受而視之,止見太清二字,忽隱去。翌日,師有書至,魔事漸消。又瞽者羅生橫生非毁,一日墮馬觀前,折其脛,即自悔曰:「我之過也。」對道衆服罪。

40 This passage recalls a day trip into the mountains, setting the scene for the exchange that follows. Readers at that time would recognize the passage as a standard narrative device of writing about day excursions to provide a natural stage for the more philosophical dialogue that follows. Such asides are regularly interspersed in diary chronicles.

41 The "correct Way" is Quanzhen Daoism.

42 One of Three Purities (or Clarities) in Daoist doctrine ("jade purity," "highest purity" and "great purity") which refer to the realm of the transcendents. See Book I, n. 28.

43 Healer Luo was probably a local shaman who promoted the efficacy of his healing over that of ritual. This follows naturally from the preceding passage about the necessity of the Way in curing people of belief in malignant animistic spirits.

merges into an intense windstorm that stirs up the dust and sets stones rolling, tears apart homes and uproots trees. With a force pounding like a hundred rivers, it finally abates in the southeast. Likewise, to the southeast, behind the ravine streams, there are three or four watermills. As the ravine water approaches level land, the flow gradually dribbles out and then stops.

The mountains produce coal. To the east are two springs that suddenly overflow in the last month of winter, as if they were huge underground rivers or lakes that suddenly burst forth full of fish and shrimp, sometimes inundating peoples' homes. In the middle month of spring the water gradually recedes, leaving the ground a dangerous mire.

Over a thousand *li* to the northwest is Kemkemji'ut Prefecture,[vii] which produces excellent iron and is home to many squirrels. Grain is also grown there. A thousand Chinese artisans live there to weave silk textiles.

From the Daoist monastery one can gaze southwest on the Jinshan. It often hails in those mountains, and there can sometimes be a foot of heavy snow in the fifth or sixth month. There are also deserts that produce *Cistanche*, which the Mongols call *suoyan*.[viii] Water is called *wusu* (Mo. *uusun*), and grass is called *aibusu* (Mo. *ebesün*).

We went deep into the northern flanks of the mountains, where the pine trees all grow a hundred feet tall.[40] The congregations reported to the Master, saying, "This region is deep in foreign territory. From ancient times they have not been exposed to the correct Way, and there are only mountain sprites and ghostly wights that delude the people.[41] Since the Master had the monastery built, established the *jiao* rituals and attendant offerings of food, and held gatherings on the first and fifteenth of every month, most people have come to observe the prohibition against the taking of life. How could this have been possible without transformation by the Way?"

Earlier, in the *renwu* year (1222), the Daoist congregation had suffered harm from the jealousy of bad people in its midst, which caused turmoil in the ranks. Song Dao'an was asleep one day in the abbot's chamber, when suddenly through a ceiling window, he saw the deceased Master Xujing, Zhao Jiugu, who said, "A letter has arrived." Dao'an asked, "From where?" "From Heaven," was the reply. He looked at it and saw only the two words "Great Purity," when suddenly everything disappeared as he awoke.[42] The next day a letter indeed arrived from the Master and all former impediments to the group disappeared. A certain healer Luo, who had been saying slanderous things, fell off his horse in front of the monastery and broke his shinbone. He immediately repented, saying, "I was wrong," and acknowledged his guilt before the Daoist congregation.[43]

師東行，書教語一篇示衆云：

萬里乘官馬，
三年別故人。
干戈猶未息，
道德偶然陳。
論氣當秋夜（對上論養生事，故云），
還鄉及暮春。
思歸無限衆，
不得下情伸。

阿里鮮等白師曰：「南路饒沙石，鮮水草。使客甚繁，馬甚苦，恐留滯。」師曰：「分三班以進，吾徒無患矣。」

五月七日，令宋道安、夏志誠、宋德方、孟志温、何志堅、潘德沖六人先行。

十有四日，師挈尹志平、王志明、于志可、鞠志圓、楊志靜、綦志清六人次之。餞行者夾谷妃、郭宣差、李萬户等數十人。送二十里，皆下馬再拜泣別。

師策馬亟進。

十有八日，張志素、孫志堅、鄭志脩、張志遠、李志常五人又次之。

師東行十六日，過大山。山上有雪，甚寒，易騎於拂廬。

十七日，師不食，但時時飲湯。東南過大沙場，有草木，其間多蚊虻。夜宿河東。

又數日，師或乘車。尹志平輩諮師曰：「奚疾？」師曰：「余疾非醫可測。聖賢琢磨故也。卒未能愈，汝輩勿慮。」

44 See Appendix 10 for a full list of the disciples.

When the Master resumed his journey east, he showed the congregation a poem on "Words of Instruction":

[43. "Writing Out Words of Instruction to Show to the Congregation"]

For ten thousand miles I rode in carts drawn by post horses,
And parted for three years from old friends.
Shield and spear have yet to cease,
But the Way and its power had a chance to unfold.
To discuss *qi*, I braved autumn nights;
Referring to the discourse on nourishing life for His Highness.
To get back to my native country will take until late spring.
Thoughts of return form an endless bundle;
I cannot explain them one by one.

Alixian and others explained to the Master, "The southern route is full of sand and rocks, water and grass are scarce, and the route will be crowded with travelers. It will be very hard on the horses, and we may be delayed." The Master thereupon suggested, "If we divide into three traveling groups then we will not be troubled." On the seventh day of the fifth month, he directed six disciples to depart first: Song Dao'an, Xia Zhicheng, Song Defang, Meng Zhiwen (1186–1261), He Zhijian, and Pan Dechong (1190–1256). Then on the fourteenth, the Master himself departed with six more disciples: Yin Zhiping, Wang Zhiming, Yu Zhike (1184–1256), Ju Zhiyuan, Yang Zhijing, and Qi Zhiqing (1190–1255).[44] Lady Jiagu (former consort of Jin Emperor Zhangzong), Imperial Envoy   1223.06.14
Guo Dequan, Myriarch Li, and several dozen people accompanied them for twenty *li*. Dismounting, they bowed twice and bid farewell in tears.

The Master spurred his horse to go faster. On the eighteenth day,   1223.06.30
the remaining five disciples—Zhang Zhisu (1188–1269), Sun Zhijian, Zheng Zhixiu, Zhang Zhiyuan, and Li Zhichang—followed. After traveling east for sixteen days, the Master crossed a large mountain covered in snow. It was extremely cold. They changed mounts at a   1223.07.01
post station tent.[ix]

On the seventeenth day, the Master ate nothing and drank a little boiled water. To the southeast we crossed a vast sandy battleground. There were grasses and trees as well as many horseflies.[x] At night we camped east of the river. For several days afterward, the Master traveled at times on the cart. Yin Zhiping and the other disciples respectfully inquired of the Master, asking, "How is your illness?" The Master replied, "My illness is not something a doctor can diagnose; rather, it is the sages and worthies who are testing me. The healing will not come quickly, so you should not be concerned." The disci-

衆揪然不釋。是夕，尹志平夢人曰：「師之疾，公輩勿
憂，至漢地當自愈。」

行又經沙路三百餘里，水草絕少，馬夜進不息，再宿
乃出。地臨夏人之北倕。廬帳漸廣，馬易得。後行者乃
及師。

六月二十一日，宿漁陽關，師尚未食。

明日，度關而東五十餘里，豐州元帥以下來迎。宣差
俞公請泊其家，奉以湯餅。是日輒飽食。繼而設齋，飲食
乃如故。道衆相謂曰：「清和前日之夢，驗不虛矣。」

時已季夏，北軒涼風入坐。俞公以璽紙求書，師書
之云：

身閒無俗念，
鳥宿至鷄鳴。
一眼不能睡，
寸心何所縈。
雲收溪月白，
㞷爽谷神清。
不是朝昏坐，
行功扭捏成。

---

45 Crossing the northwestern border of Tangut territory from north of Yumen (Jade Gate) Pass and traversing the large sand desert between modern Jiuquan and Baotou.
46 In the Daqing mountains, northeast of modern Hohhot.
47 Fengzhou, or Tiandejun 天德軍 under the Jin, just southeast of Hohhot, the capital of Inner Mongolia, had a long history as a frontier fortification.
48 That is, the Great Way of emptiness. Compare *The Way and Its Power*, stanza 6: "The valley's daemons never die, / The valley called the dark world womb; / The portal of the dark world womb / They call tree root of sky and land." See Laozi, Roberts, trans., 2019, 35–36.

ples' expressions turned somber, and they remained concerned. That evening Yin Zhiping dreamed that a man said to him, "Do not worry over your Master's illness; as soon as he returns to the land of the Han, it will cure itself."

We traveled through desert for more than three hundred *li*, with little water and grass to be found. At night we advanced without resting the horses and did the same the next night before we made it out of the desert. We skirted the northern borders of the Xia.[45] Tent dwellers grew in number and horses became easier to acquire. Those disciples traveling behind finally caught up with the Master's group.

On the twenty-first day of the sixth month, we camped at Yuyang Pass.[46] The Master had still not taken food. The next day we went through the pass and proceeded eastward for some fifty or more *li*, at which point the commander of Fengzhou came out to greet us.[47] His Excellency Imperial Envoy Yu invited the Master to stay at his home and offered him noodle soup. That day he finally ate his fill. Afterward they served us a meal, and we ate and drank as we used to. The disciples said to each other, "That dream that Qinghe (Yin Zhiping) had the other night came true!"

1223.07.20

Late autumn was already upon us, and a cool breeze blew through the north-facing veranda onto those seated within. His Excellency Yu brought forth a piece of fine silky paper and begged the Master to compose something for him. The Master's composition read,

[44. "Imperial Envoy Sir Yu of Fengzhou Brings Fine Paper to Request Calligraphy"]

With body at ease and no thoughts of the mundane,
Birds roost until the cock crows.
Even the briefest of shuteye, I cannot sleep.
What is it that tangles my thoughts?
Clouds gather away, mist disperses, the moon in the stream is white;
Night *qi* grows cool, the demon of the valley is purified.[48]
It is not morning and evening meditation,
But action that shapes and creates our completion.[49]

---

49 One must activate the body as an instrument to circulate the body's *qi* and create the vital elixir (*neidan*內丹); one must partake of the wholeness of *qi* that circulates within the cosmos. For *qi*, Qiu uses the character 炁, which refers to the vital energy of the body and the cosmos, as opposed to 氣, which refers to ordinary "breath."

　　七月朔，復起。三日至下水。元帥夾谷公出郭來迎，館於所居。來瞻禮者，無慮千人。

　　元帥日益敬。有鸂鶒三，七夕日，師遊郭外，放之海子中。少焉翔戲於風濤之間，容與自得。師賦詩曰：

養爾存心欲薦庖，
逢吾念善不爲肴。
扁舟送在鯨波裏，
會待三秋長六梢。

　　又云：

兩兩三三好弟兄，
秋來羽翼未能成。
放歸碧海深沈處，
浩蕩波瀾快野情。

　　翌日乃行。是月九日，至雲中。宣差總管阿不合與道眾出京以步輦迎歸于第。樓居二十餘日。總管以下，晨參暮禮。雲中士大夫日來請教，以詩贈之云：

得旨還鄉早，
乘春造物多。
三陽初變化，
一氣自沖和。

50　Lake Daihai 岱海, about 100 kilometers east-southeast of Hohhot.

51　A reference to a myth about a herd boy (the star Vega) and a weaving maiden (the star Altair) who are separated in Heaven by the Milky Way. Once a year, on the seventh of the seventh month, magpies fly up to heaven to form a bridge across the Milky Way so that they may meet. This day is also known as the festival of "beseeching skills," (*qiqiao* 乞巧), in which women seek the skill of the weaving maiden and participate in various games to divine their future.

52　To record his act of "liberating life" (*fangsheng* 放生), originally a Buddhist practice for accumulating good karma through the release of animals destined to die, and also to personally celebrate his own liberation into the familiar cultural environment of home.

53　The first lunar month.

We set out again at the beginning of the seventh month. Within three 1223.07.30–08.02 days we reached the Lower Water (that is, Daihai).[50] Commander Jia-gu[xi] came out from the city wall to meet us and gave us lodging in his residence. About a thousand people came to pay homage to the Master, while the commander became more deferential by the day. We had three wild fowl, and on the evening of the seventh day of the seventh month, 1223.08.05 the Master strolled beyond the city outskirts to release them at Lake Dai-hai.[51] For a while they soared and sported between the windblown waves, happy and carefree, whereupon the Master composed a few poems:[52]

[45. "Two Poems on Roaming Outside the City on the Eve of the Seventh" I]

I thought when raising them that you wanted to send them to the
     cook,
But encountering my thoughts of doing good, they do not seem
     like food.
In a little skiff I send them into the leviathan's waves,
And give them three years to grow their "six wing pinions."

[46. "Two Poems on Roaming Outside the City on the Eve of the Seventh" II]

Now two, now three, fine little brothers;
As autumn approaches, their wings have yet to mature.
Released back to the azure sea's secluded places,
They find happiness in the wildness of endless waves.

The next day we set out again and on the ninth day of that month 1223.08.07 reached Yunzhong (the Datong region). The imperially commissioned Route Commander[xii] Abuqa came out from the city with the Daoist congregation and had the Master conveyed in a palanquin back to his personal residence. The Master resided there in the upper story for more than twenty days. From the Route Commander on down, everyone came to visit and pay homage from morning until night. The elite of Yunzhong flocked to him daily to seek instruction, and the Master presented them with a poem:

[47. "Presented to the Elite of Yunzhong"]

Given permission to go home early,
I took advantage of the Shaper of Things' plenitude of spring.
The first transformations began in the Third Yang phase;[53]
And all *qi* settled naturally into harmony.

驛馬程程送，

雲山處處羅。

京城一萬里，

重到即如何？

十有三日，宣差阿里鮮欲徃山東招諭。懇求與門弟
子尹志平行。師曰：「天意未許，雖徃何益。」阿里鮮再
拜曰：「若國王臨以大軍，生靈必遭殺戮，願父師一言垂
慈」。師良久曰：「雖救之不得，猶愈於坐視其死也。」
乃令清和同徃，即付招諭書二副。

又聞宣德以南諸方道衆來參者多，恐隨庵困於接待。
令尹公約束，付親筆云：「長行萬里，一去三年。多少道
人，縱橫無賴者。尹公到日，一面施行，勿使教門有妨道
化。衆生福薄，容易轉流。上山即難，下坡省力耳。」

宣德元帥移剌公遣專使持書至雲中，以取乘馬奉師。

八月初，東邁楊河。歷白登、天城、懷安，渡潰河。
凡十有二日，至宣德。元帥具威儀出郭西遠迎師入，居州
之朝元觀，道友敬奉。遂書四十字云：

萬里遊生界，

三年別故鄉。

迴頭身已老，

過眼夢何長。

54 Qiu has in mind the Mandate of Heaven given to a new state as Heaven's imprimatur.
   With warfare still going on, the will of Heaven itself was not yet clear.
55 "Prince of State" is title Chinggis granted to Muqali, commander of Mongol operations
   in north China, in 1217. His son Bōl inherited the position and title when Muqali died
   in the third month of 1223 (YS 1.19; 119.2936).
56 The Yang is a tributary of the Sanggan River; the Kui River is also a tributary of the
   Sanggan.

The post-route mount brought us stage by stage,
Clouds and mountains spread out everywhere.
The capital city was ten thousand *li* away.
Reaching it again, what shall we do?

On the thirteenth day, Imperial Envoy Alixian was about to go to Shandong to encourage people to give up any resistance. He requested to take the disciple Yin Zhiping along, but the Master said, "The will of Heaven is yet unclear, so what good would it do were he to go?"[54] Alixian again bowed and said, "If the Prince of State brings a great army to bear, then the people will meet annihilation.[55] I would like the Master to spread his compassion with just a single word." After a long while, the Master said, "I may not be able to rescue them, but it is better than sitting by and watching them die." With that he bade Qinghe (Yin Zhiping) to go with Alixian and entrusted with him two missives counseling surrender.

1223.08.11

We also heard that a great many Daoist congregations from various quarters south of Xuande had already come to see him, and the Master feared that would create problems for the various monasteries that would receive them. He ordered Sir Yin to bring order to the situation and gave him a personal message to deliver: "I have been away on a long journey of ten thousand *li* for three years. So many followers are unruly hooligans. When Sir Yin arrives, he will bring them under control. Do not allow our sect to be hindered in the transformative teachings of the Way. The congregations have been unlucky, so it is easy to change course and flow into heterodoxy and deviancy. 'Climbing the mountain is difficult but coming down takes little strength!'" Xuande Regional Commander Yila (Yelü Tuhua) sent a special envoy to Yunzhong, with a letter saying he was to select a horse to present as a gift to the Master.

At the beginning of the eighth month, we forged ahead to the Yang River, passed through Baideng, Tiancheng, and Huai'an; then crossed the Kui River, and after twelve days reached Xuande.[56] The Commander (Tuhua) prepared a formal entourage and went out beyond the city walls to receive the Master some distance to the west. The Master took up residence in Chaoyuan Monastery in that prefecture. Friends in the Way received him with respect, whereupon the Master penned a verse for them:

~1223.09.09

[48. *"A Poem on Chaoyuan Monastery in Xuande Prefecture"*]

For ten thousand *li* I roamed to unfamiliar boundaries;
For three full years I parted from my home.
In this short while, my body has aged;
A blink of the eye—how long did this dream last?

浩浩天空闊，
紛紛事杳茫。
江南及塞北，
從古至今常。

　　道衆且云：去冬有見虛靜先生趙公牽馬自門入者，衆
爲之出迎，忽不見。又德興、安定亦有人見之。河朔州府
王官將帥及一切士庶，爭以書疏來請，若輻輳然，止迴答
數字而已。有云：

王室未寧，
道門先暢。
開度有緣，
恢弘無量。
群方帥首，
志心歸向。
恨不化身，
分酬衆望。

　　十月朔，作醮於龍門川。望日，醮於本州朝元觀。
　　十一月望，宋德方等以向日過野狐嶺見白骨所發願
心，乃同太君尹千億醮于德興之龍陽觀，濟度孤魂。前數
日稍寒，及設醮二夜三日，有如春。醮畢，元帥賈昌至自
行在，傳旨：

神仙自春及夏，道途匪易。所得食物馹騎，好否？
到宣德等處，有司在意館穀否？招諭在下人户，得
來否？朕常念神仙，神仙無忘朕。

57　A short message from Chinggis to Qiu Chuji, delivered by Alixian, is dated to this
　　day and preserved as an appendix to the text. See Appendix 5 for a translation.
58　When passing through the area in March 1221, Song Defang made a vow to hold a
　　Golden Tablet Retreat during the party's return journey, for the souls of soldiers who
　　had died in the battle of 1211 (see Book I, p. 35).
59　The original text of the edict is more colloquial and was included as an appendix to
　　the text; it is translated in Appendix 6.

Vast and wide, the void of the sky stretches on;
Countless and complicated, human affairs seem boundless.
Yet from south of the Yangzi to north of the Wall,
A constancy runs from past through the present.

The congregation then recounted, "The winter of your departure, someone saw Master Xujing, Zhao Jiugu, leading a horse through the monastery gate. They went out to meet him, but he disappeared. Likewise, people reported sighting him in Dexing and Anding (Hebei, Daming county)."

Throughout the region north of the Yellow River, officials who served Mongol princes, commanders, clerks, and commoners all wrote to invite the Master to visit them. The requests flowed in like spokes to an axle hub, and the Master could only respond with a few words, for example:

[The Fourth Gāthā*]*

With rulership still unsettled,
Let our sect first flourish.
If opening the way to salvation is predetermined,
Its great expansion will be immeasurable.
Military leaders everywhere
Fully pledge their faith by heart and will.
Would that I could multiply myself,
To respond to each congregation's hopes.

On the first day of the tenth month, the Master performed a *jiao* ritual at the Longmen River.[57] On the fifteenth day, he performed a *jiao* ritual at Chaoyuan Monastery here in Xuande. Because Song Defang and others had made an oath when they saw the bleached bones on Wild Fox Ridge, they performed a *jiao* ritual with Lady of Patent Yin Qianyi[xiii] at Longyang Monastery in Dexing on the fifteenth day of the eleventh month, to deliver the soldiers' orphaned souls to salvation.[58] It had been colder for several days, but when they began the ceremony—two nights and three days long—the weather turned springlike. After the ceremony concluded, Commander Jia Chang arrived from the Imperial Camp to convey an edict:

1223.10.26
1223.11.09
1223.12.08

The Divine Transcendent has been traveling a difficult road from spring into autumn. Were you provided with good food and horses? When you reached Xuande and other prefectures, did the officials take special care with your meals and lodging? Have you recruited people of lower stations? I think often of the Divine Transcendent. Sir, do not forget me.[59]

十二月既望，醮于蔚州三館。師於龍陽住冬，旦夕常往龍岡閑步，下視德興。以兵革之後，村落蕭條，作詩以寫其意云：

昔年林木參天合，
今日村坊徧地開。
無限蒼生臨白刃，
幾多華屋變青灰。

又云：

豪傑痛吟千萬首
古今能有幾多人。
研窮物外閑中趣，
得脫輪迴泉下塵。

甲申之春二月朔，醮於繇山之秋陽觀。觀在大翮山之陽，山水明秀，松蘿煙月，道家之地也。以詩題其楔云：

秋陽觀後碧崗深，
萬頃煙霞插翠岑。
一徑桃花春水急，
彎環流出洞天心。

又云：

羣山一帶碧嵯峨，
上有羣仙日夜過。
洞府深沈人不到，
時聞巖壁洞仙歌。

---

60 That is, their enclosing walls are now torn down or in complete disrepair.
61 That is, poems of mourning.
62 In modern Yanqing County 延慶縣, northwest of Beijing.

On the sixteenth day of the twelfth month, the Master performed 1224.01.08 ceremonies at Sanguan ("the three lodges") in Yuzhou (Hebei). The Master passed the winter at Longyang Monastery, and during the day regularly strolled to Longgang, where he had a bird's eye view of Dexing. After the ravages of war, all the villages lay in ruins. To express his impressions, he wrote several poems:

[49. "Two Poems Written at Longgang to Express My Feelings," I]

In the past a forest of trees converged to a point in the sky;
Today villages and districts lie exposed across the land.[60]
Countless souls faced unsheathed blades,
And innumerable buildings were turned to blackened ash.

[50. "Two Poems Written at Longgang to Express My Feelings," II]

How many heroes bitterly chanting myriad poems[61]
Have there been through history?
Revel in the delight of leisure in a world beyond this world of
    phenomena,
And you can escape a karmic cycle ending as ashes in hell.

On the first day of the second month of spring in the *jiashen* year, the 1224.02.21 Master performed ceremonies at Qiuyang (Autumn Yang) Monastery in Jinshan.[62] The monastery is located on the southern flank of the Dahe Mountains amid enchanting scenery, and the moss hanging from the pines turns the moon misty—truly a land made for Daoists. The Master captured its essence in two poems:

[51. "Two Poems Written in Qiuyang Monastery in Jinshan" I]

Behind Qiuyang Monastery the azure cliffs are a deep
Huge swath of mist pierced by jade green hills.
By a path of peach blossoms, surging spring waters
Wind and twine from the heart of the grotto heavens.[63]

[52. "Two Poems Written in Qiuyang Monastery in Jinshan" II]

The mountains are a single expanse of towering azure,
Over which transcendent beings fly day and night.
Grotto precincts sunken so deep the uninitiated cannot reach
    them,
Yet now and again from the cliffs you can hear songs of grotto
    transcendents.

---

63 One of seventy-two underground grotto heavens that are filled with Daoist transcendent beings.

燕京行省金紫石抹公、宣差便宜劉公以下諸官，遣使
者持疏懇請師住大天長觀，許之。既而以驛召，乃度居庸
而南。燕京道友來迎於南口神游觀。明旦，四遠父老士
女，以香花導師入京。瞻禮者塞路。

初師之西行也，衆請還期，師曰：「三載歸，三載
歸。」至是果如其言。

以上七日入天長觀，齋者日千人。

望日，會衆請赴玉虛觀。是月二十五日，喝剌至自行
宮傳旨：

> 神仙至漢地以清淨道化人。每日與朕誦經祝壽，甚
> 好。教神仙好田地內愛住處住。道與阿里鮮，神仙
> 壽高，善爲護持。神仙無忘朕舊言。

仲夏，行省金紫石抹公、便宜劉公再三持疏，請師住
持大天長觀。是月二十有二日，赴其請。空中有數鶴前
導，俟西北而去。自師寓玉虛，或就人家齋，常有三五鶴
飛鳴其上。北方從來奉道者鮮。至是，聖賢欲使人歸向，
以此顯化耳。入會之衆，皆稽首拜跪，作道家禮，時俗一
變。玉虛井水舊鹹苦，甲申、

---

64 See Appendices 7 and 8 for translations.
65 Where Qiu had lodged on his outbound sojourn in Yanjing, in 1220.
66 See Appendix 9 for translation. The received text appears to misdate the request to
1226.

[Return to Yanjing]

The Governor of Yanjing, Grandee of the First Class, Shimo Xiandebu and Imperial Envoy and Plenipotentiary Liu Min,[xiv] as well as other officials, sent an envoy with a letter beseeching the Master to manage the Great Tianchang Monastery (in Yanjing), to which the Master acquiesced.[64] With authorization to use fast courier horses, the Master thereupon proceeded through the Juyong Pass and headed south. The Daoist followers of Yanjing came out to meet him at Shenyou Monastery at the southern debouchment of the pass. At daybreak the next morning, everyone from village elders to young men and women came from all directions, carrying flowers and burning incense, to lead the Master into the city. Crowds of worshippers blocked the road. When the Master first departed to travel west and his followers asked when he would return, he had told them, "I will return in three years, I will return in three years!" And indeed, it turned out to be just as he said. On the seventh day of the second month, he entered Tianchang Monastery, and that very day hosted a thousand people at a vegetarian meal. On the fifteenth day, the congregation requested that the Master visit Yuxu Monastery.[65] 1224.03.06

On the twenty-fifth day of the second month, Qara arrived from the Imperial Traveling Camp to deliver an edict, which read, 1224.03.24

> The Divine Transcendent has arrived in the land of Han, and now in tranquility transforms people with the Way. It would be wonderful if you, Sir, would read scripture and pray for my long life each day. Let those who would like to live in your fine fields live there. And tell Alixian that since the Divine Transcendent is of advanced age, he should be vigilant in his support and protection. Divine Transcendent, do not forget my former words.

In the second month of summer, Governor of Yanjing, Grandee of the First Class Shimo and Plenipotentiary Liu for the third time delivered a request that the Master be the resident Abbot of the Great Tianchang Monastery.[66] On the twenty-second day of that month the Master fulfilled their request. Several cranes appeared in the sky to guide his way, then turned and flew off to the northwest. When the Master lodged at Yuxu Monastery, whenever he took a meal at someone's home, a few cranes could often be seen flying and calling out above him. There had been few Daoist believers in the north; now the sages and worthies used this clear manifestation to turn people to the Way. Those who entered the covenant of a congregation all bowed and knelt in obeisance and performed the rituals of the Daoists—this was a change of the common custom. The water in the well at Yuxu used to be bitter, but in the *jiashen* 1224.05.20–06.18 1224.06.10 1224–1225

乙酉年，西來道衆甚多，水味變甘，亦善緣所致也。季夏
望日，宣差相公劄八傳旨：

> 自神仙去，朕未嘗一日忘神仙，神仙無忘朕。朕所
> 有之地，愛願處即住。門人恒爲朕誦經祝壽則嘉。

自師之復來，諸方道侶雲集，邪説日寢。京人翕然歸
慕，若户曉家諭。教門四闢，百倍往昔。乃建八會於天
長，曰平等，曰長春，曰靈寶，曰長生，曰明真，曰平
安，曰消灾，曰萬蓮。

師既歸天長，遠方道人，繼來求法名者日益衆。嘗以
四頌示之。其一云：

> 世情無斷滅，
> 法界有消磨。
> 好惡縈心曲，
> 漂淪奈爾何。

其二云：

> 有物先天貴，
> 無名不自生。
> 人心常隱伏，
> 法界任縱橫。

---

67 This phrase in the imperial edict could easily be construed as authorization to confiscate territory and temples from the Buddhists, or anyone else, for that matter.

68 It became standard Chinggisid (Yuan) policy to require all religious clerics of whatever
stripe to pray for the Qan and the royal family, an obligation that generally exempted
them from other more strenuous or taxing impositions. See the Introduction, Atwood
2004b, and Jackson 2005.

69 The "realm of law": borrowed from Buddhist doctrine, "the realm of dharma," where
the law of the Way operates in its primal form.

70 QXYJ05 (166, n. 14) explains this as meaning "Let things you find good or bad per-
colate in your mind, let them go where they will: do not try to rationalize them or
discriminate between them."

and *yiyou* years, a great number of Daoists flocked there from the west, and the well water turned sweet. This was another result of the Master's good karma.

On the fifteenth day of the sixth month, Imperial Envoy Minister Ja'far 1224.07.03
Khwāja[xv] presented a decree from Chinggis, which read, "Since you left, my Divine Transcendent, not a day has passed that have I forgotten you. Do not forget me either. If there is anywhere you would like to reside in my lands, you may do so.[67] I commend those disciples who persevere in chanting scripture and praying for me."[68]

After the Master's return from his journey, friends in the Way from all over flocked to Yanjing, and unorthodox doctrines were daily put to rest. People in the capital come together in accord to render homage to the Master as though his name and instruction were known in every household. The gates of the Master's teachings opened to the four corners of the world, more than ever before. Thereupon the Eight Congregations—called Equality, Eternal Spring, Efficacious Treasure, Eternal Life, Luminous Perfection, Contented Ease, Averting Calamity, and Myriad Lotuses—were established at Tianchang Monastery.[xvi]

When the Master returned to Tianchang Monastery, increasing numbers of people arrived daily from distant places, and those requesting religious names became ever more numerous. The Master would reveal to them these four encomia:

["Four Encomia to Show to Daoists from Afar" I]

If worldly attachments are not severed and extinguished,
They will be ground away in the Realm of the Law.[69]
Let what you love and hate twine about in your innermost heart.
Why not just let it all float and drift as it will?[70]

["Four Encomia to Show to Daoists from Afar" II]

There are things valued prior to (being revealed by) Heaven;[71]
There are no names not produced by themselves.[72]
The human mind is always hiding away,
Yet the Realm of the Law allows it to move freely.

71 The Way exists prior to materiality; it is neither born nor perishes.
72 This couplet cleverly contrasts "being" 有 and "absence" 無 in the first words of each line. We believe Qiu's point to be that being and absence are undifferentiated in the Way before being revealed and, like their names in human discourse, are self-generated. "Being" and "absence" refer to the second couplet of *The Way and Its Power*, "Absence is the name applied to the beginning of all things; being is the mother of the myriad things" 無名天地之始，有萬物之母. See Laozi, Chen Guying, comm., 1983, 53–54.

其三云：

徇物雙眸眩，
勞生四大窮。
世間渾是假，
心上不知空。

其四云：

昨日念無蹤，
今朝事亦同。
不如齊放下，
度日且空空。

　　每齋畢，出遊故苑瓊華之上。從者六七人，宴坐松陰，或自賦詩，相次屬和。間因茶罷，令從者歌《游仙曲》數闋。夕陽在山，澹然忘歸。由是行省及宣差劄八相公以北宮園池并其近地數十頃爲獻，且請爲道院。師辭不受。請至于再，始受之。既而又爲頒文牓，以禁樵採者。遂安置道侶，日益脩葺。後具表以聞，上可其奏。
　　自爾佳時勝日，師未嘗不往來乎其間。寒食日，作春遊詩二首。其一云：

十頃方池間御園，
森森松栢罩清煙。

73　Blinded by the multiplicity of things that seem to exist, one forms attachments to the world.

74　See Book II, n. 31.

75　Because it is created by the human mind, divorcing one from the realm of Law. Things (*wu* 物) are created by the mind as mental images produced by perception, but they change over time and obscure the constant Way that produces them.

76　See the Table of Weights and Measures. This indicates a sizeable but unspecific area of at least fifty acres or more.

["Four Encomia to Show to Daoists from Afar" III]

Pursue external things, and the eyes are dazzled.[73]
Weary the body, and the Four Greats are exhausted.[74]
Everything in the world of time is false,[75]
Wherein the mind knows no emptiness.

["Four Encomia to Show to Daoists from Afar" IV]

No traces of yesterday's thoughts,
And the same for the affairs of today.
Better to put them all down,
So that you can pass your days in emptiness.

After his daily vegetarian meal, the Master would go strolling on the Island of Gemlike Flowers in the old imperial park.[xvii] Six or seven people would accompany him. They would sit and relax under the shade of the pines, the Master perhaps composing some verses, and then they would take turns writing poems that matched each other's rhymes. Or after drinking a cup of tea, the Master would have his companions sing several stanzas of "Songs of Roaming Transcendents." It was so peaceful as the sun set over the mountain, that they would forget about going back. The head of the Branch Secretariat and Imperial Envoy Minister Ja'far offered him several dozen *qing* of gardens and ponds around the old Jin northern palace, along with several dozen *qing* of adjacent lands, and he requested that the Master build a Daoist monastery there.[76] The Master at first refused the gift, but after being approached a second time, he finally accepted. Soon after this, proclamations were issued that banned wood gatherers on those lands. Daoist followers settled there, and the construction work proceeded apace. After its completion a detailed description was sent by memorial to the Emperor, and His Majesty approved the project. Thereafter, the Master never missed a stroll there on beautiful or auspicious days. During the Cold Food Festival, the Master composed the following:[77]

[53. "Roaming in Spring" I]

Ten *qing* of rectangular ponds are set amid the imperial garden,
And dense pine and cypress are covered by pure mists.

---

77 Held for three days around the Clear and Bright Festival, the Cold Food Festival originally celebrated the death of the hermit Jie Zhitui, who was burned to death rather than come down from his mountain retreat to serve in office. For the period of the festival, it was forbidden to light stove fires. For the Clear and Bright Festival, see Book I, n. 67.

亭臺萬事都歸夢，
花柳三春卻屬仙。
島外更無清絕地，
人間唯有廣寒天。
深知造物安排定，
乞與官民種福田。

其二云：

清明時節杏花開，
萬戶千門日往來。
島外茫茫春水闊，
松間獵獵暖風迴。
遊人共嘆斜陽逼，
達士猶嗟短景催。
安得大丹冥換骨，
化身飛上鬱羅臺。

乙酉四月，宣撫王公巨川請師致齋于其第。公關右人也，因話咸陽、終南竹木之勝，請師看庭竹。師曰：此竹殊秀。兵火而後，蓋不可多得也。我昔居于磻溪，茂林修竹，真天下之奇觀也。

All human affairs in pavilions or on terraces fade into dreams;
At spring's end, flowers and willows belong only to transcendents.
Beyond this island lies no other place of perfect purity,
This is precisely a Heaven of Spreading Cold in the human world.[78]
Certain that the Shaper of Things has fixed all firm,
I beg to cultivate fortune's field with officials and commoners.[79]

[54. "Roaming in Spring" II]

At the Clear and Bright Festival, apricot blossoms open,
And thousands of families mill about all day.
Beyond this island, spring waters spread boundless and vast,
And amid the pines that rustle and whisper, warm winds return.
Visitors sigh together as the setting sun intrudes.
Wise men still mutter, hurried by the shortening rays.
How can I get the great elixir to change my bones in secret,[80]
And transform my body to fly up to Yuluo Terrace?[81][xviii]

In the fourth month of the *yiyou* year, His Excellency Pacification   1225.5.09–06.07
Commissioner Wang Juchuan invited the Master to his residence for a
prayer service and a meal. Wang came from west of the Tong Pass, and
could converse about the superiority of the bamboo trees from around
Xianyang and the Zhongnan Mountains.[82] He invited the Master to
view the bamboo plants in his courtyard. The Master remarked, "This
bamboo is exquisite. After all the warfare it will probably be difficult
to obtain more of it. I used to live at Panxi, an area of thick forests
and tall bamboo, truly one of the marvelous places under Heaven.

---

void (*buxu* 步虛), a meditative practice in which the practitioner circumambulates
the Big Dipper, moving from star to star as different stages of enlightenment occur.

79 Like the Buddhists, the Daoists believed in the accumulation of a good reward for
good actions, a good fortune, which could be delivered in several ways, including a
rich harvest reflecting the richness of good deeds.

80 That is, to transform through ingesting or creating a magic elixir made of real or imagined cinnabar to turn oneself into a transcendent. In earlier times, the use of real
drug compounds was called "outer elixir" *waidan* 外丹, as opposed to Quanzhen's
emphasis on refining oneself from the constituents already in the body, called "inner
elixir" *neidan* 內丹. Here the idea is to transform oneself through a series of meditative
practices that involves actualizing elements of the microcosmic world (the cinnabar
fields, *dantian* 丹田) that lie within the body to make one a transcendent being.

81 A place in inner elixir practices that lies at the edge of the brain. See Book II, n. xviii.

82 Tong Pass or Tongguan (in Shaanxi), a historically crucial pass in the mountains just
east of Xi'an, marking the divide between the Yellow and Wei River valleys. Whoever
held the pass could control access to and from the north China plain to its east. Wang
Ji was from Fengxiang, Shaanxi.

思之如夢，今老矣，歸期將至。當分我數十竿，植寶玄之
北軒，聊以遮眼。」宣撫曰：「天下兵革未息，民甚倒懸。
主上方尊師重道，賴師真道力保護生靈，何遽出此言邪。
願垂大慈以救世爲念。」師以杖叩地，笑而言曰：「天命
已定，由人乎哉？」衆莫測其意。

夏五月終，師登壽樂山巔，四顧園林，若張翠幄。行
者休息其下，不知暑氣之甚也。因賦五言律詩云：

地土臨邊塞，
城池壓古今。
雖多壞宮闕，
尚有好園林。
緑樹攢攢密，
清風陣陣深。
日遊仙島上，
高視八紘吟。

一日師自瓊島迴，陳公秀玉來見。師出示七言律
詩云：

蒼山突兀倚天孤，
翠柏陰森遶殿扶。
萬頃煙霞常自有，
一川風月等閑無。
喬松挺拔來深澗，
異石嵌空出太湖。
盡是長生閑活計，
脩真薦福邁京都。

---

83 That is, seek to be screened from the world.
84 Such scholar rocks from Lake Tai, vented with curved openings, had been imported
   into the Song capital of Bianliang (Kaifeng) by the notorious "Convoys of Flower
   and Stone" (花石綱) of Emperor Huizong, the penultimate ruler of the Northern

I recall it as if in a dream. I am old now, and my final return approaches. You should divide a dozen stalks so that I can plant them in the north veranda of the Baoxuan Hall as a screen." The Pacification Commissioner replied, "The war is still going on and the people are in dire straits. His Majesty esteems the Master's devotion to the Way and relies on the Master's efficacy in protecting living beings. What makes you suddenly say this?[83] I want you to spread your great compassion and focus on saving those in distress." The Master knocked his walking stick on the floor and explained with a laugh, "The command of Heaven is fixed. What can man do about it?" No one there understood what he really meant.

In summer, at the end of the fifth month, the Master climbed up to the summit of Mt. Shoule ("Mountain of Longevity and Happiness," on the Island of Gemlike Flowers) and gazed at the gardens arrayed on all sides like emerald tents under which walkers could rest to forget the summer heat. There he composed a poem: 1225.06.28–07.06

[55. "Climbing to the Peak of Mt. Shoule"]

The land here abuts the border passes;
The walls and ponds are the most magnificent of all times.
Although now mostly crumbling palaces and pylons,
There are still fine garden plots.
Green trees cluster densely,
Cool breezes come in powerful gusts.
Every day we saunter about this transcendent isle,
Chanting as we gaze high into the distance.

One day, when the Master returned from the Island of Gemlike Flowers, Chen Xiuyu came to see him. The Master brought out a regulated verse to show him:

[56. "To Show to Chen Xiuyu"]

A dark green mountain juts up, orphaned against the sky.
Virid cypress encircle the hall in deep shade.
Ten thousand *qing* of sunset's aura seem ever present;
The stream of windblown clouds is mostly absent.
Towering pines grow straight up from deep ravines;
Strange rocks, delicately vented, emerge from Lake Tai.[84]
All a leisurely lesson for learning eternal life—
Perfect authenticity and sacrificial offerings that reach far beyond
    Yanjing.

Song. When the Jin took Kaifeng in 1126, they shipped some of these stones into the Jin capital at Zhongdu (Yanjing).

　　九月初吉，宣撫王公以熒惑犯尾宿，主燕境灾，將請師作醮。問所費幾何。師曰：一物失所，猶懷不忍，況闔境乎？比年已來，民苦徵役，公私交罄，我當以觀中常住物給之。但令京官齋戒，以待行禮足矣，餘無所用也。於是約作醮兩晝夜。師不憚其老，親禱于玄壇。醮竟之夕，宣撫喜而賀之曰：熒惑已退數舍，我輩無復憂矣。師之德感，一何速哉。師曰：余有何德，所禱之事，自古有之，但恐不誠耳。古人曰至誠動天地，此之謂也。

　　重九日，遠方道衆咸集，或以菊爲獻。師作詞一闋，寓聲《恨歡遲》云：

一種靈苗，
　體性殊。
待秋風，
　冷透根株。
散花開，
　百億黃金嫩，
　　照天地清虛。

九日持來，
　滿座隅。
坐中觀，
　眼界如如。
類長生，
　久視無凋謝，
　　稱作伴閑居。

85　Festival of the Double Ninth, or "doubled Yang." "Nine," a homophone in Chinese for "a long time," is associated with long life, and in this context the search for eternal life. Chrysanthemum blooms in autumn so it is a symbol of endurance and hardiness in the face of the season's cold. Chrysanthemum tea is thought to bestow long life. The festival is also an occasion for ascending mountains and writing poetry.

On the first day of the ninth month, because Mars had entered the Sixth   1225.10.04
Lunar Mansion, which governed disaster in the Yanjing area. Pacification
Commissioner Wang came to request that the Master perform a *jiao*
ceremony. Wang asked how much it could cost. The Master replied, "If
one thing out of place is unbearable, how much worse if it is an entire
area? In the past several years people have suffered from taxation and
corvée labor, and public and private resources have been exhausted.
I will make do with the monastery's regular provisions for this sacrifice. Just order the capital officials to observe a fast beforehand, and
that will suffice. There will be no need for anything else." Thereupon,
it was arranged that he would perform the ceremony for two days and
nights. Undaunted by his age, the Master himself officiated at the altar.
The evening when the *jiao* was finished, the Pacification Commission
happily congratulated the Master, saying, "Mars has retreated several
stages in the progression of the stars.[xix] We need fear it no more. The
Master's virtue had such a quick effect!" The Master responded, "My
virtue? From antiquity it has always been about the sincerity of praying.
One fears only a lack of sincerity. The ancients said, 'Perfect sincerity
moves Heaven and earth.' That is what happened here!"

On the day of "double ninth," Daoists from far away all gathered at   1225.10.12
Tianchang Monastery, some contributing chrysanthemums, and the
Master composed a verse to the lyric pattern "Resenting That Joy Is
Slow to Come":[85]

[e. "Resenting That Joy Is Slow to Come"]

One kind of noumenal sprout
   has a special nature—
It waits for autumn's wind
   to be cold enough to penetrate root and stem.
Then its scattered blossoms open,
   a profusion of golden delicacy,
     shining in the clear void of Heaven and earth.

It is brought here on the ninth
   to fill the corner of the dais.
I observe from my seat,
   eyes open to the world as it is.
A match to long life,
   it never withers no matter how long you look.
     It is acclaimed "companion of the quiet life."[86]

---

86 Another name for the chrysanthemum.

繼而有奉道者，持璽紙大軸來求親筆。以《鳳棲梧》詞書之。云：

得好休來休便是。
贏取逍遙，
　　免把身心使。
多少聰明英烈士。
忙忙虛負平生志。

造物推移無定止。
咋日歌歡，
　　今日愁煩至。
今日不知明日事。
區區著甚勞神思。

　　一日，或有質是非于其前者。師但漠然不應，以道義釋之。復示之以頌曰：

拂拂拂。
拂盡心頭無一物。
無物心頭是好人，
好人便是神仙佛。

　　其人聞之，自愧而退。
　　丙戌正月，盤山請師黃籙醮三晝夜。是日天氣晴霽，人心悅懌，寒谷生春。將事之夕，以詩示眾云：

詰曲亂山深，
山高快客心。

---

87 Its creation of material phenomena is unceasing since each material thing will pass away in time.
88 The Way transcends right and wrong. This way of stating the matter suggests that the Master does not directly respond to the speaker but makes a general comment.

One devotee had brought a large scroll of fine silk paper and asked for something written in the Master's own hand. On it, the Master wrote another lyric to the lyric pattern "The Phoenix Perches on the Parasol Tree":

[f. "The Phoenix Perches on the Parasol Tree" III]

When finding a good place to stop, stopping is right.
After winning a free and unfettered life,
   avoid exercising your mind.
How many clever heroes
Have worked and worked only to lose their life's aspiration?

The movements of the Shaper of Things have no fixed stopping
   place.[87]
Yesterday you sang of your joy;
   today you confront sorrow.
What happens tomorrow is unknown today.
Why wear yourself out over meaningless and trivial things?

One day someone ventured to question the nature of right and wrong right in front of the Master. The Master was silent and did not respond directly to the person, but he used the occasion to explain right and wrong using the principles of the Way.[88] He reinforced this by showing him an ode of praise:

Brush, brush, brush.
Brush your mind clean until there is nothing there.
Nothing on the mind: that is a good person.
A good person is a divine transcendent and a Buddha.

When the questioner heard this, he felt ashamed and withdrew.

In the first month of the *bingxu* year, followers on Mt. Pan asked the Master to perform a Yellow Register *jiao* on behalf of the dead for three days and nights.[89] That day, the weather had just cleared, and the people were in high spirits. Spring was coming to the cold valleys. The evening that he finished, the Master shared a verse with the congregation: 1226.01–02

[57. "The Yellow Register Jiao at Mt. Pan Finished, a Poem to Show to the Congregation"]

Twisting and turning chaotic mountains deepen,
But the high mountains please this sojourner's mind.

89 Mt. Pan is a scenic mountain near the Great Wall.

羣峰争挺拔，
巨壑太蕭森。
似有飛仙過，
殊無宿鳥吟。
黃冠三日醮，
素服萬家臨。

五月，京師大旱。農不下種，人以爲憂。有司移市，
立壇懇禱。前後數旬無應。行省差官賷疏，請師爲祈雨醮
三日兩夜。當設醮請聖之夕，雲氣四合，斯須雨降，自夜
半及食時未止。

行省委官奉香火來謝曰：「京師久旱，四野欲然。五
穀未種，民不聊生。賴我師道力感通上真，以降甘澍。百
姓僉曰：『神仙雨也。』」師荅曰：「相公至誠所感，上聖
垂慈，以活生靈，吾何與焉。」使者出，復遣使來告曰：
「雨則既降，奈久旱未霑足。何更得滂沱大作，此旱可
解。願我師慈悲。」師曰：「無慮，人以至誠感上真，上
真必以誠報人，大雨必至。」齋未竟，雨勢海立。

是歲有秋。名公碩儒皆以詩來賀。一日，有吳大卿德
明者，以四絕句來上。師復次韻荅之，其一云：

燕國蟾公即此州，
超凡入聖洞賓儔。

90 This is a gesture to the story of the transcendent Ding Lingwei 丁令威, who went
into the mountains outside of Liaoyang to perfect the Way. He was transformed into
a crane and flew back to the city, where he sat atop an ornamental column (華表). As
a young man was about to shoot him with a crossbow pellet, he flew away, singing,
"A bird, a bird: Ding Lingwei, / A thousand years since departing home, I return
today. / The city walls and outskirts exactly of old; the people not so much. / Learn
to be a transcendent, for the tombs pile one on another." 有鳥有鳥丁令威。去家千
年今始歸。城郭如古人民非。何不學仙冢壘壘。
91 Officials moved the markets from central markets into neighborhoods to try to control
the prices of goods and provide the necessities of life.

Layers of peaks vie to be taller,
And huge valleys are gloomy and shaded.
It seems as if a flying transcendent had passed through,
But there is no roosting bird to sing.[90]
In a yellow cap, I performed a three-day *jiao*;
In plain funeral garb, an audience of thousands came.

In the fifth month, a great drought hit the capital. Farmers were unable   1226.05.28–06.25
to plant their crops, and the people grew very anxious. Officials moved
the markets and set up altars.[91] They prayed continuously for several
weeks, without any result. The Branch Secretariat sent an official with a
formal request that the Master perform a *jiao* ritual for rain for three days
and nights. On the very evening that they set up the altar and summoned
the Master, clouds formed from all quadrants and within minutes rain
began to fall. It did not stop from midnight until mealtime the next day.

In thanks, the Branch Secretariat sent officials with offerings of incense, saying, "The capital has long suffered drought, the countryside
is about to burn up, the crops are not yet planted, and the people have
no means of survival. We relied on our Master's potent virtue to affect
the Perfected above, who have sent us this sweet timely rain. The people
declare this a Divine Transcendent rain." The Master replied, "Moved
by the Minister's perfect sincerity, the sages above have let fall their
compassion to give succor to humanity. What part could I have played
in it?" The envoys left, but another emissary came to report, "Rain has
started falling, but what if it is not enough to moisten the soil after the
long drought? If we get a real downpour, the drought can be alleviated.
We hope our Master will keep showing compassion." The Master said,
"Do not worry. If people can move the Perfected above through perfect
sincerity, the Perfected will respond in kind, and a great rain will arrive."
Before the ceremony ended, rain was coming down in a deluge.

There was a good harvest that year, and prominent literary men and
great scholars came to congratulate the Master with poems. One day the
great minister Wu Deming came bearing four quatrains, and the Master
replied with four of his own, following the same rhyme-word sequence:[92]

*[58. "Repeating the Rhymes of Great Minister Wu Deming, Four
Poems" I]*

Lord Moonlight[xx] of the state of Yan[xxi] is from this place,
Transcending the mundane to become a sage, a companion to Lü
    Dongbin.[xxii]

---

92 The quatrains, *jueju*, consisted of four lines each of five or seven syllables, with a
    specified tone pattern and rhyme scheme.

一時鶴駕歸蓬島，
萬劫仙鄉出土丘。

其二云：

我本深山獨自居，
誰能天下眾人譽。
軒轅道士來相訪，
不解言談世俗書。

其三云：

莫把閑人作等閑，
閑人無欲近仙班。
不於此日開心地，
更待何時到寶山。

其四云：

混沌開基得自然，
靈明翻小大椿年。
出生入死常無我，
跨古騰今自在仙。

93 A *kalpa* is a cosmic eon in Buddhism 16.8 million years in length. There is a playful pun in the last three words of this line: Qiu, a burial mound, is also Qiu Chuji's surname, which renders the last line, "And after a myriad *kalpas* as the transcendents' home, it produces a rustic Qiu."

94 This is a complex allusion to the famous account by Han Yu 韓愈 (768–824) of the creation of the "Linked Verses on a Stone Tripod Pot" 石鼎聯句. See Hightower 1984, 17–19. Briefly, an aged priest visits a lay friend who is drinking with another person. They dismiss the priest as an old bumpkin, and the priest challenges them to a contest of composing poems on the stone tripod. He claims he does not recognize their "mundane script" (he writes in the script of the Way), asks his lay friend to write down his words, and completes a series of lines that subtly make fun of the two who had dismissed him so lightly.

95 Where the Daoist transcendents dwell.

96 As QXYJ03 (266, n. 7) explains, "what is naturally so" (*ziran* 自然) involves three concepts: "(1) It is the source of the creation of the Way. (2) It is the basic nature of

Suddenly, guiding their cranes, they returned to
    Penglai Island,
And after a myriad *kalpas* in *this* transcendent realm, burial
    mounds emerged.[93]

*[59. "Repeating the Rhymes of Great Minister Wu Deming, Four
Poems" II]*

I once lived alone, deep in the mountains.
Who can match the praises of those under Heaven?
When the Daoist Master Xuanyuan came to visit,
They did not understand his speech, and he knew nothing of their
    "mundane script."[94]

*[60. "Repeating the Rhymes of Great Minister Wu Deming, Four
Poems" III]*

Do not consider the man of leisure ordinary,
Shorn of desire, a man of leisure approaches the ranks of
    transcendents.
If you do not open your consciousness today,
Will you ever reach these precious mountains?[95]

*[61. "Repeating the Rhymes of Great Minister Wu Deming, Four
Poems" IV]*

Undifferentiated chaos began, acquiring "what is naturally so,"[96]
Its own immediacy making the longest lives seem short.[97]
Emerging in birth and re-entering in death, constantly without a
    self,[98]
Straddling the past and soaring across the present—the free
    roaming transcendent.[99]

---

all things in the cosmos. All material objects take the Way as pattern and rule and
thus take *ziran* as their pattern and rule. (3) *Ziran* is the originating nature of the Way,
and since it resides within the Way itself, there is no need to strive to emulate it."

97 Literally, "making the years of the great *chun* tree short." In the first chapter of *Zhuangzi*, Master Zhuang insists that all things are relative, bounded by their own nature. He
cited as an example "In high antiquity was the Great Chun tree, which took 5,000
years as its spring and 5,000 years as its fall." See Zhuangzi, Guo, ed., 1995, 11.

98 Qiu has in mind the Buddhist concept of self as a changing bundle of matter, perceptions, sensation, mental formations, and consciousness, always in flux and lacking any
entity that one can point to as a self. Self, here, is "I," which is a state of temporary
consciousness that is not one of an infinite number of independent selves but stands
in distinction to otherness, as expressed in the common binary contrastive phrase
"all other things—'I'" 無我.

99 Freed from the limitations of a created subject and from time itself, realizing that
what he "is" is a forever changing materiality that will return to the undifferentiated
cosmic power of the Way.

又題支仲元畫得一、元保、玄素《三仙圖》云：

得道真仙世莫窮，
三師何代顯靈蹤。
直教御府相傳授，
閱向人間類赤松。

又，奉道者求頌，以七言絕句示之云：

朝昏忽忽急相催，
暗換浮生兩鬢絲。
造物戲人俱是夢，
是非嚮日又何爲？

師自受行省已下眾官疏以來，憫天長之聖位殿閣、常住堂宇，皆上頹下圮，至於窗戶堁砌，毀撤殆盡。乃命其徒日益修葺，罅漏者補之，傾斜者正之，斷手于丙戌，皆一新之。又創修寮舍四十餘間，不假外緣，皆常住自給也。凡遇夏月，令諸齋舍不張燈，至季秋稍親之，所以預火備也。

十月下寶玄，居方壺。每夕召眾師德以次坐，高談清論，或通宵不寐。

仲冬十有三日夜半，振衣而起，步於中庭。既還坐，以五言律詩示眾云：

100　Red Pine was a fabled transcendent of antiquity.
101　Fanghu Chamber was named after one of the three mountain-islands where transcendents dwelt, along with Penglai and Yingzhou.

The Master also inscribed a poem on *Portrait of the Three Tran-scendents*, by Zhi Zhongyuan,[xxiii] which portrayed Deyi, Yuanbao, and Xuansu:

[62. "Inscribed on Zhi Zhongyuan's Portrait of the Three Tran-scendents, Deyi, Yuanbao, and Xuansu"]

True transcendents who attain the Way are countless through time.
In what era did these three Masters reveal their noumenal traces?
Tell the court to keep this painting in circulation,
To circulate for perusal the likes of Red Pine in the human
   world.[100]

When a Daoist devotee begged for a hymn, he replied with a quatrain:

[63. "A Quatrain for an Adept"]

Dawns and dusks hurry past in a blur,
Our floating lives transform unnoticed until our temple locks are
   but threads.
The Shaper of Things plays with people, but it's all just a dream.
Those rights and wrongs of the past—what of them now?

After the Master had received petitions (to reside at Tianchang Mon-astery) from the officials of the Branch Secretariat and other officials as well, he was deeply concerned about the halls and galleries that held the statues of the patriarchs. And the roofs and walls of their living quarters were in complete disrepair. The windows and steps were also crumbling. He commanded his disciples to institute a daily repair schedule, to fill in leaking seams and make everything level and plumb. They ceased work in the *bingxu* year (1226) when everything had been renewed. They also built or renovated over forty disciples' cells, without availing themselves of outside aid. Everything was provided by the regular inhabitants of the monastery. In the summer months, the Master ordered that no lamps be used in the rooms, and at the end of autumn he personally inspected any lamps in use, to prevent fires.

In the tenth month the Master moved out of Baoxuan Pavilion and into Fanghu Chamber.[101] Every evening he summoned the congregants of exemplary virtue to sit in order of rank to discourse freely on ab-stract and refined topics, sometimes through the whole night. On the thirteenth day of the second month of winter, the Master rose in the night, shook the dust off his clothing, and went for a walk in the courtyard. He then returned and sat down to write a verse to show his followers:

1226.10.23–11.06

1226.12.03

萬象彌天闊，
三更坐地勞。
參橫西嶺下，
斗轉北辰高。
大勢無由過，
長空不可韜。
循環誰主宰，
億劫自堅牢。

丁亥自春及夏，又旱。有司祈禱屢矣，少不獲應。京師奉道會衆，一日請師爲祈雨醮。既而消灾等會，亦請作醮。師徐謂曰：「我方留意醮事，公等亦建此議，所謂好事不約而同也。公等兩家，但當慇懃。」

遂約以五月一日爲祈雨醮，初三日爲賀雨醮。

三日中有雨，是名瑞應雨。過三日雖得，非醮家雨也。或曰：「天意未易度。師對衆出是語，萬一失期，能無招小人之訾邪？」師曰：「非爾所知也。」及醮竟日，雨乃作。翌日，盈尺。越三日，四天廓清，以終謝雨醮。事果如其言。

時暑氣煩燠，元帥張資胤者，請師遊西山。再四過勤，師赴之。翌日齋罷，雨後遊東山庵。師與客坐于林間，日夕將還以絕句示衆云：

102 From 11 pm to 1 am.

103 *Dou* is the first manor, or constellation, in the northern (second) quadrant of the 28 constellations. Described here is the seasonal, nightly movement of the stars around the Polestar.

104 The Buddhist temples in the Western Hills west of Beijing remain a popular tourist attraction to this day.

[64. "Written at Midnight on the Thirteenth Day of the Eleventh Month, to Show to the Congregation"]

Images of everything fill the vastness of the heavens,
But I sit on the ground, working in the third watch of night.[102]
The constellation Shen[xxiv] (Orion) lies in the western sky behind
    the Western Hills,
While the constellation Dou (Big Dipper) rotates as the Polestar
    rises high.[103]
Such great forces cannot be impeded;
In infinite emptiness nothing can be hidden.
Who governs these cyclical rotations?
They have remained steady over countless *kalpas*.

From spring to fall of the *dinghai* year there was another drought. The authorities continuously offered prayers but got little response. One day the Daoist faithful in the capital requested that the Master perform a *jiao* ceremony for rain. Immediately, Averting Calamity and another congregation also requested that he perform a *jiao*. The Master slowly said, "I recently have been considering a *jiao*. That you gentlemen have also made this suggestion shows that 'good things come together on their own.' Your two congregations should attend to the matter." Thereupon they agreed to hold the *jiao* ritual for rain on the first day of the fifth month, and on the third day to perform the *jiao* ceremony for celebrating drought-relief rain. 1227.01.19–08.14 1227.05.17, 19

If rain fell during the three days, it would be called Auspicious Response rain. Any rain that fell after those three days would not be associated with the *jiao*. Someone remarked, "Heaven's intent is not easy to discern. If you, Master, tell this to the congregation and, if by some chance, we miss the appointed period, will that not attract censure by small-minded people?" The Master replied, "This is not for you to understand." After the first full day of the rite, the rain did fall, and by the following day a foot had fallen. After the three days had passed, the entire heavens had been swept clean by the rain, so we could finish with the *jiao* for celebrating drought-relief rain. It all turned out just as the Master had said.

At that time, the summer heat was unbearable. Commander Zhang Ziyin invited the Master to go strolling around his residence in the Western Hills.[104] He persistently insisted until the Master went with him. As soon as the rain abated the day after the *jiao*, they strolled around the East Hill Cloister, and the Master lounged amid the cooling trees with his guests. Toward sunset, as they were preparing to return, he composed a regulated verse to show them:

西山爽氣清，
過雨白雲輕。
有客林間坐，
無心道自成。

　　既還元帥第，樓居數日，來聽道話者，竟夕不寐。

　　又應大谷庵請，次日清夢庵請。其夕大雨自北來，雷
電怒合，東西震耀。師曰：此道之用也。得道之人威光烜
赫，無乎不在，雷電莫能匹也。夜深客散，師偃息草堂。
須臾風雨駭至，怒霆一震，窗戶幾裂。少焉收聲，人皆異
之。或曰：「霹靂當游至，何一舉而息邪？」有應者曰：
「無乃至人在茲，雷師為之霽威乎？」

　　既還，五月二十有五日，道人王志明至自秦州，傳
旨：

　　改北宮仙島為萬安宮，天長觀為長春宮，詔天下出
　　家善人皆隸焉。且賜以金虎牌，道家事一仰神仙
　　處置。

　　小暑後，大雨屢至，暑氣愈熾。以七言詩示眾云：

溽暑熏天萬里遙，
洪波拍海大川潮。
嘉禾已見三秋熟，
旱魃仍聞五月消。

105　The sixteenth day of the fifth intercalary month (1227.07.01). An intercalary month
is a month inserted to rectify the Metonic cycle and bring lunar months and the
solar year in sync. The fifteen-day period of lesser heat usually starts around the
beginning of the seventh month, when the sun at noon is at 105° northern latitude.
106　Signs of good fortune: good harvest, no drought, peace, and happiness, all done in
a subtle manner to aid a court in harmony with the Way.

[65. "Roaming in the Eastern Hill Cloister after the Rains, a Quatrain to Show to the Group."]

The cool air in the Western Hills is fresh.
After the rain, the white clouds are light.
Guests sit among the trees,
And without intention, the Way becomes complete.

He returned to Commander Zhang's residence and stayed for several days. People came to listen to him discourse on the Way, keeping him up all night. He then agreed to a request from Dagu Cloister and on the next day accepted an invitation from the Qingmeng Cloister. That evening a great rainstorm rolled in from the north, with thunder and lightning, rumbling and flashing, from east to west. The Master remarked, "This is an application by the Way. One who has obtained the Way possesses an awe-inspiring radiance. Mere thunder and lightning are no match." Late that night, the guests dispersed, and the Master lay down to rest in a thatched cottage. A great gust of wind and rain came, and a thunderclap boomed, rattling the windows until they almost broke. After a moment, all was quiet again. Everyone marveled at that turn of events, one saying, "Thunder comes in waves; why did it cease after just one peal?" Someone responded, "Is it not because the Perfected is here that the thunder god restrained himself?"

After he returned to the monastery, on the twenty-fifth day of the fifth month the Daoist Wang Zhiming arrived from Qinzhou (in Gansu), transmitting an order from the Qan: "Change the name of Transcendent's Isle in the Northern Palace to Wan'an Palace and the name Tianchang Monastery to Changchun Palace. Tell all who have left home and are good people that they should be registered there. Also, bestow the Golden Tiger Tally on the Divine Transcendent so that all affairs of the Daoist realm are left to him to adjudicate." 1227.06.10

After the solar period of Lesser Heat, much rain fell, and the weather became very hot and muggy.[105] The Master composed a regulated verse to share with his followers:

[66. "After Lesser Heat, a Poem to Show to the Group"]

Summer humidity suffuses the heavens for ten thousand *li* and
   more.
Huge waves beat the oceans, rivers surge with the tides.
Auspicious awns of wheat have appeared and will ripen by
   autumn;[106]
The still-perceptible demon of drought vanished in the fifth
   month.

百姓共忻生有望，
三軍不待令方調。
寔由道化行無外，
暗賜豐年助聖朝。

自瓊島爲道院，樵薪捕魚者絕迹數年。園池中禽魚蕃
育，歲時遊人往來不絕。

齋餘，師乘馬日凡一往。

六月二十有一日，因疾不出，浴於宮之東溪。

二十有三日，人報巳、午間，雷雨大作，太液池之南
岸崩裂，水入東湖，聲聞數十里，黿鼉魚鱉盡去，池遂枯
涸。北口山亦摧。師聞之初無言，良久笑曰：山摧池枯，
吾將與之俱乎！

七月四日，師謂門人曰：昔丹陽嘗授記於余云：

「吾沒之後，教門當大興，四方徃徃化爲道鄉。公正
當其時也。道院皆勅賜名額，又當住持大宮觀，仍
有使者佩符乘傳，勾當教門事。此時乃公功成名遂，
歸休之時也。丹陽之言，一一皆驗，若念符契。況
教門中勾當人內外悉具。吾歸無遺恨矣。」

---

107 Three Armies is a synecdoche for the imperial forces.
108 Daoists ate only two meals a day, like Buddhist monks.

Ordinary people delight together, living now with hope;
No opposing armies, the Three Armies wait on redeployment
      orders.[107]
All this, without external action, is due to the transformation to
      the Way;
The Way, unseen, bestows a bountiful year to aid the sagely
      dynasty.

After the Island of Gemlike Flowers became a Daoist monastery, the
wood gatherers and fishermen disappeared, and after a few years the
birds and fish in the gardens and ponds burgeoned. Sightseers come
year-round to enjoy the scenery.

[Death and Apotheosis]

The Master often took a horseback ride after his mid-morning meal.[108]
On the twenty-first day of the sixth month, he was ill and did not go   1227.08.04
out. He bathed in a creek on the east side of Changchun Palace. On
the twenty-third day, someone reported that a great thunderstorm in   1227.08.06
the late morning and early afternoon hours caused the southern bank
of the imperial Taiyi Pond to collapse and its water to empty into East
Lake, with a sound that was audible for dozens of *li.* The large turtles,
Yangzi alligators, fish, and soft-shelled turtles all escaped, and the pond
dried up. A mountain also collapsed at a northern pass.[xxv] When the
Master heard this, he was silent at first, but after a while, he laughed and
remarked, "A mountain has collapsed, and a pond has dried up; I may
soon be in their company!"
      On the fourth day of the seventh month, the Master spoke to his   1227.08.17
disciples, saying,

In the past, Danyang, the adept Ma Yu, once gave me a prediction.
He told me, "After my death, our sect will greatly flourish; in all
directions the land will be transformed into a Daoist realm. You
shall be there at that time. All the monasteries will be graced with
a name plaque in the imperial hand, and you will manage a great
palace monastery. Officials bearing imperial insignia and riding
on government post horses will support your management of the
Daoist community. When you have achieved this great success
and renown, that will be the proper time for your return to rest."
Every word that Danyang spoke has come true; his words and
events match like the two halves of a tally stick. Moreover, all the
administrators within the Daoist community are fully prepared.
I can pass on with no regrets!

師既示疾于寶玄。一日數如偃中，門弟子止之。師
曰：「吾不欲勞人，汝等猶有分別在。且偃、寢奚異哉。」
七月七日門人復請曰：「每日齋會，善人甚眾。願垂大慈
還堂上，以慰瞻禮。」師曰：「我九日上堂去也。」是日
午後，留頌云：

生死朝昏事一般，
幻泡出没水長閑。
微光見處跳烏兔，
玄量開時納海山。
揮斥八紘如咫尺，
吹噓萬有似機關。
狂辭落筆成塵垢，
寄在時人妄聽間。

遂登葆光堂歸真焉。異香滿室。門人捻香拜別，眾
欲哭。臨侍者張志素、武志攄等遽止眾曰：「真人適有遺
語，令門人宋道安提舉教門事，尹志平副之，張志松又其
次，王志明依舊勾當，宋德方、李志常等同議教門事。」
遂復舉似《遺世頌》，畢，提舉宋道安等再拜而受。

---

109   The disciples probably were suggesting that he use a chamber pot that they would
       empty, so that he did not have to move from his room.
110   The raven is the sun; the hare the moon.
111   To quote *Zhuangzi*, "Those who are perfected can rise as peaks into the blue sky, can
       hide themselves away in the Yellow Springs (the underworld). They move freely in
       the eight furthest directions, yet their divine ether never changes." See Zhuangzi,
       Guo, ed., 1995, 175.
112   An alternate version of his death recounts that Qiu was stricken with dysentery and
       spent the last days of his life in the privy, refusing to be moved by disciples. These
       accounts feature in later extremely imaginative and polemical anti-Quanzhen texts
       written by Buddhist rivals. See Appendix 13.

After the Master began to show symptoms at Baoxuan Hall, he visited the privy several times a day. When some disciples tried to stop him from going, he said, "I do not wish to make work for anyone. You are still distinguishing between better or worse. What is the difference between a bedroom and a privy anyway?"[109] On the seventh day of the   1227.08.20
seventh month, the disciples again asked, "Every day at the dinner assembly, a sizable crowd of benefactors gathers. We yearn for you to display great compassion and come back into the hall, so that people may find comfort in showing reverence to you." The Master replied, "On the ninth day I will go to the hall." On the afternoon of that day,   1227.08.22
he sent them a hymn:

[67. "A Hymn Left Behind in the Afternoon of the Ninth Day of the Seventh Month"]

Birth and death are like mornings and evenings:
Illusory bubbles that emerge and sink while the water stays calm.
Where dim rays are seen, there hop the raven or the hare;[110]
When the mysterious capacity (of the Way) unfolds, it
    encompasses seas and mountains.
I will indulge myself in the eight extremities as though they were a
    foot away;[111]
I will puff and blow within phenomena as though I controlled their
    movements.
Crazy words that flow from my brush will turn into dust and
    grime,
To be cast among my contemporaries, who will doubt the truth of
    what they hear.

Then he ascended to the Baoguang Hall, where he returned to the final perfection. A strange perfume filled the room.[112] The disciples lit incense to bid him goodbye, and the congregations were on the verge of weeping. His deathbed attendants—Zhang Zhisu, Wang Zhishu, and others—quickly stopped them, saying, "The Perfected recently made a last testament, ordering the disciple Song Dao'an to take over as supervisor of the sect, with Yin Zhiping as his second and Zhang Zhisong next after that. As before, Wang Zhiming will remain manager. Song Defang, Li Zhichang, and the others shall consult on affairs concerning the sect." After they finished once again displaying the Master's "Hymn on Leaving This World," supervisor Song Dao'an and the others bowed twice and accepted the testamentary orders.

黎明，具麻服，行喪禮，奔走赴喪者萬計。宣差劉仲祿聞之愕然歎曰：「真人朝見以來，君臣道合。離闕之後，上意眷慕，未嘗少忘。今師既昇去，速當奏聞。」

首七之後，四方道俗，遠來赴喪，哀慟如喪考妣，於是求訓法名者日益多。一日提舉宋公謂志常曰：「今月上七日，公暨我同受師旨，法名等事，爾其代書，止用吾手字，印此事已行，姑泌襲之。」

繼而清和大師尹公至自德興，行祀事。既終七，提舉宋公謂清和曰：「吾老矣，不能維持教門，君可代我領之也。」讓至于再，清和受其託，遠邇奉道。會中善衆，不減往往昔。

戊子春三月朔，清和建議爲師構堂于白雲觀。或曰：工力浩大，粮儲鮮少，恐難成功。清和曰：

「凡事要人前思，夫衆可與樂成，不可與慮始。但事不思已，教門竭力，何爲而不辦。況先師遺德在人，四方孰不瞻仰。可不勞行化，自有人贊助此緣，公等勿疑。更或不然，常住之物，費用靜盡，各操一瓢，乃所願也。」

113 Funerary customs involved seven periods of seven days of mourning, each period punctuated by special services.
114 It was customary to accept important commissions, gifts, etc., only on the third request.
115 An allusion to *Analects* 6.11, where Confucius praises Yan Hui for remaining happy and content despite his impoverished daily diet of a single bamboo dish of food and a single gourd dish of water.

At daybreak, they dressed in hempen garments and performed the funeral rituals. So many hurried to the funeral that they were counted by the tens of thousands. When Imperial Envoy Liu Zhonglu heard the news, he was stunned and sighed, "Ever since the Perfected was presented at court, monarch and subject shared the Way. After departing the Imperial Camp, His Majesty has nourished a tender regard for him and never forgot him. Now that the Master has ascended to Heaven, we will quickly notify His Majesty."

After the first seven days of mourning,[113] Daoists and laypeople, grief-stricken as though for their own parents, came from all over to participate in the mourning rites. The numbers of those requesting religious names grew by the day. One day, supervisor Song Dao'an said to Li Zhichang, "On the first seventh day of this month, we both received a parting directive from the Master. From here on, in conferring religious names and other such matters, you should write the letter for me and use my personal seal. This is already the practice, and we will continue it for now."

Soon after, the Qinghe Master Yin Zhiping arrived from Dexing to perform mourning prayers. Then in the final seven days, the supervisor Song Dao'an said to Qinghe, "I am old now, and cannot continue to have responsibility for our whole community. You should replace me to lead them." Qinghe refused twice,[114] then accepted the duty entrusted to him. Near and far, those who served the Way, congregations, and benefactors remained just as numerous as before.

In spring of the *wuzi* year, on the first day of the third month, Qinghe   1228.05.06
proffered the idea of building a memorial hall for the Master at Baiyun (White Cloud) Monastery.[xxvi] Someone remarked, "That would require immense effort, and our supplies are scarce. I fear it will be difficult to accomplish." Qinghe replied,

"All things require careful planning. Our congregations can accomplish this if we do it with joy, but not if we begin with worry. It is simply that it has not been thought through; if the whole community exerts its strength, what can it not accomplish? Moreover, the legacy of our old master's virtue remains in people's hearts. Who around us does not want to pay homage to him? Must we go out to round up resources? There are already those to assist and support this cause—of that you should have no doubt. If it turns out to be otherwise, and we exhaust our provisions to cover expenses, we can each content ourselves with a single gourd dish of water.[115] This is my wish.

宣差便宜劉公聞而喜之，力贊其事，遂舉鞠志圓等董
其役。自四月上丁，除地建址。歷戊、己、庚，俄有平
陽、太原、堅、代、蔚、應等羣道人二百餘，賚粮助力，
肯構是堂，四旬告成。其間同結茲緣者，不能備紀。議者
以爲，締構之勤，雖由人力，亦聖賢陰有以扶持也。

期以七月九日，大葬仙師。

六月間，霖雨不止，皆慮有妨葬事。既七月初吉，遽
報晴霽，人心翕然和悅。前一日，將事之初，乃炷香設
席，以嚴其祀。及啓柩，師容色儼然如生。遠近王官、士
庶、僧尼、善衆，觀者凡三日，日萬人，皆以手加額，嘆
其神異焉。繼而喧播四方，傾心歸嚮，來奉香火者，不可
勝計。

本宮建奉安道場三晝夜，預告齋旬日。八日辰時，玄
鶴自西南來，尋有白鶴繼至，人皆仰而異之。九日子時
後，設靈寶清醮三百六十分位，醮禮終，藏仙蛻于堂，異
香芬馥，移時不散。臨午致齋，黃冠羽服，與坐者數千
人。奉道之衆，又復萬餘。既寧神，翌日大雨復降，人皆
嘆曰：「天道人事，上下和應。了此一大事，非我師道德
純備，通于天地，達于神明，疇克如是乎，諒非人力所能
致也。」

---

116 This description of the project is confirmed by Chen Shikein in a funerary record
found in Chen Yuan 1988, 458.
117 At this rite, offerings were made to 360 divinities. The rite entailed dozens of sacrificial masters to carry out the ritual and to chant the scriptures.

Imperially Commissioned Plenipotentiary Liu Zhonglu rejoiced when
he heard about the project, strongly supporting it. He appointed Ju
Zhiyuan and others to direct the construction. In the three days after
the first *ding* day of the fourth month, when they cleared the ground to   1228.05.09
lay the foundation, more than two hundred people from Daoist groups
in Pingyang (Shanxi), Taiyuan (Shanxi), Jian (Shanxi), Dai (Shanxi),
Yu (Hebei), Ying (Shanxi), and elsewhere, eager to build the hall, came   1228.07.27
to contribute provisions and labor. Within forty days the project was
completed.[116] Those who united with us in this purpose are too numerous to record. Those who discussed the matter thought that the human
effort required to complete the construction benefited from the Divine
Transcendent's invisible succor.

It was agreed that the Transcendent Master would be buried on the
ninth day of the seventh month (a year after his death). In the sixth   1228.08.10
month, heavy rain fell continuously, and everyone was concerned that
it would prevent the burial ceremony. Then on the first day of the sev-   1228.07.31
enth month, it was reported that the rain was clearing, and everyone
was delighted. The day before the funeral began, incense was burned,
and seating mats were arranged to lend dignity to the service. When
the coffin was opened, the Master's countenance appeared no different
than when he was alive. For three days, princes and officials, scholars
and commoners, monks and nuns, and benefactors came from near and
far to gaze upon him, many each day, all touching their hands to their
foreheads in reverence and marveling at his miraculous appearance. As
the news continued to spread, numerous people came to burn incense
to pay their respects.

For three days and nights, the home monastery (Changchun Palace)
carried out the rituals for "providing rest," and announced ahead of
time a ten-day vegetarian fast. On the morning of the eighth day, a black
crane came flying from the southwest, soon followed by a white crane.
Everyone gazed up at them in wonder. At midnight on the ninth day,
a Noumenal-Treasure Purification *jiao* was held in three hundred and
sixty positions.[117] At the conclusion of this rite, the Master's transcendent
husk was laid to rest in the hall, and a strange fragrance filled the air and
did not disperse for many hours. At the noon vegetarian feast, those
capped in yellow and in feathered clothing sat among the thousands
who participated. There were scores of congregations of believers in
the Way. The day after his soul was laid to rest, it rained heavily again.
Everyone sighed and remarked, "The Way of Heaven and the enterprise
of men have been in perfect accord to bring this great event to an end.
Who else but the Master, whose pure virtue penetrated through Heaven
and earth and reached even the deities, could have accomplished this?"

權省宣撫王公巨川，咸陽巨族也，素慕玄風，近歲又
與父師相會于燕，雅懷昭映，道同氣合，尊仰之誠，
更甚疇昔，故會茲葬事，自爲主盟。京城內外，屯以甲
兵，備其不虞。罷散之日，略無驚擾。於是親榜其堂曰處
順，其觀曰白雲焉。師爲文，未始起槀，臨紙肆筆而成。
後復有求者，或輒自增損，故兩存之。嘗夜話謂門弟子
曰：「古之得道人，見于書傳者，略而不博[vi]，失其傳者
可勝言哉。余屢對汝衆，舉近世得道之士，皆耳目所親接
者，其行事甚詳，其談道甚明。暇日當集全真大傳，以貽
後人。」師既没，雖嘗口傳其槩，而後之學者，尚未見其
成書，惜哉。

The acting governor, Pacification Commissioner Wang Juchuan, from a prominent Xianyang clan, had always admired the import of the Master's discussions on the Way. In recent years he had met with the revered Master in Yanjing, and they were alike in their elegant interests and in their perfect harmony in the Way. He venerated the Master with even deeper sincerity, so he took on the role of sponsor of the funeral event on his own. To ensure that there would be no unexpected disturbances, he stationed armored troops inside and outside the city. There was not the slightest trouble during the funeral. Wang himself presented a name plaque for the hall inscribed "Residing in Compliance," and one for the monastery inscribed "White Clouds."

When the Master wrote, he never made drafts, but would complete a work as soon as he set brush to paper. If anyone asked for a given work again, he might quickly make a few additions or deletions, and both copies would be kept. Once, during an evening conversation, he said to the disciples,

Information about ancients who attained the Way and who appear in texts is often very thin, and too many lives have gone unrecorded. I have frequently brought to your attention our contemporaries who have attained the Way, all of whom I have met. How they conducted themselves is known in detail, and their discussions on the Way are extremely lucid. In my free time, I should compile a *Complete Biographies of the Quanzhen Daoists* to bequeath to posterity.

Now the Master is gone, and although he orally transmitted his knowledge in broad outline, later scholars will not have the opportunity to read the book he intended to write. It is indeed unfortunate.

Endnotes

Text Critical Notes to Preface, and Book I

i. The Monastery of the Jade Void, located in the northern part of the old Jin capital of Yanjing (now southwest Beijing). Originally a Daoist monastery occupied by the Authentic Great Way (Zhen Dadao 真大道) sect. See Huang Taiyong 2016; QXYJ03, 19 n. 6; Wu Cheng 1999, in QYW vol. 15, 510.370–372; Song Lian 1939. On the Authentic Great Way sect, see Bussio 2017.

ii. Longyang (Dragon Yang Power) Monastery, in Dexing, Hebei, modern Zhuolu county (northwest of Beijing), on the north side of Mt. Chanfang (see Book I, n. xxii).

iii. Tianchang (Perpetual Heaven) Monastery, the monastery that Qiu Chuji took charge of after his return to Yanjing in 1224. Later combined with Baiyun (White Cloud) Monastery (白雲觀), which has endured over the years as the main Daoist temple complex in Beijing. See Li Yangzheng 2020, 5–14, 403–432, 461–463.

iv. Sun Xi, bynames Tianxi 天錫 and Zhongxi 仲錫, a native of Changping 長平 (modern Gaoping, Shanxi). Held a *jinshi* degree from the Jin dynasty and befriended Yuan Haowen's friends Xin Yuan 辛愿 and Liu Angxiao 劉昂霄 (1186–1223). See "A Record of the Daoist Monastery of Audience with the Three Primes" ("Chaoyuan guan ji") in Yuan Haowen 2012, vol. 2, 959.

v. Panxi and Longmen are in Shaanxi. See Xiao Jinming 2003, 3–4.

vi. Qiu was summoned to the capital in the spring of 1188 and attended Emperor Shizong of the Jin. He seems to have returned to Shaanxi in September of that year and then gone back to Shandong in 1192. See Qiu's biography in Qin zhi'an 2004, in ZHDZ vol. 47, 46–47.

vii. Li Quan 李全 led a peasant rebellion, the "Red Coat" (*hong'ao* 紅襖) uprising, at the end of the Jin. At the time of *Journey to the West*, he had surrendered to the Song and led their forces in the North. Li later surrendered to the Mongols and was slain leading an expeditionary force into South China. See Franke 1994, 256–257, and Davis 2009, 824–825, 847–851.

viii. Peng Yibin 彭義斌 (d. 1225) attached himself to Li Quan and surrendered to the Song, where he served under Li. While Li surrendered to the Mongols, Peng remained allied with the Song and led their armies in Shandong. See Davis 2009, 847–851.

ix. On the golden tiger tablet, see Hsiao 1978, 73; West 1977, 278–280; and Atwood 2004a, 433–434.

x. Zhang Lin had been enticed to defect from the Jin to the Song side in 1219. In 1221 he went over to the Mongols for two years. On Zhang's fluctuating allegiances, see Davis 2009, 825–826, 850.

xi. Yin Zhiping, byname Taihe 太和, religious name Qinghezi 清和子 (Master of Pure Harmony). See EOT 1171–1172.

xii. Shimo Xiandebu 石抹咸得不 (Sendeb, d. 1235), a Kitan, the elder son of Shimo Ming'an 石抹明安 (1164–1216), from whom he inherited the position of *darughachi* (governor, or resident Mongol agent) and head of the Branch Secretariat (行尚書省) established to govern the Yanjing area after it came under Mongol control. Shimo Ming'an and his descendants held sway over the Yanjing region for decades. See ISTK 115–116, 119–120, 140, 145, 147–148; YS 150.3555–3557; Atwood 2004a, 501; Biran 2015.

xiii. Wang Juchuan (Wang Ji 檝, 1181–1240), an old acquaintance of Qiu Chuji and an official in the Mongol government of Yanjing from ca. 1220. See ISTK 176–184 and Xiao Qiqing (Hsiao Ch'i-ch'ing) 2007, 117–124.

xiv. Yan Liben 閻立本 (d. 673), a renowned Tang court painter who specialized in portraiture of people and celestial beings. This lost painting is sometimes referred to as *Laozi Leaving the Pass*. See QXYJ03 46, n. C1, Pan Yungao 1999, 30–34, and Ning 2008.

xv. Little is known of Zhang Tiandu, apart from a poem he wrote praising Qiu for allegedly restoring a long-dead cypress tree to life.

xvi. Sun Zhou held the post of Official of Confucian Learning in Yanjing. See Li Daoqian 2004a, in ZTDZ vol. 33, 139a.

xvii. Liu Zhong and several others listed here were selected by Yelü Chucai to be tax officials in ten newly established routes in North China, an indication of their former status under the Jin, and their positions of trust in the new regime. See YS 2.30 and 146.3458.

xviii. In addition to authoring a sacrificial writ for Qiu Chuji (see ZHDZ vol. 47, 128, and QYW vol. 22, 694.287), Wu Zhang was Vice Director of the Court of Judicial Review, according to a Yuan gazetteer. See Xiong Mengxiang 1983, 85.

xix. Jin poet-scholar Yuan Haowen remarks that Zhongli "passed the advanced scholar examination and had quite a reputation for writing." See Yuan Haowen 2018, vol. 7, 2150.

xx. A Wang Rui is listed as a tax official assigned to the Dongping area in Shandong during the reign of Ögödei Qan. See YS 2.30.

xxi. Zhao Fang, a figure who rose to prominence as a student in the National Academy, unsuccessfully argued against giving up the capital at Yanjing to the Mongols (see JS 14.304, 39.2232). He was later selected by Yelü Chucai to oversee tax collection in North China. See YS 2.30 and 146.3458.

xxii. Mt. Chanfang, the area known as Longmen, where the Sanggan River debouches into the Zhuolu plain on the southwestern boundary of modern Zhuolu County, has an abundance of artesian springs and was once graced with a beautiful three-tier waterfall known as "the layered bluish-green of Longmen" 龍門疊翠. It was blasted to build a dam in 1958, and the dam itself was destroyed because of the danger of breaching in 1964, leaving no further sign of the waterfall. See Anon. 2017 and QXYJ03 54, n. C4.

xxiii. In Daoist views of the body, "essence" is a seed of materiality formed out of the Way and sustained by the ingestion of food. In turn, it nourishes the physical body and is refined by circulating within the body, traveling up along the backbone and down an anterior meridian. It thus creates "breath," transforming matter into a physical and mental energy, a process called "refining essence so it transforms into pneuma" (*lian jing hua qi* 鍊精化氣). See EOT 767–772. Pneuma is then refined into "spirit" (*lian qi hua shen* 鍊氣化神), and spirit transforms into Nothingness (*lian shen hua xu* 鍊神化虛).

xxiv. Literally, "has leakage," a term Quanzhen Daoism borrowed from the Buddhist Sanskrit term *sāsrava*. One's actions, even if pure in the doing, have some sort of directed goal, which taints the action. The term contrasts well with the Daoist ideal of nonaction.

xxv. Modern Xuanhua, Hebei. On Tuhua, see the Introduction, p. xxxv.

xxvi. Shifting sands is a conventional reference to the deep sand and sand dunes of the Taklamakan Desert near the modern Tian Shan. It is used consistently in texts to mean a large area difficult to cross because of deep sand and lack of water. It is also a geographical metonym for all the deserts in Xinjiang. See Yule 1913–1916, 212, for a description.

xxvii. Our interpretation is from notes to the passage "Zou Yan's blowing on the pitch pipe" 鄒衍之吹律 in the Daoist work *Liezi*. "Note: There was a beautiful but cold land in the north that could not grow the five cereals. Master Zou blew on his pitch pipes to make it warm, and the millet and broomcorn millet were nourished" 注: 北方有地, 美而寒, 不生五穀。鄒子吹律煖之。而禾黍滋也 (Yang Bojun 1979, 177). For the context of the statement and note, see Graham 1960, 108.

xxviii. On Chinggis's younger brother Temüge-otchegin or Otegin, see Rashīd-ad-Dīn 1998, vol. 1, 137–139. On efforts to identify the Tangut Alixian, see Yang Zhijiu 1985, 163–170. Otegin's ambitious chafing against his overlord-brother eventually resulted in his execution by Güyük Qan (r. 1246–1248) in 1246, for presenting a claim to the throne after the death of his nephew Ögödei (r. 1229–1241). Following Chen Dezhi (QXYJ03 5), we locate his camp near the Hui River, south-southeast of Hulun Buir. As it was due north, not west, of Yanjing, the following reference to Qiu traveling west means "to the Qan."

xxix. Now Mt. Yantong 煙筒山, located about twenty kilometers north-north-east of modern Xuanhua County.

xxx. The three masters of the lineage that came before Qiu are, in order, Ma Yu, Tan Chuduan, and Liu Chuxuan. Ma Yu 馬鈺 (1122–1184), original name Congyi 從義, original byname Yifu 宜甫; name changed to Yu, byname to Xuanbao 玄寶, Daoist name Danyang zi 丹陽子 (Master Cinnabar Yang). Tan Chuduan 譚處端 (1123–1185), original name Yu 玉, original byname Boyu 伯玉; name changed to Chuduan, byname to Tongzheng 通正, Daoist name Changzhen zi 長真子 (Master Perpetual Perfection). Liu Chuxuan 劉處玄 (1147–1203), byname Tongmiao 通妙, Daoist name Changsheng zi 長生子 (Master Perpetual Life).

xxxi. The Cuiping Mountains, just southwest of Wild Fox Ridge, north of Xuande.

xxxii. Song Defang (1183–1247), one of the eighteen disciples who accompanied Qiu part way to Afghanistan (EOT 915–916). He later oversaw the compilation of the *Precious Storehouse of the Mysterious Abode of Laozi* 玄都寶藏 in 1244 and a printing of the Daoist Canon "nearly without state support, in a very short period of time and under troubled conditions" (Schipper and Verellen 2004, vol. 2, 1131). See also Li and Zhao 2006 and Zhang Fang 2012.

xxxiii. Known to the Mongols as Yeke Derusün (great grasslands), today known as the Hunshan Dake. See Jia Jingyan 2004, 34.

xxxiv. On Yu'erpo, see Chen Zhengxiang 1968, 18, and 1994, 70, n. 69. Shiraishi 2012, 29–32, argues that Yu'erpo was Lake Kòl/Khür-Chaghan in Abag Banner, Inner Mongolia. For the lake's importance, see Landa 2020, 137–167, 151.

xxxv. The "sandy river" refers to the Khalkh river of eastern Mongolia, part of which forms the boundary between China and Mongolia. QXYJ03 81, n. C23, locates this desert in the present-day Hulun Buir Sandy Land (*shadi* 沙地), in northeastern Inner Mongolia.

xxxvi. Qiu Chuji's party saw the full eclipse, which is recorded in the Jin and Song dynastic histories (see QXYJ03 83, n. C1). A detailed scientific account can be found in Stephenson and Yau 1992.

xxxvii. Peng Daya et al. 2014, 22–23, describes this type of tent: "In the steppe construction, willow wood is woven into an inflexible cylinder and felt is stretched tightly over the top. This cannot be rolled and unrolled. They are carried on carts." See also Andrews 1999. Called *ger* in Mongolian, the nomadic tent is called *yurt* in the West, which comes via the Russian *yurta* from the Turkic *jurta* (Starostin et al. 2003, 542–543).

xxxviii. Identified as the archaeological site of Chintolgoi Balgas in Mongolia, coordinates 47°52'30.70"N, 104°14'47.15"E (QXYJ03 88–89, n. C6). Some scholars identify it with the Liao garrison city of Zhenzhou 鎮州, also known as Kedun.

xxxix. Only five Kitan royals ascended the Qara Khitai throne before the Naiman refugee prince Güchülüg usurped it in 1211. The Qara Khitai capital lay northeast of Samarkand, in the environs of Balasaghun in the Chu River valley, not far from where the Chu flows into Issyk Kul (Biran 2005, 39, 80–81).

xl. Changsong Range, the Undur narsu ("tall pines"), was a section of the eastern Khangai Mountain range of central Mongolia west of Ulaanbatur (QXYJ03 92, n. C1).

xli. Liu Xiao (2004, 15–21) speculates that this may be the *ordo* of Chinggis Qan's Jurchen wife, titled Qiguo, the Princess-*qatun* and head of his fourth *ordo*. A devout Quanzhen patron, the Princess-*qatun* issued two decrees, in 1245 and 1250, protecting Daoist temples belonging to the Quanzhen main branch temple in Yanjing. See Chen Yuan 1988, 486, 508; Broadbridge 2018, 74–95. QXYJ03 95, n. C3, reviews the evidence and adopts Wang Guowei's identification of the river as Chaghan-olon.

xlii. Chinggis Qan customarily demanded a royal woman in marriage from rulers whose kingdoms he subordinated or conquered. Little is known about the Xia (Tangut) princess, Chaqa; the Yuan history "Table of Consorts" places her in Chinggis's Third *Ordo*. The four *ordos* headed by his principal *qatuns* were near each other, permitting easy visiting.

xliii. Chen Zhengxiang (1968, 21, and 1994, 72, n. 86) suggests that this is Mt. Otgontenger, which rises 13,225 feet, or 4031 meters, high.

xliv. Wang Guowei considers Helaxiao to have been Uliastai, but QXYJ03 98–99, n. 4, is skeptical on phonetic grounds.

xlv. On Chinqai City and the identity of Chinqai, see ISTK 95–111; Atwood 2004a, 103, and 2020; and Muraoka and Nakata 2020. Chinggis Qan ordered Chinqai to build the settlement that bore his name, at a place called Aluhuan, as a supply depot, granary, and agricultural colony behind the lines of the Western Campaign, to support the Mongol army. Thousands of prisoners of war were transported there to ply their trades and skills as farmers, artisans, etc. (YS 120.2963–2964). We understand that this is where the travelers stopped for a prolonged stay.

xlvi. Lady Tudan and Lady Jiagu, two of the Jin emperor Zhangzong's five consorts who were unable to escape from Yanjing when it fell to the Mongols (JS 56.1267, 101.2228). After ten years at her daughter's *ordo*, Madame Yuan (Lady Qinsheng) became a Daoist nun, returned to Yanjing, and befriended Yin Zhiping, Qiu Chuji's successor. See Liu Xiao 2004, 20–21.

xlvii. The Abuhan Mountains have been variously identified. They are probably identical to the "Aluhuan" 阿魯歡 mountains in the *Yuanshi* biography of Chinqai (YS 120.2964). Atwood (2020, 424–425, n. 25) identifies them as the Khasagt Khairkhan (Xasagt Xairxan) ridge in the Altai Mountains.

xlviii. Little else is known about Song Dao'an. The commemorative stele written for Li Zhichang by Wang E 王鶚 (1190–1273) claims that Qiu left Li Zhichang behind with Song Dao'an, and that the abbey was constructed at the request of the local Chinese inhabitants. See Li Daoqian 2004a, ZHDZ vol. 47, 138, and ZTDZ vol. 19, 744. None of the other texts in the *Daoist Canon of the Zhengtong Reign* lists anyone else's name with Song Dao'an, nor is Li Zhichang mentioned in these sources in affiliation with this Daoist abbey. The stele inscription by Li Ding 李鼎 for Meng Zhiyuan 孟志源 (1187–1261) says specifically that Qiu had an abbey built here because "it was the first time (since leaving the Central Plain) that they encountered Han people engaged in agriculture." See Li Daoqian 2004a, in ZTDZ vol. 33, 193a, and ZHDZ vol. 47, 165.

xlix. Qixia was the name of Qiu's ancestral home in Shandong. The monastery was probably not completed before Qiu's party resumed its journey, so this description comes from their visit on the way home. According to Wang E's stele, Qiu wrote a celebratory name plaque for the monastery before he departed for the West.

l. *Jishu* was a kind of millet distinct from the grains (barley, wheat) mentioned earlier under cultivation by the first Uyghurs they encountered, and again mentioned in the next sentence. It is unclear whether barley or millet or wheat, or all, were cultivated here, or even whether the writer cared to specify. See QXYJ03 105, n. C3.

li. Zhao Jiugu, religious name, Master Xujing 虛靜子 (Empty Stillness); also known by a formal name, Daojian 道堅, given by Qiu (see Appendix 10). Born in 1163, he died in 1221 during the journey, aged 58. See Li Daoqian 2004b, in ZHDZ vol. 47, 90–91.

lii. Ulungur (in western Mongolia and northeastern Xinjiang), transcribed as *longgu* 龍骨 in Liu Yu's *Embassy to the West*, and identified as the Öröngö River in Allsen 2019, 148. See QXYJ02 A.24a.

liii. The Armantai range, where a fault line lies on the northeast side of the Jungar Basin (QXYJ03 111, n. C11).

liv. The Aibiwula and Hulumulin mountains south of the Armantai range, both reddish in tint (QXYJ03 112, n. C3).

lv. This range, the Bogdo Range (Bogdo Ula), is the eastern arm of the modern Tian Shan range, seventy kilometers from Urumchi (Chen Zhengxiang 1968, 23, and 1994, 75, n. 100).

lvi. Dushan Cheng 獨山城 (Solitary Mount City). The Chinese name is a direct translation of the city's Turkic name, Bir-baliq (QXYJ03 115, n. C2, citing Dai Liangzuo 1984, sans page number). The city is located just south of Mulei City, Mori Khazak Autonomous County, Changji Hui Autonomous Prefecture, east of Urumchi. See Hamilton 1958, 147; Dai Liangzuo 1984, passim; and Boyle 1964, 181.

lvii. See the discussion in Pelliot 1959, 161–165, of the many names for Hezhou/Qocho and its Chinese name's derivation from the Turkic. This Uyghur city lay south of Besh-Baliq (literally "five towns"), and so was off our travelers' route. Its ruler surrendered to Chinggis in 1209.

lviii. The ruins of Besh-Baliq are near the seat of today's Jimsar (Jimusa'er 吉木薩爾) County, Changji Prefecture, about 100 kilometers northeast of Urumchi. See Chen Zhengxiang 1968, 24, and 1994, 75–76, n. 103; Chen Dezhi 2015, 76.

lix. Yang He is unattested in Tang sources. Xue Zongzheng (2009, 4–5) speculates about his identity almost entirely on the basis of this reference.

lx. Xiliang, modern Wuwei 武威, is in Gansu, at the eastern end of the Hexi Corridor. Yelü Chucai (1981, 2, 6, n.13) refers to Luntai in his travel record (see de Rachewiltz 1962, 20). Dickens (2020, 18) locates Luntai "between Turfan and Aqsu on the northern edge of the Taklamakan desert." See also Zhong Xingqi 2008, 604–605.

lxi. *Diexie*, from the Persian *tarsā*, meaning "Christian." Eastern Christianity had spread widely among the Turkic peoples of Central Asia in the first millennium. See Dickens 2020, 18, and also Fu Ma 2019 (Chinese) or 2020 (English).

lxii. The Bogdo Range (Bogdo Ula), east of Urumchi. The travelers had already sighted it before when crossing the Plain of White Bones (see n. lv above). See Chen Zhengxiang 1968, 25, and 1994, 76, n. 110.

lxiii. Some walls and gates of this city (variously transcribed as Changbali 昌八里, Chanbali 掺八里, and Zhangbali 彰八里) remain in the area of the Public Park just north of the Changji 昌吉 central district in Xinjiang. See Zhong Xingqi 2008, 181.

lxiv. A sand desert between Lake Ebi (Ebinur) and Jinghe 精河, today a county seat south of the lake (Chen Zhengxiang 1968, 25, and 1994, 77, n. 114).

lxv. Lake Sairam (Sayram), in Bortala Prefecture, Xinjiang, across the Tian Shan from Ili to the south, and approaching the border of Kazakhstan. See Chen Zhengxiang 1968, 25, n. 115, but compare Chen Zhengxiang 1994, 77. Another Sayram lies in southeast Kazakhstan (see Book I, n. 112).

lxvi. Almaliq, in the upper Ili River valley, north of the Tian Shan slopes, on the border of today's Kazakhstan and Xinjiang, west of the Chinese city of Yining (Gulja/Kuldja). The Qarluq Turk ruler had surrendered to Chinggis Qan in 1211. See QXYJ03 128–130, n. C2, and Chen Dezhi 2005, 81, for many sources on medieval Almaliq.

lxvii. Kazakhstan and the Tian Shan mountains were covered with forests of *Malus sieversii*, a wild apple tree that was probably the source of most domesticated apples. The local name for apple was *alima*. They were (and are) called *alma* in Kazakh and several other Altaic and Turkic languages.

lxviii. *Taohuashi*, from the Turkic Tabgach/Tavgach, used as far back as the eighth century in Old Turkic inscriptions as a term denoting the Chinese and their lands. For two recent contributions to the long-running debate on the etymology of the term, see Xushan Zhang 2010 and Liu Yingsheng 2022.

lxix. This river was not the Talas but the Ili. In the Chinese of North China at this time, 沒輦 was probably pronounced *molian* by the writer, a transliteration of *müren*, the Middle Mongolian word for river (Starostin et al. 2003, 935).

lxx. Eastern Xia, an autonomous Jurchen regime set up in Liaodong in 1215; finally suppressed only in the 1230s. See YS 1.19 and 149.3515.

lxxi. Muhammad Jalal-ad-Din, under whose auspices the killing of a Mongol embassy at Otrar precipitated Chinggis's invasion of the Khwarazm realm in Central Asia in 1219. For a succinct overview, see Allsen 1994, 352–357.

lxxii. *Dashi*, a short-hand reference to the Qara Khitai state and its founder (Biran 2005, 39, 106–107, 215, maps). *Linya* was a Kitan word meaning "scribe" and the title of an office in the Liao government dealing with compositions in the Kitan script, a position once held by Yelü Dashi in the Liao Northern Region (JS 121.2636; LS 45.695–696). Sugiyama (2011, 138) suggests that *dashi* means either "great teacher" or "heir apparent."

lxxiii. For the usurpation of the Qara Khitai throne by the Naiman prince Güchülüg, see Biran 2005, 74–86.

lxxiv. Probably the Wels catfish (*Silurus glanis*), a sheatfish native to the Syr Darya, which can grow to fifteen feet in length and three hundred pounds, or the Turkestan catfish (*Glyptosternon reticulatum*), also native, but which ranges up to only ten inches.

lxxv. The Kyzylkum Desert in Uzbekistan, between the Syr Darya and Amu Darya, the region known formerly as Transoxiana (*Oxus* is the Greek name of the Amu Darya) or Sogdiana.

lxxvi. Probably the Western Pamirs, two arms of which, the Turkestan and Zerafshan ranges, taper out to the southwest of Samarkand. They would have crossed the river at modern Bekabad/Bekobod, in Uzbekistan, close to the Syr Darya, where it makes its final turn toward the northwest.

lxxvii. Also transliterated as *Xunsigan* earlier in the text, and later as *Xiemisigan*. All three forms are derived from *Semizkent*, the Turkic form of the city's name.

lxxviii. The Zeravshan River (from the Persian "spreader of gold") in Uzbekistan flows east out of the Pamirs between Kyrgyzstan and Tajikistan, turns southwest on the west side of Samarkand, and flows down into the desert north of the Amu Darya.

lxxix. Kong Yingda (574–648), reputedly a direct descendant of Confucius (Kong-zi/Kong Qiu), was an early Tang classical scholar and the author of this influential commentary on *The Zuo Commentary* (*Zuozhuan*

左傳). *The Zuo Commentary* was regarded as a commentary on the famously laconic *Spring and Autumn Annals*, traditionally attributed to Confucius. Kong's work is also known as the *Correct Meaning of the Zuo Commentary to the "Spring and Autumn Annals"* (*Chunqiu Zuozhuan zhengyi* 春秋左傳正義).

lxxx. The author mistakes the date. The vernal equinox occurred in Central Asia on 1222.03.20, or the sixth day of the lunar second month.

lxxxi. Bo'orchu was one of Chinggis Qan's earliest *nökör*, or trusted companions, and one of his "four steeds." For the tale of how he met Temüjin, helped him to retrieve horses stolen from the family encampment, and was later entrusted by Chinggis with command of the right wing of the army as a myriarch in 1206, see de Rachewiltz 2004, para. 90–93, 205, and Atwood 2004a, 44. Tiemen (Iron Gate) is a strategic mountain pass about 160 kilometers south of Samarkand.

lxxxii. Perhaps the giant reed (*Arundo donax*), native to Central Asia and south China but not north China.

lxxxiii. Hela-bode, possibly the Buda (Buda Noyan) described by Rashīd al-Din as a Tangut taken captive as a boy, around the same time as the Tangut Chahan (Chaghan), commander of Chinggis Qan's personal guard of a thousand soldiers, a post Buda Noyan later inherited (Rashīd-ad-Din 1998, 73–74, 272). The two boys were renamed, Qara (Buda), meaning "black," and Chaghan, meaning "white."

Notes to the Chinese Text

i. Since he already accounted for events in the second lunar month, this may be an original miscription for 三月上旬.

ii. 暗 is the character used in ZTDZ. Wang Guowei changed it to a near antonym, *lang* 朗 and attached it to the previous line, resulting in *bieshi yiban* qinglang 別是一般清朗: "is a different sort of clear brightness." However, while the "He shengchao" is a tune of many metrical and tonal variations, in no case can the structure vary between the two stanzas, and both should end with a five-syllable line.

iii. This might be an original miscription for 二十九日.

iv. Replacing 于 with 于.

v. Replacing 床 with 禾.

vi. Replacing 愽 with 博.

Text Critical Notes to Book II

i. QXYJ03 181, n. C11, suggests that this is Supervisor Li De 提控李德 mentioned in an inscription that Yelü Chucai composed for a Buddhist temple in Yanjing in 1233 (see Yelü Chucai 1986, 198). However, Li is such a common surname, and "supervisor" (*tikong*) such a common term for referring to low-level functionaries, that there is no compelling reason to link two men separated by such a gap in both distance and time.

ii. Zheng Shizhen, byname Jingxian 景賢, dates uncertain. A close friend of Yelü Chucai and a fine poet and painter. See Yelü Chucai 1986, vi.

iii. Hezhu, tentatively identified by QXYJ03 99, n. C7, as the Qaju mentioned in Yuan sources as having served under Ögödei as a junior interpreter (*xiao tongshi* 小通事), which fits his function here perfectly (see Farquhar 1990, 32).

iv. Kishliq Darqan, a loyal horse herder who warned Chinggis of betrayal by Ong Qan and his son. Later rewarded with command of his own army of a thousand and the status of *darqan*—a free man with special privileges (de Rachewiltz 2004, 87–88, 108, 295; Atwood 2004a, 133).

v. Zhang Rong surrendered to the Mongols in 1214 and in 1218 was appointed supervisor of carpenters for the Mongol Western Campaign. He solved the problem of crossing rivers by building boats for the Mongols and their animals, for which service Chinggis dubbed him Usuchi ("water master"). He died in 1230 at age 73. See YS 151.3581; QXYJ02 B.10b.

vi. Wang E remarks, "Once the Master had continued on to the west, Li Zhichang led the congregations in building the monastery, and it was done in record time; he also established the two congregations of Changchun (Eternal Spring) and Yuhua (Jade White Flower), which exist to the present day." See Li Daoqian 2004a, in ZHDZ vol. 47, 138.

vii. The Kemkemji'ut (modern Khemchik) River, now in the Republic of Tuva, flows eastward, meeting the Yenisei River as it turns north to empty into the Arctic Ocean. The prefecture was 9,000 *li* from Dadu (Beijing), with a population of several thousand Mongols, Uyghurs, and artisans transported from China early in the conquest period (YS 63.1574–1575). See Rashīd-ad-Dīn 1998, 23, 58, 77 *passim*; QXYJ03 221, n. C1; and Dardess 1972–1973, 122–123.

viii. *Cistanche* is called *tsoliin argamjin tsetseg* in Mongolian. The transliteration of the Mongolian term in Chinese, *suoyan*, is related to its Chinese nomenclature of *suoyang* 鎖陽, literally "locking away Yang power," a clue to its mushroom-like shape and its use as an aphrodisiac (supposedly accounting for Chinggis's prodigious stamina).

ix. Called *fulu* in the text, a word used in Tang sources to transcribe the Tibetan word for the finely woven felt cloth for tents used by the Tibetan empire in the seventh to ninth centuries. See QXYJ03 230, n. C12, citing the work of the Tibetologist Wang Yao.

x. Possibly the desert area northeast of Lake Barkol in the Barkol Kazakh autonomous county (QXYJ03 231, n. C2).

xi. Probably Jiagu Tongzhu 通住, elder paternal uncle of Jiagu Tangwudai 唐兀歹 (1216–1262.04.17). The Jurchen Jiagu family lived in the Lower

Water area. See QXYJ02 B.11b and Li Ting 李庭 (13th c.) 1999, in QYW vol. 2, 55.161.

xii. Route Commander, following Hucker's translation, to highlight the military nature of the office at this early time (Hucker 1985, 531). A Route was an administrative region. A *zongguan* typically operated alongside the imperial agent (Mo. *darughachi*, Ch. *daluhuachi*). The Mongols had occupied Yunzhong in their operations against the Jin by the start of the Western Campaign (1219).

xiii. QXYJ06 176, n. 1443, identifies this figure as the abbot of the Longyang Monastery in Dexing. QXYJ03 241, n. C3, suspects that it is another reference to Yin Zhiping, who may have returned from his mission with Alixian by this time. But the phrase literally translated "together with the Lady (mother) of the County, Yin Qianyi," refers to the recipient of a patent title bestowed on the mothers of officials. Her inclusion demonstrates the Quanzhen openness to female patrons and activists.

xiv. Liu Min, a native of Xuande, was abandoned during the Mongols' first invasion, captured at age twelve, and reared in the Mongol camp, like many youths left in the wake of Mongol forays. He favorably impressed the Qan, accompanied him to Central Asia, and had returned by 1223 to assume office in the Yanjing Route. See YS 153.3609–3611.

xv. Zhaba'er huozhe (Ja'far Khwāja), a *sayyid* (one claiming descent from the Prophet Muhammad) and Muslim trader who allied with Chinggis early in his struggle against the Kereit. Later he held prominent military and diplomatic positions and helped administer Yanjing after its fall. His biography (YS 120.2960–2961) reports several conversations between him and Qiu Chuji. See Yihao Qiu 2020.

xvi. "Stele of the Deeds of Changchun the Perfected" (*Changchun zhenren benxing bei* 長春真人本行碑), by Chen Shike 陳時可, a contemporary, makes it clear these Eight Congregations were formed from adepts in Yanjing. Preface dated 1228.09.05. See Li Daoqian 2004a, in ZHDZ vol. 47, 127.

xvii. In the Separate Northern Palace (*Beili gong* 北離宮) of the Jin, located northeast of the capital itself, now Beihai Park in Beijing. The site escaped destruction in the Mongol pillaging of the capital and was later incorporated into the palace complex in Yuan Dadu. See Wang Shiren 2013, 294–296. Another "northern palace," located just outside of the northeastern gate of the capital (the Guangtai Gate), was also used as a summer palace.

xviii. Yuluo Terrace, located on Jade Capital Mountain (*Yujing shan* 玉京山) in the 32 heavens that comprise the Great Canopy Heaven (*Daluo tian* 大羅天) of Lingbao and Shangqing Daoism. Inner elixir Daoism features a microcosmic reproduction of the heavens within the body. According to Chen Zhixu 2004, Yuluo Terrace is located at the edge of the brain (*naoji* 腦際). See Bokenkamp 1997, 373–402, and Despeux 2018, chap. 1.

xix. The progression of the stars refers to the twelve divisions of the heavens, as calculated by Jupiter's movement through stars along the equatorial plane, which takes twelve years for the full journey. Within these twelve divisions are twenty-eight fixed stars, called "lunar mansions." As the planets move through these mansions, they are thought to signal fortunate or baleful events. In a system called "division of fields" (*fenye* 分野) each of these twelve divisions governs a corresponding land area in China, linking Heaven and earth in a symbolic correlation.

xx. Liu Haichan, who lived in the Five Dynasties period (10th c.) in northeastern Hebei, the Yan region. He was a master of inner alchemy and one of the Five Northern Patriarchs retroactively adopted by the Quanzhen school. See Jinping Wang 2018, 97; Marsone 2001. The term *haichan* (toad of the sea) is a metaphor for the bright moon.

xxi. Either northern Hebei, the traditional area of Yan, or the short-lived state of Yan (911–913), with its capital near modern Beijing.

xxii. Lü Dongbin, of the latter half of the Tang (9th–10th c.), is subject of many legends and texts in the Daoist canon. He was later made a Quanzhen patriarch, probably after Qiu Chuji's death, and became the best known of the Eight Transcendents (*baxian* 八仙), subsequently popularized by the sect. See Marsone 2001; Jinping Wang 2018, 97–100; Katz 1999.

xxiii. Zhi Zhongyuan, an early painter of the Five Dynasties period and a specialist in portraits of Daoist priests and transcendents. On Zhi, see Pan 1999, 68–69, esp. n. 8. On his *Portrait of the Three Transcendents*, see Huang Taiyong 2015.

xxiv. Shen (Orion), seventh mansion or constellation in the third or western quadrant of the 28 lunar mansions (*xingxiu* 星宿), which are divided among the east, north, west, and south quadrants. It has three main stars (the Chinese graph for *shen* 参 originally meant "three"), forming the belt of Orion and said to represent three generals.

xxv. Probably Gubeikou, northeast of Beijing. An earthquake occurred on the 23rd of July in that year and was listed among a series of omens foretelling the fall of the Jin (JS 23.544). While QXYJ03 280, n. C7, suggests it was the proximate cause of the collapse of the pass and ponds, there is a gap of some two weeks. This narrative has probably conflated the two events to heighten the drama of Qiu's death.

xxvi. In 1227 Yin Zhiping proposed changing the eastern side of Changchun Palace, the old Baoxuan Hall, by constructing the Baiyun Monastery on the site where Qiu had died. Inside the monastery he built the Chuxun Hall to house the bones of the deceased Master. In the Ming dynasty, Baiyun Monastery became the official headquarters of the Quanzhen sect. See the sources listed in QXYJ03 287, n. C2.

Additional Note

The earliest edition of *Changchun's Journey*, a manuscript found in the *Daoist Treasury of the Zhengtong Era* (*Zhengtong Daozang*), provides the following lists of disciples and those assigned by the Mongols to travel with Qiu Chuji (Figure 1). The list of "Disciples Who Served Him on the Journey" (found in Appendix 10) is rather straightforward, listing eighteen disciples, first by their Daoist names, then by their surnames, and finally by their given names. The next list is ambiguous. This short list at the end of Figure 1 is titled "Four Mongols Especially Appointed to Follow the Master to Protect and Support Him." The term "Four Mongols," while it can be used to describe ethnicity, here evidently implies a division based on allegiance or affiliation. In the case of Liu Zhonglu, for instance, we know that he was of Parhae (Bohai) ethnic origin and was a long-trusted personal attendant to Chinggis, and Alixian (elsewhere identified as a Tangut from Xi Xia) was also a trusted deputy. The ambiguity arises with the three terms Mengguda, Hela, and Bahai in the first column. In an early word list, "Translation Terms from the Zhiyuan

FIGURE 1 Lists of travelers from the *Daoist Treasury of the Zhengtong Era*

Era (1264–1294)" (*Zhiyuan yiyu* 至元譯語), we find 達達蒙古歹 (Dada Menggudai), which Ligeti and Kara 1990, 263, translate as "*mongɣuldai* (*mong-kou-tai*) «Tatar, Mongol»." The term *menggudai* is often used as an ethnic marker in texts of dramas (particularly early Ming dramas). Plays also use *menggudai* or *menggutai* in a variety of written forms, 蒙古歹，蒙古帶，蒙古岱，蒙古台 , as well as the close phonetic relative *manggudai* 莽古歹，忙古歹, as a personal name, often specifically to denote servants. The use of *manggudai* as an ethnic marker to mean "a Tatar" or "Mongolian" has a long history that goes back to the Southern Song (see Fang Linggui 2001, 239–244).

Thus, the list *Mengguda Hela Bahai*, with no punctuation except the typical use of blank space in manuscripts to imply separation of terminology, is inherently ambiguous, leaving two possible distinct interpretations: "Mongols (servants?) (1) Hela and (2) Bahai, (3) Imperial Envoy Alixian, and (4) Imperial Envoy Plenipotentiary Liu Zonglu," or "(1) Mengguda (name), (2) Hela-Bahai, (3) Imperial Envoy Alixian, and (4) Imperial Envoy Plenipotentiary Liu Zhonglu."

In his 1926 edition of *Changchun's Journey to the West*, Wang Guowei (Figure 2, Appendix 3b) leaves the separation between Hela and Bahai, indicating that he probably understood the phrase in the first sense as "The Mongols Hela and Bahai." All modern editions of the text ignore the implications of the manuscript spacing and interpret it in the second

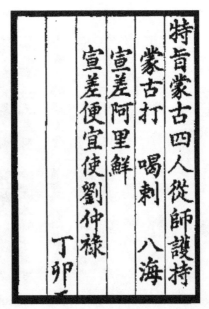

FIGURE 2 "Four Mongols" list in Wang Guowei's edition

sense: (1) Mengguda and (2) Hela-Bahai. The names occur together one more time in the text (see Figure 3), but that instance offers no actual help because the same problem of ambiguity persists, because 因命阿里鮮河西也為宣差，以蒙古帶喝剌八海副之，護師東還 can also be read as "he consequently ordered Alixian (a Tangut) to be the Imperial Envoy, (1) taking the Mongols Hela and Bahai as his seconds, *or* (2) taking Menggudai and Hela-Bahai as his seconds." While we have opted to follow modern editions and adopt the second reading, we cannot completely dismiss the other reading offered by the original *Daoist Treasury* text and Wang Guowei's edition. This is also an excellent demonstration of the kinds of problems that arise in deciphering foreign words that were at that time completely understandable to the writer and the audience. It also reinforces the need to avoid relying on modern commentaries as authorities of interpretation without first looking at the original source.

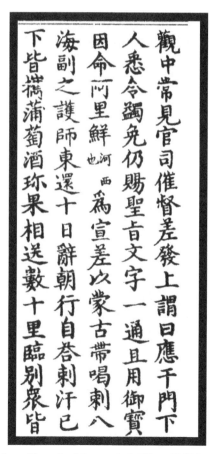

FIGURE 3 A passage from *Changchun's Journey to the* West with "Menggudai Hela Bahai"

重陽萬壽宮聖旨碑 [i]

碑高六尺四寸，分四截，正書。

成吉思皇帝賜神仙手詔。

制曰：

天厭中原驕華太 [ii] 極之性，朕居北野嗜慾莫生之情，反朴還淳，去奢從儉，每一衣一食，與牛豎馬圉，共弊同饗。視民如赤子，養士若兄弟，謀素和，恩素畜。

練萬衆以身人之先，臨百陣無念我之後，七載之中成大業 [iii]，六合之內為一統。非朕之行有德，蓋金 [iv] 之政無恆，是以受之天祐 [v]，獲承至尊。南連蠻宋，北接回紇，東夏西夷，悉稱臣佐。念我單于國千載百世以來未之有也。

然而任太守，重治平，猶懼有闕。且夫刳舟剡楫，將欲濟江河也，聘賢選佐，

---

i   Cai Meibiao 1995, 115 (hereafter CMB): 1219 年盩厔重陽萬壽宮聖旨碑.
ii CMB, 115: 大.
iii Ibid.: 帝業.
iv Ibid.: 鑒.
v   Ibid.: 天之祐.

---

1   Probably composed by Yelü Chucai.
2   We are following the inscriptions as recorded in Chen Yuan 1988; comparisons are made to Cai Meibiao 1955, 115. These are not titles of the stele but are identifying references to the place where the stele was found and separately recorded by Chen Yuan and Cai Meibiao. Cai titles his selection 1219 Stele of the Imperial Command at Chongyang Wanshou Monastery in Zhouzhi County. The monastery, one of three major sites of the Quanzhen sect, which also includes the White Cloud Daoist Monastery in Beijing and the Monastery of Perpetual Happiness in Shanxi, is where Wang Chongyang perfected the Way and where he was buried. As mentioned in the Introduction, Wang Chongyang was the founder of the Quanzhen sect.
3   A paraphrase of Stanza 19 of Laozi's *The Way and Its Power*, "Make your appearance plain and embrace simplicity, diminish selfish thoughts and have fewer desires" 見素抱樸，少私寡欲.
4   Cai Meibiao 1955, 115: "the imperial enterprise."
5   The term *man*, here translated as "barbarian," was usually used for peoples on the southern peripheries of Sinitic states. In this context, it appears to denigrate the Southern Song, a practice also seen in Jin literati writings of the early thirteenth century.
6   *Chanyu* was the title held by rulers of the Xiongnu confederation, the first steppe empire in history. The rescript's author places the Mongol empire in a long lineage of such steppe empires, stretching back some fourteen hundred years.

Appendix 1: *Chinggis Qan's Rescript Requesting Qiu Chuji to Journey to the West*[1]
Stele of the Imperial Edict at the Chongyang
Wanshou Palace[2]

The August Emperor Chinggis Qan bestows an edict in his own hand upon the divine transcendent being.

His command says,
Heaven detests the excessive arrogance and indulgence
in the Central Plain. I live in the Northern wilds, in a state
of freedom from sensuous desires. I return to the
uncarved block, return to purity, dispel excess, and follow
frugality.[3] In all my clothes and meals, I share the good
and the bad with cowherds and stable boys. I look upon
the people as innocent children; I nurture men of worth as
though they were my brothers. My plans have long been for
peace and harmony; my grace has long been held in store to
be used.
I have trained a multitude for war while leading them at the
front; I have faced a hundred battles without concern for my
progeny in the rear. Within seven years, I have completed
the Grand Enterprise;[4] at the center of the six directions, I
have forged a unity. It is not that my actions are so virtuous,
but that there was no constancy in Jin governance. Through
this I received Heaven's aid and took it upon myself to bear
the title of Most Revered. In the south, we linked up with
the barbarian Song;[5] in the north, we connected with the
Uyghurs. The Chinese in the east and barbarians in the
west all proclaim themselves my vassals. This, I believe, is
something that has never existed among those countries
headed by a *qan* (*chanyu*).[6]
Nonetheless, the responsibility we bear is great and weighty,
and we still fear that our methods for achieving order and
peace are imperfect. Now, hollowing out wood for boats
and carving it into oars is for the purpose of crossing rivers;
employing worthies and selecting able assistants for the

將以安天下也。朕踐祚 ⁶ⁱ 已來，勤心庶政。而三九之位，未見其人。

訪聞丘師先生，體真履規，博物洽聞，探賾窮理，道沖德著。懷古君子之肅風，抱真上 ⁷ⁱⁱ 人之雅操。久棲巖谷，藏聲 ⁷ⁱⁱⁱ 隱形，闡祖宗之遺化，坐致有道之士。雲集仙徑 ⁱˣ，莫可稱數。

自干戈而後，伏知先生，猶隱山東舊境，朕心仰懷無已。豈不聞渭水同車，茅廬三顧之事。奈何山川懸闊，有失躬迎之禮。朕但避位側身，齋戒沐浴，選差近侍官劉仲祿，備輕騎素車，不遠千里，謹邀先生暫屈仙步，不以沙漠悠遠為念，或以憂民當世之務，或以恤朕保身之術。朕親侍仙座，欽惟先生將咳唾之餘，但授一言斯可矣。

今者，聊發朕之微意萬一，明於詔章。誠望先生既著大道之端要，善無不應。亦豈違眾生之願哉。故茲詔示，惟宜知悉。

五月初一日筆。ˣ

vi   Ibid.: 阼.
vii Ibid.: 正.
viii Ibid.: 身.
ix   Ibid.: 遯.
x   Chen Yuan, 1988 (Hereafter CY), 445 original note:第一截右方.

7   A direct quotation from "The Biography of Liang Yi" 良頡傳 in HHS 30b.1168.
8   Cai Meibiao 1955, 115: "hiding your body away."
9   A happy confluence of reality and legend. Jiang Taigong was eighty years old when he was fishing in the Wei River with a straightened hook when King Wen encountered him. When King Wen asked why he did not bend it into a hook shape, Jiang replied that the fish he wanted would take his hook out of desire. King Wen understood the double entendre and asked Jiang to be his mentor. In another tradition, Jiang was fishing in the very same Panxi creek where Qiu studied. So the story represents a perfect homology for Chinggis (as King Wen) asking Qiu Chuji from Panxi (Jiang Taigong) to be his mentor.
10 A reference to the famous story of Liu Bei making three visits to the hut of Zhuge Liang to enlist his help in the years leading up to the Three Kingdoms period. See "The Triple Visit" in Idema and West 2016, 73–78.
11 1219.06.18. "On the right side of the first section of the stele." (Chen Yuan 1988, 445 n.)

ruler is for the purpose of bringing security to all under
Heaven. Since I have assumed the position of Great Qan,
I have "thought carefully about all aspects of governance,
and for the positions of the Three Noble Ones and Nine
Grandees, I have yet to see the right candidates."[7]

I have inquired about you, Master Teacher Qiu, one who
embodies perfection and treads within correct ambits, who
is widely learned and broadly experienced, who probes the
abstruse and exhaustively studies the principles of things,
and whose Way soars upward and whose Virtue is manifest.
You adopt the stern air of Superior Men of the past; you
embrace the elegant integrity of Perfected Ones on high.
Long have you perched among cliffs and valleys, hiding your
voice away and keeping out of sight.[8] You expound on the
transformative powers bequeathed by the patriarchs, easily
giving rise to men of the Way. They are like innumerable
clouds gathering on the path to transcendence.

After battles had ceased, when I came to know that the Master
was still hidden away in Shandong, I constantly thought of you
with admiration—have you not heard about riding in the same
cart at the Wei River?[9] Or making three visits to the thatched
hut?[10] Alas, we are separated afar by mountains and rivers,
and I have failed in the personal ritual of inviting you. All I
can do is to come down off my throne to salute you, fast, and
purify myself with bathing. I have sent my personal attendant
Liu Zhonglu to prepare light cavalry and an unadorned
cart and, hoping you find a thousand *li* not too far to travel,
I respectfully invite you, Sir, to temporarily bend your
transcendent steps, to not worry about the long distances over
deserts, to perhaps take on this worldly duty out of concern for
the people, or to share, perhaps out of sympathy, techniques
to help me protect my own person. I will wait upon the dais of
the transcendent one, and hope that from the leftover scraps of
your discourse, you will bestow upon me a single word.

I have expressed in this edict only a few of my deepest thoughts.
I sincerely hope that once you have made manifest the
beginning principles of the Great Way, everything will
respond with goodness. And how could this proposal go
against the desires of the multitudes? Therefore, you should
understand what this edict expresses.

Written on the first day of the fifth month.[11]

丘真人

登州棲霞縣志道丘處機近奉宣旨,遠召不才。海上居民,心皆悅惚。處機自念謀生太拙,學道無成,辛苦萬端,老而不死。名雖播於諸國,道不加於眾人。內顧自傷,衷情誰測。前者南京及宋國屢召不從,今者龍庭一呼即至,何也?

伏聞皇帝天賜勇智,今古絕倫,道協威靈,華夷率服。是故便欲投山竄海,不忍相違,且當冒雪衝霜,圖其一見。兼聞車駕只在桓撫之北,及到燕京,聽得車駕遙遠,不知其幾千里,風塵澒洞,天氣蒼黃,老弱不堪,切恐中途不能到得。假之皇帝所則,軍國之事,非己所能,道德之心,令人戒欲,悉為難事。遂與宣差劉仲祿商議。不若且在燕京德興府等處盤桓住坐, 先令人前去奏知。其劉仲祿不從,故不免自納奏帖。念處機肯來歸命,遠冒風霜,伏望皇帝早下寬大之詔,詳其可否。

---

1   Quoted in Tao Zongyi 1959, 10.121–122.

Appendix 2: *Qiu Chuji's Request to Remain in the Yanjing and Dexing Area*[1]

April–May 1220

I, Qiu Chuji, adherent to the Way from Qixia County of Dengzhou, have recently received your imperial directive. From afar you have summoned me, one lacking in talent, and the people who live here along the coast now feel distressed. I, Chuji, reflect that my plans in life have been too dull-witted, that I have studied the Way without success. I have borne bitter troubles from countless sources and, having grown old, somehow have yet to die. Though my fame has spread to many countries, my Way has not yet been taught to many. I am deeply moved (by your trust), but am also sick at heart; can anyone understand my innermost feelings? Prior to this the southern capital of the Jin and the state of Song summoned me several times, but I did not heed them. Now suddenly a call arrives from your dragon court. Why is that?

I have long heard that you, the August Emperor, received Heaven's gift of bravery and wisdom and have no equal among rulers both past and present. The Way has united with your awe-inspiring divine power, and both Chinese and barbarians obey you. For this reason, even should I wind up in a remote and distant place, I could not bear to be kept apart from you, and so I now brave the snow and frost in hopes of a single audience. Moreover, I had heard that your carriage was in the north at Huanzhou and Fuzhou, but when I reached Yanjing, I learned that it had left for somewhere distant. Dust blows everywhere, Heaven's ethers constantly shift, and I, being old and weak, cannot take it. I fear I will fail midway and never reach you. You, August Emperor, are a model for military and state affairs, which are beyond my capabilities. The heart and power of the Way is to make people abstain from their desires, which is difficult to accomplish. So I told Imperial Envoy Liu Zhonglu that it would be better to stop somewhere like Yanjing or Dexing prefecture for the time being, and that he should send someone to inform you of this request of mine. But Liu Zhonglu did not agree, so I am forced to send this request myself. I am willing to come as ordered, to brave the snow and frost across the vast distance. Yet I humbly hope that you, August Emperor, will soon send down a magnanimous edict, clarifying whether my request is possible.

兼同時四人出家，三人得道，惟處機虛得其名，顏色
顦頓，形容枯槁，伏望聖裁。龍兒年三月日奏 i。

i Tao Zongyi 1959, 10.121–22.

2 1220.04.05–05.03.

Moreover, of the original four of us who left our families to become Daoists, three have already attained the Way and passed on. It is only I, Chuji, who have falsely gained a reputation. I have grown haggard and frail. I humbly await your sagely decision.

> Sent on the [*unspecified*] day of the third month of the year of the dragon.[2]

重陽萬壽宮聖旨碑 i

成吉思皇帝敕真人丘 ii 師：

省所奏應詔而來者，具悉。惟師道逾 iii 三子，德重多方。命臣奉厥玄纁，馳傳訪諸滄海，時與願適，天不人違。兩朝屢詔而弗行，單使一邀而肯起，謂朕天啟，所以身歸。不辭暴露於風霜，自願跋涉於沙磧 iv。書章來上，喜慰何言。軍國之事非朕所期，道德之心誠云可尚。

朕以彼酋不遜，我伐用章 v；軍旅試臨，邊陲底定。來從去背，實力率之故然，久逸暫勞，冀心服而後已。于 vi 是用載揚威德，略駐車徒。

---

i CMB, 116: 1220 年盩厔重陽萬壽宮聖旨碑.
ii Ibid.: 邱.
iii Ibid.: 踰.
iv Ibid.: 磧.
v Ibid.: 張.
vi Ibid.: Missing this character.

---

1 Chen Yuan 1988, 445. Cai Meibiao 1955, 116, gives the title as "1220 Stele of the Sagely Directive at Chongyang Wanshou Monastery in Zhouzhi County."
2 In response to the last paragraph of Qiu's request.
3 Black and maroon cords were a symbolic gift given by emperors to worthy people they recruit.
4 This phrase may simply be an idiom.
5 In response to a line in Qiu's request, citing part of the original.
6 The chieftan is Khwarazm-shah Muhammad, who had put to death a group of Mongol merchants and envoys. Here following Cai Meibiao 1955, 116, and replacing 章 with 張.
7 "Force and benevolence": that is, both quick punishments and rewards for loyalty.

Appendix 3: *Chinggis Qan's Response to Qiu Chuji's Request for Delay*

Stele of the Imperial Command at Chongyang Wanshou Monastery[1]

The August Emperor Chinggis commands Master Qiu the Perfected to consider:

I have scrutinized what you sent in response to my edict and am clear on the details. It is precisely because the Master's Way surpassed that of the other three masters that your virtue is valued everywhere.[2] I ordered an official to take black and maroon cords and hurry by relay mount to call on you by the sea.[3] "The timing accorded with my wish; Heaven did not turn its back on men."[4] Two courts have often summoned you by imperial edict, and you did not travel to either, yet with a single envoy and invitation, you were willing to begin the journey to me. You say that I have been blessed by Heaven, and that this is the reason you have given your allegiance. You do not shirk exposure to wind and frost, and you are willing to trudge through sand and gravel. Your written report was received on high, and my delight and relief were beyond words. "Military and state affairs" are not what I expect;[5] it is the heart and power of the Way that I sincerely esteem.

When I found that chieftain recalcitrant, I confronted him with a range of military forces, and now the frontiers are safe and secure.[6] Compliant when they arrive, rebellious when they leave, they only respond to force. Therefore, to gain long-lasting peace through temporary effort, I will not rest until they submit completely. I showed both force and benevolence, and partially halted my chariots and troops.[7]

On second consideration, I thought, "Now that your cloud carriage has departed Penglai, you, the 'crane rider,' can roam all the way to India. Bodhidharma came east and relied on the Dharma Seal to transmit the Buddha's mind; Laozi journeyed west, perhaps to transform the barbarians and complete the Way. Though the

重念雲軒既發於蓬萊，鶴馭可遊於天竺。達磨東邁，
元印法以傳心；老氏西行，或化胡而成道。顧川途之
雖闊，瞻几 vii 杖以非遙。爰答來章，可明朕意。
秋暑，師比平安好，指不多及。

十四日　［御寶］。viii

vii　Ibid.: 幾.
viii　CY, 445 note: 第一截左方.

8　"On the left side of the first section of the stele" (Chen Yuan 1988, 445 n.).

rivers and roads appear far, look to your armrest and staff, and they will not seem so remote."

Now I have answered your writ and made my wishes clear. In the autumn heat, Master, I wish you peace and security. I have nothing else to say in this directive.

The fourteenth day [*space for imperial seal*][8]

重陽萬壽宮聖旨碑 [i]

成吉思皇帝聖旨，道與諸處官員每：

丘神仙應有底修行底 [ii] 院舍等，係逐日念誦經文告天底人每 [iii]，與皇帝祝壽萬萬 [iv] 歲者。所據大小差發賦稅，都休着者。據丘神仙應係出家門人等隨處院舍，都教免了差發稅賦者。其外詐推出家，影占差發底人每，告到官司治罪，斷按主者。[v]

　　奉到如此。不得違錯。須至給付照用者。

右付神仙門下收執照使。

所據神仙應係出家門人、精嚴住持院子 [vi] 底人等，並免差發賦稅。准此。

　　癸未羊兒年三月　　日［御寶］.[vii]

i   CMB, 1: "1223 年盩厔重陽萬壽宮聖旨碑."
ii   CMB: Missing this character.
iii CMB: 人等.
iv   CMB: Missing this character.
v   Following the punctuation of CMB.
vi   CMB: Missing these characters.
vii CY, 446 note: 第二截右方.

---

1   Cai Meibiao 1955, 2, titles this passage, "1223 Stele of the Sagely Directive Located at Chongyang Wanshou Palace in Zhouzhi County, No. 1." The language and tone of this and the next two edicts reproduced here are direct word-by-word translations of the Qan's Mongolian oral instructions into a form of Chinese that follows the word order of Mongolian. They are quite different from the elegant texts compiled by his highly educated secretaries. See Tong Laga 2007.

2   The expression *duan an zhu*, in which the owner of a transgressing slave must also be punished, is defined in Peng and Xu 2014, 114, thus: "For those who commit robbery: execute them and confiscate their wives and children and their livestock to turn over to the family that was robbed. If person A's servant steals person B's possessions, or if he steals the possessions of person B's servant, in every case the wives and children of both person A and his servant shall be confiscated, and both person A and his servant shall be executed. This is called *duan an zhu*." 其犯寇者, 殺之, 沒其妻子、畜產以入受寇之家。或甲之奴盜乙之物, 或盜乙之奴物, 皆沒甲與奴之妻子、畜產而殺其奴及甲, 謂之 斷案主。 See also Liu Xiao 2008.

3   1223.04.03–05.01. The imperial seal was "On the right side of the second section" (Chen Yuan 1988, 446, n.).

Appendix 4: *Chinggis Qan's Sagely Directive to All Officials*

Stele of the Sagely Directive Located at Chongyang Wanshou Palace in Zhouzhi County, No. 1[1]

The Sagely Directive of Emperor Chinggis declaims to all officials everywhere:

> The houses that Divine Transcendent Qiu properly holds as places for self-cultivation should all be used by people who chant scriptures and pray to Heaven daily, and those who pray for the long life of the Emperor. They do not have to pay any of the various forms of levies or taxes. As for the disciples of Divine Transcendent Qiu who have left their homes and who live in these houses, they too are exempt from levies and taxes. Apart from them, all who falsely claim to be monks or otherwise have evaded levies must be reported to the authorities. They will be subject to execution, and their possessions confiscated.[2]
> Make it so. Let there be no transgressions. Upon arrival this document must be presented by the entrusted as verification.
>
> The order above should be received and retained by the Divine Transcendent's disciples.
>
> As certified by this document carried by my envoy, all those connected to the Divine Transcendent who have left their homes as well as those who are meticulous and strict in their management of abbeys are equally exempt from levies and taxes. Act in accordance with this directive.
>
> *Guiwei* year of the Sheep, third month, [*unspecified*] day [*space for imperial seal*][3]

盩厔重陽萬壽宮聖旨碑 i

宣差阿里鮮面奉成吉思皇帝聖旨：

丘神仙奏知來底公事，是也瞞好。我前時已有聖旨文
字與你來，教你 ii 天下應有底出家善 iii 人都管着者。好
底歹底 iv，丘神仙你就便理，合 v 只你識者。

奉到如此。

　　癸未年九月二十四日　[imperial seal]。vi

---

i　CMB, 2: 1223 年盩厔重陽萬壽宮聖旨碑.
ii　CMB: Missing.
iii　CMB: Missing.
iv　CMB: 好的歹的.
v　Following CMB reading of CY's 丘神仙你就便理會，只你識者.
vi　CY, 446 note: "第二截中."

1　Cai Meibiao 1955, 2, gives the title as "1223 Stele of the Sagely Directive at Chongyang Wanshou Palace Zhouzhi county, No. 1."
2　1223.10.26. The imperial seal was "in the center of the second section" (Chen Yuan 1988, 446, n.).

Appendix 5: *Chinggis Qan's Sagely Directive Delivered by Alixian*

Stele of the Sagely Directive at Chongyang
Wanshou Palace[1]

The Imperially Commissioned Alixian delivers the sagely directive of the August Emperor in person:

> Divine Transcendent Qiu, the official business that you reported in your memorial to me is excellent. I have already written a sagely directive, telling you to take charge of all those good people in the empire who have left their homes for the monastic life. As for the good and the bad, Divine Transcendent Qiu, you manage them, as only you understand how.

> Make it like so.

> *Guiwei* year, ninth month, twenty-fourth day [*space for imperial seal*].[2]

宣差都元帥賈昌傳奉：

成吉思皇帝聖旨：丘神仙，你春月行程別來，至夏日路上炎熱艱難來，沿路好底鋪馬得騎來麼，路裏飲食廣多不少來麼，你到宣德州等處官員好覷你來麼，下頭百姓得來麼，你身起心裏好麼。我這裏常思量著神仙你，我不曾忘了你，你休忘了我者。

癸未年十一月十五日 i

i　ZTDZ 34.*fulu*.500c.

1　ZTDZ 34.*fulu*.500; ZHDZ vol. 47, 22–23; QXYJo1 Appendix 4, 34.500c.
2　1223.12.08.

Appendix 6: *Imperial Edict from Chinggis Qan Conveyed by Jia Chang*[1]

Jia Chang, Imperially Commissioned Commander, hereby conveys the sagely directive of the August Emperor:

> Divine Transcendent Qiu, you left in the spring, and it is now summer, when the roads are hot and hard. On the way, did you get good horses to ride? Did you get plenty to eat and drink? When you reached Xuande and elsewhere, did the officials treat you well? Did you get people to work for you as servants? Are you well in body and in heart? I think of you often, Divine Transcendent. I haven't forgotten you, so don't forget me either!
>
> *Guiwei* year, eleventh month, fifteenth day[2]

燕京行尚書省石抹公

謹請

真人長春公住持天長觀者

竊以必有至人而後可以啓箇中機，必有仙闕而後可以
待方外士。天長觀者，人間紫府，天上福田。[i] 若非真
神仙人，誰稱此道場地。仰惟長春上人，識超群品，
道悟長生。舌根有花，木香胸襟，無塵土氣，寔人天
之眼目，乃世俗之津梁。向也乘青牛而西邁，不憚朝
天。今焉奉紫詔而南迴，正當傳道。幸無多讓，早賜
光臨。

謹疏

癸未年八月　[space for seal]　日 [ii]

---

i   The translators found that the rule of parallelism dictated a correction of *zhushang*
　　主上 to *tian shang* 天上, balancing mortal world with heaven. This variant is found
　　in five editions of the text.
ii   ZTDZ 34.*fulu*.500.

---

1   ZTDZ 34.*fulu*.500; ZHDZ vol. 47, 22–23; QXYJo1 34.500c–501a.
2   Mention of a black ox refers to an older legend that Laozi, dismayed by the decline
　　of the Zhou dynasty, went west out of Hangu Pass riding a black ox and left Chinese
　　lands. The gatekeeper at the pass persuaded him to write down his thoughts in what
　　eventually became *The Way and Its Power*.
3   1223.09.07–10.06.

Appendix 7: *Shimo Xiandebu (Sendeb) Invites Qiu Chuji to Take Charge of Tianchang Monastery*[1]

His Excellency Yanjing Chief Councilor Shimo

     respectfully invites

    His Excellency the Perfected Changchun to become Supervisor Teacher of Tianchang Monastery

In my limited understanding, only a man of supreme insight can unlock the central pivot, and only a transcendent's tower is worthy of receiving men from beyond this secular world. Tianchang Monastery is such a place, a Purple Palace in this mortal world, a field of merit in the heavens. Who but a true Divine Transcendent could be worthy of this sacred space of the Way? May I humbly suggest that the superior man Changchun has knowledge surpassing that of ordinary beings, and that his Way is one that comprehends the secrets of eternal life. His tongue emits the fragrance of flowers and his breast is free of the stench of this muddy world. He has the eyes of a heavenly being and is a bridge for mortal men to the world beyond. He rode a black ox far out west and paid homage to the Son of Heaven without fear.[2] Now he returns to the south bearing a purple edict and will commence spreading the Way. I beg him to honor us with his presence and hope that he will not decline the invitation out of an excess of modesty.

Respectfully sent

    Guiwei year, eight month, [*space for seal*] [*unspecified*] day[3]

宣撫使御史大夫王
敦請

真人師父住持燕京十方大天長觀者

竊以應變神龍，非蹄涔所能止，無心野鶴，亦何天不可飛。故蒙莊出遊，漆園增價。陳摶歸隱，雲臺生光。不到若輩人，難了如此事。伏惟真人師父，氣清而粹，道大而高。已書絳闕之名，暫被玉壺之謫。以千載爲旦暮，以八極爲門庭。振柱史之宗風，提全真之法印。昔也三朝之教主，今茲萬乘之國師。幾年應詔北行，本擬措安於海內。一旦迴轅南邁，可能獨善於山東。維太極之故宮，寔大燕之宏構。國家元辰之所在，遠近取則之所先。必欲立接人之基，

1 ZTDZ 34.*fulu*.501; ZHDZ vol. 47, 23; QXYJ01 34.501a.

2 Zhuangzi once served "as a minor official in the Lacquer Garden in Meng" (from the biography in Sima Qian's second century BCE *Records of the Historian*, translated in Ames and Nakajima 2015, 3). Chen Tuan was a prominent tenth century Daoist who settled on Mt. Hua in Shaanxi and restored the Cloud Terrace Abbey (Yuntai Guan). For what is known of his life and work, which were very influential in the Song, see EOT 257–259.

3 The "jade kettle" refers to the biography of Fei Changfang in the *History of the Later Han* (HHS 82). He encountered an herbal medicine peddler in the market that he supervised. The peddler had a magic kettle made of jade, which he could jump into to find a beautiful banquet hall. Wang Juchuan uses the allusion to refer to a transcendent's magical abode.

4 The term *zhushi* refers to an official post, *yushi* 御史, ancient royal scribes, and from the Han dynasty on, investigating censors. Laozi allegedly held such a position; thus the term also functions as a reference to Laozi.

5 Probably referring to the reigns of the Jin emperors Shizong, Zhangzong, and Xuanzong.

Appendix 8: *Wang [Juchuan] Invites Qiu Chuji to Take Charge of Tianchang Monastery*[1]

Wang [Juchuan], Pacification Commissioner and Censorial Grandee,

    warmly requests

    The Perfected Master [Changchun] to become Supervisory Teacher of Tianchang Monastery

    In my limited understanding, no mere puddle in a hoofprint can impede a divine dragon of many transformations rising from the water collected therein; no corner of the heavens is beyond the soaring range of a carefree wild crane. Hence, the wanderings of Zhuangzi of Meng only enhanced the Lacquer Garden's value, and when Chen Tuan went into seclusion, Cloud Terrace Monastery emitted a brilliant light.[2] Such things can hardly occur unless the right kind of man appears. May I humbly observe that you, Perfected Master, possess *qi* that is pure and refined and a Way that is great and lofty. Now that your name has been inscribed on the crimson gates [of the imperial palace], I beg you to condescend to temporary exile from your jade kettle home.[3] To you, a thousand years are as a single day, and the entire world is but a single house. You have revived the lineage of the Censor;[4] you bear the dharma seal of Complete Perfection (Quanzhen). You were the leader of your teaching for three imperial reigns;[5] now you are the preceptor of a great country of ten thousand chariots. For several years, you journeyed in the north in answer to an imperial edict, hoping to bring peace to all the lands within the seas. Then your carriage returned south, where you planned to dwell in solitary virtue in Shandong. But Tianchang Monastery is the former palace of the Supreme Ultimate, a magnificent monument in the great city of Yan. It is where the state celebrates its auspicious occasions and the place that people near and far first look to as a model. If you wish to establish the foundations for a place where people will gather under your tutelage, there is nowhere better than

莫如宅首善之地。敢輒伸於管見，冀少駐於霓旌。萬
里雲披，式副人天之望。四方風動，舉聞道德之香。
謹疏

　　癸未年八月　[space for seal]　日 [i]

---

i　ZTDZ 34.*fulu*.501.

here in the empire's preeminent city. May I be so bold as
to express my limited opinion and hope that you will plant
your cloud-fashioned banner here for a while? Behold, the
clouds are parting over a thousand *li* as a sign of the hope
of all humanity and Heaven alike; the winds in the world's
four quarters are rising, longing to carry the fragrance of the
Way's virtue far and wide.

Respectfully notified

Guiwei year, eighth month, [*space for seal*] [*unspecified*] day[6]

燕京尚書省石抹公

謹請

丘神仙久住天長觀

竊以時止時行，雖聖人不凝滯於物，爰居爰處。而君子有恒久之心，於此兩端，存乎大致。長春真人，重陽高弟，四海重名，爲帝者之尊師，亦天下之教父。昔年應聘，還自萬里，尋思于今日接人，久住十方天長觀。

上以祝皇王之聖壽，下以薦生靈之福田。項因譏察於細人，非敢動搖於仙仗。不圖大老，遂有退心。

況京師者，諸夏之本根，而遠近取此乎法則。如或舍此而就彼，是謂下喬而入幽，輒敢堅留幸不易動。休休莫莫，無爲深山窮谷之行。

1   ZTDZ 34.*fulu*.501; ZHDZ vol. 47, 23; QXYJ01 34.501b.
2   A reference to a line in the "Fisherman" chapter from *Songs of the South* (*Chuci* 楚辭):
    "The sage does not become fixated on things, but is able to evolve with the world)"
    聖人不凝滯於物，而能與世推移.

Appendix 9: *Shimo Xiandebu (Sendeb) Invites Qiu Chuji to Reside Permanently in Tianchang Monastery*[1]

His Excellency Yanjing Chief Councilor Shimo

      respectfully invites

   Divine Transcendent Qiu to reside permanently in Tianchang Monastery

In my limited understanding, though sages do not fixate on material things and stay and go at will, superior men nonetheless have constancy in their hearts when it comes to where they choose to dwell.[2] Between these two poles, one seeks only to maintain a general principle. You, the Perfected Changchun, are Master Chongyang's leading disciple and are renowned within the four seas. You are the honored teacher of emperors and a teacher and father to all under Heaven. Some years ago, you responded to a summons from the Qan, and now you have returned from Samarkand across ten thousand *li*. Today you are gathering people to you and have taken up permanent residence in the Universal Tianchang Monastery.

You will first pray for the emperor's longevity, and you will next guide all living souls to plant themselves in fields of merit. Before, the security around you was so tight that the people dared not even shake your transcendent being's walking staff. They had no hope of approaching such a revered personage and thus felt distant from you.

Moreover, the capital city is the root of the Chinese lands, and people near and far take it as their model. Abandoning it for some other place would be like descending from the treetops into a dark valley. Hence, we dare presume to enjoin you to stay. How fortunate we would be if you ceased your travels and gave up your journeys deep into

永永長長，而作太極瓊華之主。

謹疏

丙戌年八月　[*space for seal*]　日 ⁱ

i　ZTDZ 34.*fulu*.501.

3　1226.08.25–09.22.

mountains and valleys. May you forever be the lord of the Supreme Ultimate Palace and the Island of Gemlike Flowers.

Respectfully noted

Bingxu year, eighth month, [*space for seal*] [*unspecified*] day[3]

侍行門人:

虛靜先生趙道堅

冲虛大師宋道安

清和大師尹志平

虛寂大師孫志堅

清貧道人夏志誠

清虛大師宋德方

葆光大師王志明

冲虛大師于志可

崇道大師張志素

通真大師鞠志圓

通玄大師李志常

頤真大師鄭志修

玄真大師張志遠

悟真大師孟志穩

清真大師綦志清

保真大師何志清

通玄大師楊志靜

冲和大師潘德冲

1 ZTDZ 34.*fulu*.501; ZHDZ vol. 47, 23; QXYJ01 34.501b–c.
2 Wang Guowei notes that this name is written as 孟志溫 in the main text. Meng's epitaph, composed in 1261, gives his name as Zhiyuan 志源, suggesting a later name change. See Li Daoqian *Ganshui xianyuan*, 770.
3 Wang Guowei notes that this disciple is named He Zhijian 何志堅 in the main text.

Appendix 10: *Disciples Who Accompanied the Master*[1]

Master Xujing (Empty Stillness) Zhao Daojian
Great Master Chongxu (Ascending the Void) Song Dao'an
Great Master Qinghe (Pure Harmony) Yin Zhiping
Great Master Xuji (Empty Silence) Sun Zhijian
Daoist Master Qingpin (Pure in Poverty) Xia Zhicheng
Great Master Qingxu (Pure Void) Song Defang
Great Master Baoguang (Luxuriant Brilliance) Wang Zhiming
Great Master Chongxu (Ascending the Void) Yu Zhike
Great Master Chongdao (Esteemed Way) Zhang Zhisu
Great Master Tongzhen (Reaching the Perfected) Ju Zhiyuan
Great Master Tongxuan (Reaching the Arcane) Li Zhichang
Great Master Yizhen (Nourish the Perfected) Zheng Zhixiu
Great Master Xuanzhen (Perfected in the Arcane) Zhang Zhiyuan
Great Master Wuzhen (Perfected in Understanding) Meng Zhiwen[2]
Great Master Qingzhen (Perfected in Clarity) Qi Zhiqing
Great Master Baozhen (Preserved Perfected) He Zhiqing[3]
Great Master Tongxuan (Reaching the Arcane) Yang Zhijing
Great Master Chonghe (Peace in Tranquility) Pan Dechong

特旨蒙古四人從師護持：

蒙古打　喝剌　八海
宣差阿里鮮
宣差便宜使劉仲祿 [i]

1　QXYJ01 34.501c.
2　On the problem of interpreting this line, see the Additional Note above.

Appendix 11: *Four Mongols Ordered to Escort and Protect the Master*[1]

Mengguda   Hela Bahai[2]
Imperially Commissioned [Envoy] Alixian
Imperially Commissioned Plenipotentiary Liu Zhonglu

玄風慶會錄
玄風慶會錄序

國師長春真人昔承宣召，不得已而後起，遂別中土，過流沙，陳道德以致君，止干戈而救物。功成身退，厭世登天。自太上玄元西去之後，寥寥千百載，唯真人一人而已。

1　Yelü Chucai 1986, 14.

Appendix 12: Record of the Felicitous Encounter with the Mysterious Wind of Daoism

Translators' note   The author of the preface to this text is unknown but is likely to have been a Quanzhen adherent. The text itself was probably published without the permission of its putative author, Yelü Chucai, whose attitude toward Qiu Chuji and the Quanzhen sect had turned decidedly negative by 1229. In that year Chucai published *Record of a Journey to the West* (*Xiyou lu*), the bulk of which is a polemic (framed as a dialog between Chucai and a guest) aimed at exposing Qiu and his sect as charlatans and absolving himself from charges of having aided them in deceiving Chinggis. *Record of a Journey to the West* contains only a brief reference to the sermon recorded in *Record of the Felicitous Encounter with the Mysterious Wind*, and it dismisses the sermon's contents as banal:

> The Guest asked, "May I hear what Master Qiu said when he went into the imperial presence to speak of the Way?" 客曰：「丘公進奏談道之語，可得聞歟？」
>
> The Householder (that is, Chucai) said, "In the tenth month of the winter of the *renwu* year (1222), the Emperor summoned Master Qiu to ask him about the Way of achieving immortality. His response was commonplace talk about such things as essence, spirit, and *qi*. He also told tales like that of Lin Lingsu taking Song Huizong on a tour of the Divine Empyrean Palace in a dream. That was the best of Master Qiu's preaching on the Way!"[1] 居士曰：「壬午之冬十月，上召丘公以問長生之道。所對皆平平之語言及精神氣之事。又舉林靈素夢中絜宋徽宗遊神霄宮等語。此丘公傳道之極致也。」

Preface

The Perfected Changchun, preceptor of the state, received an imperial summons and so reluctantly departed from the Central Plain and crossed the shifting sands, there to explicate the Way's moral power in order to assist the ruler in sagely governance and save many lives by bringing an end to warfare. This mission accomplished, he then withdrew (from the imperial court), grew weary of the world, and ascended to Heaven. From the time that the Most High Lord of Mysterious Origin (Laozi) went into the west, thousands of years had passed and only one man,

其往回事跡載於《西遊記》中詳矣，唯餘對上傳道
玄言奧旨，上令近侍錄而秘之。歲乃踰旬，傳之及外，將
以刊行於世，願與天下共知玄風慶會一段奇事云。壬辰長
至日序。

玄風慶會錄
元侍臣昭武大將軍尚書禮部侍郎移剌楚才奉敕編錄

欽奉皇帝聖議，宣請高道長春真人，歲在己卯，正元後一
日。敕朝官劉仲祿齎詔尋訪，直至東萊。適符聖意，禮迎
仙馭，不辭遠遠而來。

逮乎壬午之冬，十月既望，皇帝畋于西域雪山之陽。是
夕，御行在設庭燎，虛前席，延長春真人以問長生之道。
真人曰：

　　夫道生天育地，日月星辰、鬼神人物，皆從道生。人
　　只知天大，不知道之大也。余生平棄親出家，唯學此
　　耳。道生天地，天地開闢，而生人焉。人之始生也，
　　神光自照，行步如飛。地生菌，自有

2　During his lifetime, Chucai transcribed his surname in the Kitan form of Ila (Ch.
　　Yila), not Yelü. His given name is variously written as 楚材 and 楚才. Since the Yuan
　　dynasty was not founded until 1271, his identification here as a Yuan minister must
　　reflect later editing. Grand General of Martial Glory was a sinecure position in the
　　army, first used under the Jin dynasty and adopted by the Mongols. Yelü Chucai, a
　　civil administrator, did not hold any military command during his career

3　Although this text and Yelü Chucai's *Record of a Journey to the West* imply that the
　　sermon on November 20, 1222, was Qiu Chuji's first to Chinggis, *Daoist Master Chang-
　　chun's Journey to the West* records that Qiu had already preached to Chinggis thrice
　　in the ninth lunar month (on October 21, 25, and 29) and at least once in the tenth
　　(November 11). Perhaps November 22 was the first time that Chucai was present at
　　a sermon and tasked with recording it in Chinese.

4　In Daoist cosmogony, the Way, or the Supreme Ultimate (Taiji), produced *qi*, which
　　bifurcated into yin and yang, producing Heaven (yang) and earth (yin). Living things,
　　including human beings, were spontaneously generated by the interaction of *yin* and *yang*
　　between Heaven and earth. Each thing consists of proper proportions of yin and yang.

the Perfected, followed in his footsteps. The events of his journey there and back are recounted in detail in *Journey to the West*. The mysterious words and profound lessons from his sermons to His Majesty, additional to the *Journey*, were transcribed and kept secret by his close attendants on His Majesty's order. Now, after more than ten years, they will finally be revealed to the world in print so that all under Heaven may know of this rare event, His Majesty's encounter with the Mysterious Wind (of Daoism). This preface was written on the summer solstice of the *renchen* year (1232).

A Record of the Felicitous Encounter with the Mysterious Wind of Daoism

Compiled, by Imperial Order, by Yila Chucai,
Minister of the Yuan Dynasty, Grand General of Martial Glory, and
Vice Minister of Rites in the Department of State Affairs[2]

In reverent accordance with the Emperor's sagely wishes, a summons was sent out to the great Daoist master Changchun the Perfected on the day after New Year's in the *jimao* year (1219). The court minister Liu Zhonglu was commanded to go directly to the city of Donglai and visit him bearing an imperial edict. His wishes tallied with those of our sagely emperor, and we thus respectfully welcomed this crane-riding transcendent who deigned to come from afar.

In the winter of the *renwu* year, on the sixteenth day of the tenth month (November 20, 1222), the Emperor went hunting south of the Snowy Mountains in the Western Regions. That night, braziers were set up in the imperial encampment and the Emperor, having cleared all seats before his throne, invited Changchun the Perfected to come in and asked about the Way of achieving immortality.[3]

The Perfected said,

The Way gave birth to Heaven and earth. The sun, moon, and stars, the demons and gods, human beings, and all other living things—all are born from the Way. People know that Heaven is vast but know nothing of the vastness of the Way. I left my home and family for one purpose only: to learn about the Way. The Way produced Heaven and earth, which in turn initiated the process of creation and produced human beings.[4] When humans were first created, they glowed with a divine radiance and walked as swiftly as flying. Mushrooms grew from the ground, and they were so delicious that humans ate them raw. At that time, humans had not yet learned to cook over fire. These mushrooms were fra-

滋味，不假炊爨，人皆食之。此時尚未火食，其菌皆香，且鼻嗅其香，口嗜其味。漸致身重，神光尋滅，以愛欲之深故也。

學道之人，以此之故，世人愛處不愛，世人住處不住。去聲色以清靜為娛；屏滋味以恬淡為美。但有執著，不明道德也。眼見乎色，耳聽乎聲，口嗜乎味，性逐乎情，則散其氣。譬如氣鞠，氣實則健，氣散則否。人以氣為主，逐物動念，則元氣散，若氣鞠之氣散耳。

天生二物，曰動，曰植。草木之類為植，植而無識，雨露霑濡，自得生榮。人物之屬為動，動而有情，無衣無食何以卒歲？必當經營耳。旦夕云為，身口為累故也。

夫男陽也，屬火；女陰也，屬水。唯陰能消陽，水能剋火。故學道之人，首戒乎色。夫經營衣食，則勞乎思慮，雖散其氣，而散少，貪婪色慾，則耗乎精神，亦散其氣，而散之多。

道產二儀，輕清者為天，天陽也，屬火。重濁者為地，地陰也，屬水。人居其中，負陰而抱陽。故學道之人，知修鍊之術，去

grant and sweet; people's noses were drawn to their smell and their mouths craved their flavor. Gradually, people's bodies grew heavy, and their divine light faded out because their feelings and desires grew strong.

Consequently, those of us who study the Way do not crave what people of the world crave and do not dwell where people of the world dwell. We turn away from lovely sounds and sights, taking pleasure only in simplicity and serenity. We reject rich flavors and see the bland as beautiful. If we were to cling stubbornly to anything, we would fail to understand the Way's moral power. If our eyes fixed on human beauty, our ears listened for beautiful music, our mouths craved delicious flavors, and our spirit were driven by our emotions, then our *qi* would dissipate and be lost. It is like a ball inflated with air (*qi*). When it has enough air, it is solid and strong; if the air leaks, it goes flat. Humans are primarily composed of *qi*, and pursuing things moves their longing. Thus their primal *qi* dissipates, like a ball leaking air.

Heaven has produced two kinds of living beings: animate beings and plants. Grass and trees are plants; they are rooted in the ground and have no sentience. They are watered by rain and dew and thus can naturally obtain what allows them to grow and flourish. Humans are beings that move and can be moved. Once moved, they have emotional responses, but how can they get through a year without clothing and food? They must work to secure these necessities. They exert themselves day and night, burdened by the needs of their bodies and mouths.

Now, men are yang in their *qi* and have the characteristics of fire; women are yin in their *qi* and have the characteristics of water. Only yin can diminish yang, as only water can overcome fire. Therefore, we who study the Way must above all abstain from sexual relations. One who labors to produce clothing and food is wearied by contemplation, but though this causes one's *qi* to dissipate, the dissipation is minimal. Coveting sexual congress, on the other hand, both depletes one's spiritual essence and dissipates one's *qi* to a greater extent.

The Way produced the two parts of the cosmos: the light and pure part became Heaven, which is yang and has the characteristics of fire; the heavy and turbid part became earth, which is yin and has the characteristics of water. Human beings live between the two, carrying both yin and yang. That is why we who study the Way know the technique of internal alchemy. We do away

奢屏欲，固精守神，唯鍊乎陽。是故陰消而陽全，則升乎天而為仙，如火之炎上也。其愚迷之徒，以酒為漿，以妄為常。恣其情，逐其欲，耗其精，損其神。是以致陽衰而陰盛，則沉于地而為鬼，如水之流下也。

夫學修真者，如轉石上乎高山，愈高而愈難，跬步顛沛，前功俱廢。以其難為也，舉世莫之為也。背道逐欲者，如擲石下乎峻坡，愈卑而愈易，斯須隕墜，一去無迴。以其易為也，故舉世從之莫或悟也。

余前所謂修鍊之道，皆常人之事耳。天子之說，又異於是。陛下本天人耳，皇天眷命，假手我家，除殘去暴，為元元父母，恭行天罰，如代大匠斲，克艱克難，功成限畢，即昇天復位。在世之間，切宜減聲色，省嗜慾，得聖體康寧，睿筭遐遠耳。

庶人一妻，尚且損身，況乎天子，多畜嬪御，寧不深損？陛下宮姬滿座，前聞劉仲祿中都等揀選處女以備後宮。竊聞道經云：「不見可欲，使心不亂。」既見之，戒之則難，願留意焉。

with our excesses and desires, strengthen our essence, and protect our spirit in order to purify our yang. Therefore, when our yin is eliminated and our yang is completed, we ascend into Heaven to become transcendent beings, just as flames and heat always rise. Foolish and deluded men, in contrast, drink wine as though it were water and treat wantonness as normal. They indulge their emotions and pursue their desires, diminishing their essence and damaging their spirit. They reach the point at which yang withers and yin predominates. they then descend into the earth as ghosts, just as water always flows down.

Studying the Way and cultivating perfection are like rolling a boulder up a tall mountain. The higher one gets, the harder it is to keep going. One false step, one fall, and all that effort comes to nothing. It is so difficult that no one even tries. Turning one's back on the Way and pursuing one's desires, on the other hand, is like tossing a rock down a steep slope. The bigger the drop, the easier it is—the rock plummets like a meteor and is gone. It is so easy that everyone does it without realizing it.

The Way of internal alchemy, of which I spoke of earlier, is just for ordinary men. There is a different teaching for the Son of Heaven. Your Majesty is a divine being. August Heaven favored you and entrusted you with its mandate, working through your family to eradicate the tyrannical and violent. As father and mother to the common people, you mete out Heaven's punishments, just as an apprentice carves jade like the master craftsman. When you have overcome all difficulties, accomplished your mission, and completed your allotted time, you will ascend to Heaven and resume your place among the gods. While you are here in the mortal world, you should lessen your indulgence in music and women, and reduce your cravings and desires. In so doing, you will keep your sagely body in good health and your reputation for wisdom will spread far and wide.

If even the single wife of a commoner can damage his body, how much worse is it for the Son of Heaven, who keeps many concubines? Will you not suffer grievous damage? Your Majesty has a palace filled with serving women, and I have heard that Liu Zhonglu selected virgins from Zhongdu and elsewhere to enlarge your harem. The Daoist scriptures teach, I humbly submit, "Do not show them things they may desire, so that their hearts will not be disordered." Once you have seen them, it will be difficult to abstain. Please give this some thought.

人認身為己，此乃假物，從父母而得之者。神為真己，從道中而得之者，能思慮瘤寐是也。行善進道，則昇天為之仙；作惡背道，則入地為之鬼。

夫道產眾生，如金為眾器，銷其像則返成乎金。人行乎善則返成乎道。人間聲色衣食，人見以為娛樂，此非真樂，本為苦耳。世人以妄為真，以苦為樂，不亦悲哉？殊不知，天上至樂，乃真樂耳。

余儕以學道之故，棄父母而棲巖穴，同時學道四人，曰丘、曰劉、曰譚、曰馬。彼三人功滿道成，今已昇化。余辛苦之限未終，日一食一味一盂，恬然自適，以待乎時。其富者貴者，濟民拯世，積行累功，更為異耳。但能積善行道，胡患不能為仙乎？

中國承平日久，上天屢降經教，勸人為善。大河之北，西川江左，悉有之。東漢時，干吉受《太平經》，一百五十卷，皆修真治國之方。中國道人，誦之行之，可獲福成道。又桓帝永壽元年，正月七日，太上降蜀臨邛，授天師張道陵南斗北斗經及二十四階法籙諸經籍千餘卷。晉王纂遇太上道君

---

5 On Gan Ji, see EOT 433–434. On the *Scripture of Great Peace*, see EOT 938–940.

6 155.02.26 CE. On Zhang Daoling, see EOT 1222–1223. On the scriptures of the northern and southern dippers, see EOT 1053–1055. On the Daoist registers, see EOT 39–42.

People regard their bodies as their selves, but they are only passed down from their parents. Their spirits are their true selves, received from the Way. It is the spirit that thinks, sleeps, and wakes. If one does good and advances in the Way, then one's spirit will ascend to Heaven as a transcendent; if one does evil and turns from the Way, then one's spirit will descend into the earth as a ghost.

The Way produces all living things in the same way that metal is used to make all vessels. When vessels, whatever their shape, are melted down, they return to being raw metal. People who do good return to being the Way. People look on the sights and sounds and clothing and food of the mortal world as sources of pleasure. But that is not true pleasure; it is suffering. The people of this world treat falsehood as truth and suffering as pleasure. Is that not tragic? They do not know that true pleasure is the supreme pleasure of Heaven.

There were four of us who, to study the Way, left our parents and dwelt in cliffs and caves, spending our days studying together: I, Qiu Chuji; Liu Chuxuan; Tan Chuduan; and Ma Yu. The other three have accomplished their missions and fulfilled the Way. They have now transcended, while my time of suffering has yet to end. Each day, I eat one meal, consisting of one dish and one cup of water, content, waiting for my time to come. It is different for the wealthy and powerful, who give aid to the people and save the world from suffering, thus accumulating good works. If they can accumulate merit by practicing the Way, what fear have they of not achieving transcendence?

That the Central Plain has had many years of peace is because High Heaven has repeatedly sent down scriptures and teachings to exhort people to do good. The lands north of the Great (Yellow) River, Xichuan (Sichuan), and the lands southeast of the Yangzi River all have such scriptures. In the Eastern Han, Gan Ji received the *Scripture of Great Peace* in a hundred and fifty scrolls, all containing methods for cultivating one's true nature and bringing order to the state.[5] Daoist practitioners in the Central Plain who recite it and put it into practice can gain blessings and realize the Way. Next, in the first year of the Yongshou era, on the seventh day of the first month, under Emperor Huan, the Most High Lord of the Way (Laozi) descended to Linqiong in Shu (Sichuan) and revealed the scriptures of the northern and southern dippers and of the twenty-four grades of model registers and other scriptures, over a thousand scrolls in all, to the Celestial Master Zhang Daoling.[6] In the Western Jin, Wang Zuan encountered the imperial

法駕乘空賜經數十卷。元魏時，天師寇謙之居嵩山，
於太上等處，受道經六十餘卷，皆治心修道、祈福禳
災、掃除魑魅、拯疾疫之術。其餘經教，不可盡言。
降經之意，欲使古今帝王臣民皆令行善。

　經旨太多，請舉其要。天地之生，人為貴，是故人
身難得，如麟之角；萬物紛然，如牛之毛。既獲難得
之身，宜趣修真之路，作善修福，漸臻妙道。

　上至帝王，降及民庶，尊卑雖異，性命各同耳。帝
王悉天人謫降人間，若行善修福，則昇天之時，位踰
前職；不行善修福，則反是。天人有功微行薄者，再
令下世，修福濟民，方得高位。昔軒轅氏，天命降世，
一世為民，再世為臣，三世為君。濟世安民，累功積
德，數盡升天，而位尊於昔。

　陛下修行之法無他，當外修陰德，內固精神耳。恤
民保眾，使天下懷安，則為外行；省欲保神，為乎內
行。人以飲食為本，其清者為之精氣，

7　Wang Zuan's story is found in Chapter 15 of *Extensive Records of the Taiping Xingguo
　　Era* (*Taiping guangji* 太平廣記), which attributes it to *Biographies of Those Who
　　Encountered Immortals* (*Shenxian ganyu zhuan* 神仙感遇傳), by Du Guangting (850–
　　933). (On Du, see EOT 385–388.) However, the received versions of Du's *Biographies*
　　(preserved in the *Zhengtong Daoist Treasury*) are incomplete and do not contain this
　　story.

8　On Kou Qianzhi, see EOT 601–602.

9　In Chinese lore, a *qilin* was a fabulous creature akin to a unicorn that only appeared
　　in the world when a sage-ruler was on the throne. The idiom "like a phoenix's feather
　　or a *qilin*'s horn" describes something that is extremely rare.

10　On the Yellow Emperor, see EOT 504–506.

carriage of the Most High Lord, who came riding on air and gave him several dozen scrolls of scriptures.[7] In the Yuan Wei (Northern Wei), the Celestial Master Kou Qianzhi resided on Mt. Song and there received more than sixty scrolls of Daoist scriptures from the Most High Lord and other deities.[8] These were all techniques for regulating one's mind and cultivating one's practice of the Way, praying for blessings and dispelling calamity, driving out demons and healing the sick. There are other scriptures and teachings besides these, too many to recount. Heaven's purpose for sending down these scriptures was to make past and present rulers and subjects practice goodness.

There are too many teachings in the scriptures, so I will just summarize their essentials. Human beings are superior to all other creatures produced by Heaven and earth. That is why being born in a human body is as rare as a *qilin*'s horn, whereas the myriad other creatures are so abundant as to be like the hairs on a cow.[9] If one does receive such a rare body, then one should follow the path of cultivating one's true nature, doing good and cultivating merit, and thus gradually achieving completeness in the marvelous Way.

From rulers above to commoners below, all human beings have the same innate nature, regardless of their status. All rulers are divine beings exiled to the human world. If they do good deeds and cultivate merit, then when they ascend back to Heaven, their positions will be even higher than before. If they do not do good deeds and cultivate merit, then the opposite will happen. Divine beings whose accomplishments are meager and whose conduct is unworthy are sent down to the mortal world a second time to cultivate merit and aid people in need. Only then will they earn a high position. In ancient times, the Yellow Emperor Xuanyuan was commanded by Heaven to descend to the mortal world.[10] In his first incarnation, he was a commoner; in his second incarnation, a minister; in his third, a ruler. By saving the world and bringing peace to the people, he accumulated merit, and when his allotted time expired, he ascended to Heaven and enjoyed a more exalted position than before.

Your Majesty, there is only this way to cultivate yourself: externally, you must do good deeds; internally, you must strengthen your seminal essence and spirit. Outer cultivation consists of being compassionate and protecting the people, so that everyone is happy in their lives; inner cultivation consists of reducing your desires and guarding your spirit. As human beings, our health depends on our diet. Clear fare becomes our essence and *qi*, while

濁者為之便溺。貪慾好色，則喪精耗氣，乃成衰憊。陛下宜加珍嗇。一宵一為，已為深損，而況恣欲者乎？雖不能全戒，但能節欲，則幾於道矣。

夫神為子，氣為母。氣經目為淚，經鼻為膿，經舌為津，經外為汗，經內為血，經骨為髓，經腎為精。氣全則生，氣亡則死。氣盛則壯，氣衰則老。常使氣不散，則如子之有母，氣散則如子之喪父母，何恃何怙？

夫神氣同體，精髓一源。陛下試一月靜寢，必覺精神清爽，筋骨強健。古人云：「服藥千朝，不如獨臥一宵。」藥為草，精為髓。去髓添草，有何益哉？譬如囊中貯之金，旋去金而添鐵，久之金盡，囊雖滿，空遺鐵耳。服藥之理，夫何異乎？

古人以繼嗣之故，娶婦而立家。先聖周公、孔子、孟子各有子，孔子四十而不惑，孟子四十不動心。人生四十以上，氣血已衰，故戒之在色也。陛下聖子神孫，枝蔓多廣，宜保養戒欲，為自計耳。

昔宋上皇，本天人也。有神仙林靈素者，挈之神遊上天。入所

turbid fare becomes excrement and urine. Indulging in lust and sex drains our essence and *qi*, leaving us exhausted and sick. Your Majesty should take good care of your body. Having sex once a night is already damaging to one's health; how much worse is indulging one's desires even more? Even without complete abstinence, simply being able to regulate your desires will bring you closer to achieving the Way.

Our spirit is a child, and our *qi* is its mother. When *qi* passes through the eyes, it becomes tears; through the nose, it becomes mucus; through the tongue, it becomes saliva; externally, it becomes sweat; internally, it becomes blood; through the bones, it becomes marrow; through the kidneys, it becomes semen. When our *qi* is complete, we live; when it is depleted, we die. When our *qi* is abundant, we are in the prime of life; when our *qi* runs low, we are old. If we can constantly keep our *qi* from dissipating, it is like a child being with his mother. If our *qi* dissipates, it is like a child losing his parents. On whom can he then rely?

One's spirit and one's *qi* are the same in substance; one's semen and one's marrow come from the same source. Your Majesty should try sleeping alone for a month. You will surely feel your essence and spirit becoming pure and relaxed, and your muscles and bones becoming strong and healthy. The ancients had a saying, "Sleeping alone for one night is more effective than taking medicine for a hundred days." Medicine is made of herbs, while semen is made of marrow. Why squander one's marrow and then make up for it with herbs? That is like having a purse full of gold and replacing every piece of gold you spend with iron. Eventually the gold will run out, and although the purse is full, you are left with nothing but iron. How is taking herbal medicines any different?

The ancients took wives and started families for the sake of producing an heir. Ancient sages like the Duke of Zhou, Confucius, and Mencius all had sons, but Confucius at the age of forty was free of delusions, and Mencius at forty had an immovable heart. When a man passes the age of forty, his *qi* and blood have already begun to decline, and he should therefore refrain from sex. Your Majesty already has sagely sons and divine grandsons in abundance; the branches and leaves of your family tree have spread widely. You should now preserve your health and curb your desires, making considerations now only for yourself.

In the past, the Retired Emperor (Huizong) of Song was originally a divine being. A divine transcendent named Lin Lingsu took his spirit on a tour of the heavens. There they entered the

居宮，題其額曰神霄。不饑不渴，不寒不暑，逍遙無
事，快樂自在，欲久居之，無復往人間意。林靈素勸
之曰：「陛下天命人世，有天子功，限未畢，豈得居此
？」遂下人間。自後女真國興，太祖皇帝之將婁失虜
上皇北歸，久而老終于上京。

由是知上天之樂，何啻萬倍人間！又知因緣未終，
豈能遽然而歸也？余昔年出家，同道四人，彼三子先
已昇化，如蟬蛻然。委此凡骨而去，能化身千百，無
不可者。余辛苦萬端，未能去世，亦因緣之故也。

夫人之未生，在乎道中，不寒不暑，不饑不渴，心
無所思，真為快樂。既生而受形，眼觀乎色，耳聽乎
聲，舌了乎味，意慮乎事，萬事生矣。古人以心意莫
能禦也，故喻心為猿，意為馬，其難制可知也。古人
有言曰：「易伏猛獸，難降寸心。」乃成道昇天之捷逕
耳。

道人修真鍊心，一物不思量，如太虛止水，水之風
息也，靜而清，萬物照之，燦然悉見。水之風來也，
動而濁，何曷能鑒萬物哉？本來真性，靜如止水，眼
見乎色，耳悅乎聲，舌嗜

11　On Lin Lingsu and the Divine Empyrean movement in Daoism, see EOT 657–659,
　　889–892.

12　The Jin general Wanyan Loushi 完顏婁室 (1078–1130) played an instrumental role
　　in the Jurchen conquest of north China. The text uses a variant transliteration of his
　　name.

emperor's palace, which had a placard above the door that read "Divine Empyrean."[11] In it, the emperor neither hungered nor thirsted; he felt neither the cold of winter nor the heat of summer. He could live carefree and happy. He wished to stay forever and never return to the human world. Lin Lingsu dissuaded him, saying, "Your Majesty is a man with a heavenly mandate. How can you stay here when your work as Son of Heaven is not yet finished?" So they went back down to the human world. Later the Jurchen empire rose, and Emperor (Jin) Taizu's general Loushi captured the Retired Emperor and returned to the north with him.[12] Eventually, he died of old age in the (Jin) Supreme Capital.

From this we know that the happiness enjoyed up in the heavens exceeds that on earth many fold! It also tells us that if our destiny remains unfulfilled, we cannot just leave this world and return to Heaven. When I left my family many years ago, I was among four disciples. Now the three other masters have transformed and ascended to Heaven, like cicadas emerging from their shells and flying off. Having left their mortal bones behind and ascended into transcendence, they can now transform their bodies into hundreds of forms; there is nothing they cannot do. That I have gone through manifold sufferings and yet am still not able to leave this world is also due to my destiny.

Before birth, human beings exist in the Way. In that state, they feel neither cold nor heat, hunger nor thirst; their minds are free of thoughts and cares. That is true happiness! Once they are born and have physical form, their eyes look upon pleasant sights, their ears hear pleasant sounds, their tongues learn pleasant flavors, and they begin to think about things—and then all manner of problems arise. The ancients, knowing that our minds and thoughts are hard to rein in, likened the mind to an ape and its thoughts to a horse. That is how hard they are to control. The ancients had a saying: "It is easier to tame a ferocious beast than to subdue that little square inch of the mind." Thus, mastering one's mind is a shortcut to fulfilling the Way and ascending to Heaven.

Daoist practitioners who cultivate their true nature and refine their minds, do so by clearing their thoughts. Their minds are like the great void, or like still water. When the wind over the water subsides, it is quiet and clear and reflects everything like a mirror. But when the wind starts blowing, the water moves and grows turbid; how can it then mirror all things? Our original true nature is as quiet as still water. But when our eyes see pleasant things, our ears are delighted by pleasant sounds, our tongues

乎味，意著乎事，此數者續續而疊舉，若飄風之鼓浪
也。道人治心之初甚難，歲久功深，損之又損，至於
無為。道人一身耳，治心猶難，矧夫天子富有四海，
日攬萬機，治心豈易哉？但能節色慾，減思慮，亦獲
天祐，況全戒者邪？

昔軒轅皇帝，造弧矢，創兵革，以威天下。功成之
際，請教于仙人廣成子，以問治身之道，廣成子曰：
「汝無使思慮營營，一言足矣。」余謂修身之道貴乎中
和。太怒則傷乎身，太喜則傷乎神，太思則傷乎氣。
此三者，於道甚損，宜戒之也。

陛下既知神為真己，身是幻軀，凡見色起心，當自
思身假神真，自能止念也。人生壽命難得，且如鳥獸，
歲歲產子，旋踵夭亡，壯老者鮮，嬰童亦如之。是故
二十、三十為之下壽，四十、五十為之中壽，六十、
七十為之上壽。陛下春秋已入上壽之期，宜修德保身，
以介眉壽。出家學道之人，惡衣惡食，不積財，恐害
身損福故也。在家修道之人，飲食居處，珍玩貨財，
亦當依分，不宜過差也。

13 On the concept of nonaction, see EOT 1067.
14 On Master Guangcheng, see EOT 457–458.
15 From advice given by Gengsang Chu to Nanrong Chu in the *Zhuangzi* chapter "Geng-sang Chu." On Gengsang Chu, see EOT 445–446.

crave pleasant flavors, and our thoughts grow attached to things, everything mounts like waves stirred up by wind. The very first stage of Daoist cultivation of the mind is very difficult, but as the years pass, one's skills increase, and one's stray thoughts decrease. Finally, one arrives at the state of nonaction.[13] A Daoist practitioner is responsible merely for his own body and still has much difficulty disciplining his mind. How much harder is it for the Son of Heaven, who rules everything within the four seas and handles innumerable affairs of state each day? How could it be easy for him to discipline his mind? But if he regulated his sexual desires and limited his thoughts and cares, he would receive blessings from Heaven. And how much more so if he were to abstain entirely?

In ancient times, the Yellow Emperor Xuanyuan invented bows and arrows, swords and shields, to overawe the world. Close to accomplishing his goals, he sought advice from the transcendent Master Guangcheng on how to discipline his body.[14] Master Guangcheng told him, "Do not let your thoughts keep working anxiously. That is all I need say to you."[15] In my opinion, when it comes to the Way of self-cultivation, moderation and harmony are best. Intense anger injures our bodies, intense exhilaration injures our spirit, and intense thought injures our *qi*. These are all extremely damaging to the Way and should be avoided.

Your Majesty, since you now know that your spirit is your true self and your body is but an illusory shell, whenever you see female beauty and are stirred to desire, you should remind yourself that your body is false, and your spirit is true. You will then be able to restrain yourself. It is rare for humans to live to their allotted age. Like birds and beasts, they bear offspring year after year and are dead before they know it. Few remain healthy when old; infants and children, too, often sicken and die. That is why those who die in their twenties or thirties have a lower allotted lifespan, those who die in their forties or fifties have a medium allotted lifespan, and those who die in their sixties or seventies have a high allotted lifespan. Your Majesty has already entered a high allotted lifespan. You should cultivate your virtue and care for your body, so that you may live much longer. Those who leave their homes to study the Way loathe fine clothing and food and do not accumulate wealth and possessions, fearing that these will harm their bodies and damage their allotted fortune. But even those who study the Way at home should avail themselves of a diet, material comforts, and possessions fitting to their lot.

四海之外，普天之下，所有國土，不啻億兆，奇珍
異寶，比比出之。皆不如中原，天垂經教，治國治身
之術，為之大備。屢有奇人，成道昇天耳。山東、河
北天下美地，多出嘉禾美蔬，魚鹽絲枲，以給四方之
用。自古得之者為大國。所以歷代有國家者，唯爭此
地耳。今已為民有，兵火相繼，流散未集，宜差知彼
中子細事務者能幹官，規措勾當，與免三年稅賦，使
軍國足絲帛之用，黔黎獲蘇息之安，一舉而兩得之。
茲亦安民祈福之一端耳。自天祐之吉，無不利也。

余萬里之外，一召不遠而來。修身養命之方，既已
先言，治國保民之術，何為惜口？余前所謂安集山東、
河北之事，如差清幹官前去，依上措畫，必當天心，
苟授以非才，不徒無益，反為害也。初金國得天下，
以創起東土，中原人情尚未諳悉，封劉豫於東平，經
略八年，然後取之，此亦開創良策也。願加意焉。

修身養命要妙之道，傳之盡矣，其治國保民之術，
微陳梗槩，用之捨之，在宸衷之自斷耳。昔金國世宗
皇帝，即位之十年，色欲過度，不勝衰憊，每朝會，

16 This statement refers to the power vacuum in southern Hebei and Shandong resulting
    from the Mongol invasion and the Jin court's relocation to Henan. While Mongol
    control remained limited to northern Hebei and Shanxi, these regions came to be
    divided among many warlords and rebel groups.
17 Liu Yu, prefect of Jinan, Shandong, during the Jurchen invasion, surrendered to
    the Jurchen in 1128. In 1129 the Jin moved him to nearby Dongping Prefecture and
    entrusted him with part of north China. He was elevated to emperor of Qi in 1130
    and ruled north China as a Jin vassal until 1137, when the Jin abolished his state and
    began ruling its territory directly. Qiu Chuji seems to be advising Chinggis to appoint
    a similar Chinese puppet ruler.

In this world, there are millions of countries beyond the four seas, each one of which produces rare treasures. But none compares to the Central Plain, which Heaven has blessed with a plenitude of scriptures and teachings and techniques for governing the state and disciplining the body. That is why we have had one extraordinary man after another fulfill the Way and ascend into Heaven. Shandong and Hebei are the most beautiful lands in the empire. They produce a bounty of fine grain, vegetables, fish, salt, and silkworm cocoons to supply the whole country's needs. Since antiquity, whichever state gained control of them was counted as the greatest, so rulers through the ages have fought over these regions. Now they are in the common people's hands, and war has repeatedly ravaged the land, scattering the people into waves of refugees.[16] You should send a capable official who knows the situation well to restore order, and you should exempt the region from taxes for three years. Then your army and state would have an adequate supply of silk, and ordinary people would have the security to rest and revive themselves—two benefits from one action. This is one way to pacify the people and bring down blessings from Heaven. With the blessing of Heaven's aid, everything would go well.

Despite the distance, I have traveled here a thousand *li* in answer to your summons. Since I have already spoken of the method for cultivating the body and prolonging life, why should I not also speak of techniques for governing the state and preserving the people? As I said, stabilizing Shandong and Hebei would surely accord with Heaven's will if an incorrupt and capable official were sent to carry out Your Highness's plans. But if the man appointed is incompetent, then it would not only bring no benefit, but would also cause harm. When the Jin dynasty conquered all under Heaven, the people of the Central Plain were unfamiliar with it since it arose in the far east. So it enfeoffed Liu Yu at Dongping and let him govern the region for eight years before taking over.[17] This too is a good strategy for establishing stable rule, and I hope you will consider it carefully.

I have transmitted to you all that I know of the secret way of cultivating the body and prolonging life. I have also given a rough outline of techniques for governing the state and preserving the people. Your Majesty may judge for yourself whether to accept or reject them. In the past, Emperor Shizong of the Jin overindulged in sex during the first ten years of his reign. His body became so frail that when he attended court audiences, he had to be support-

二人掖行之。自是博訪高道，求保養之方，亦嘗請余，問修真之道，余如前說。自後身體康健，行步如故，凡在位三十年，昇退。

余生平學道，心以無思無慮，夢中天意若曰：功行未滿，當待時昇化耳。幻身假物，若逆旅蛻居耳，何足戀也？真身飛升，可化千百，無施不可，上天千歲或萬萬，遇有事，奉天命降世，投胎就舍而已。

傳道畢，上諭之曰：「諄諄道誨，敬聞命矣。斯皆難行之事，然則敢不遵依仙命，勤而行之？傳道之語，已命近臣錄之簡策。朕將親覽，其有玄旨未明者，續當請益焉。」

玄風慶會終

ed on either side as he walked. He sought out many Daoist masters to learn methods for preserving his health. He once summoned me as well and asked me about the Way of cultivating one's true self. I told him just what you have heard here. Thereafter, his body was restored to health and he could walk normally again. He reigned for thirty years before ascending to Heaven.

I have studied the Way all my life and my mind is free of cares and worries. Once, in a dream, Heaven seemed to say to me, "Your work is not yet done, so you must wait for the right time to transform and ascend to the heavens." This illusory and borrowed body is like an inn or a cicada shell to me, nothing more. Why should I feel any attachment to it? When my true self flies up to Heaven, I will be capable of thousands of transformations; nothing will be impossible. I may dwell in Heaven for a thousand or ten thousand years, but when there is an urgent need on earth, I will obey Heaven's command and descend to this world again to be reborn in a human body.

When he finished preaching, His Majesty said to him, "You have instructed me sincerely, and I have reverently paid heed. These teachings are difficult to practice, but how could I dare not follow your words, Transcendent One, to practice them diligently? I have commanded my trusted attendant to record your sermon in writing. I will read it, and if there is any mysterious teaching that remains unclear to me, I shall ask you to elaborate further."

　　End of *A Record of the Felicitous Encounter with the Mysterious Wind*

《 至元辯偽祿 》 摘錄 [i]
祥邁

良鄉縣東南張謝村興禪寺地土，棗樹林檎園并外白地，丘
公弟子孔志童強占種佃，欺侮尼眾。如此等例略有數百。
雖莊蹻狼戾於南荊，盜跖跋扈於東魯，方今剿劫未為過也。
不以道德為心，專以攘奪為務。

　　後毒痢發，作臥於廁中。經停七日，弟子移之而不肯
動。疲困羸極，乃詐之曰：「且偃之與寢何異哉？」又經二
日，竟據廁而卒。而門弟子外誑人云：「師父求福（ 編丘公錄
者李浩然集來 ），即日登葆光而化，異香滿室。」此皆人人具知，
尚變其說。

　　餘不公者例皆如此。故當時之人為之語曰：

一把形骸瘦骨頭，
長春一旦變為秋。
和灘帶屎亡圍廁，
一道流來兩道流。

　　斯良證也。（ 大道四祖之語也 ）即丁亥年七月初九日也。

---

i　　Xiangmai, *Zhiyuan Bianweilu*, 3.24.

1　　From Xiangmai 1988.
2　　Zhuang Qiao was a Chu general turned rebel in 301 BCE. Robber Zhi appears in the
　　eponymous chapter of *Zhuangzi* as an infamous and brazenly amoral bandit leader
　　who has a conversation with Confucius.
3　　That is, Li Zhichang.
4　　On the Authentic Great Way Daoist sect, which competed with Quanzhen throughout
　　the thirteenth century, see Bussio 2017; EOT 1247–1248.

Appendix 13: *Excerpt from* A Disputation of Contrived and False Records of the Zhiyuan Era[1]

Monk Xiangmai (fl. 1260–1300)

The land of Xingchan Monastery in Zhang-Xie Village in the southeast portion of Liangxiang County (near modern Fangshan, southwest of Beijing), including jujube trees and apple groves, as well as all open land, was forcefully occupied by Kong Zhitong, a disciple of Qiu, who took over the lease rights of the land to abuse the congregation of nuns. There were hundreds of cases of this type. Neither the plundering of Zhuang Qiao in southern Chu nor the violence of Robber Zhi in eastern Lu could have surpassed this recent pillage.[2] They held not to the "Way or its virtue" in their hearts but took plunder and pillage as their sole duty.

Finally, Qiu came down with dysentery and lay down in the privy; it stopped after seven days, but when his disciples wanted to move him, he refused to budge. Listless and emaciated, he still deceived them, saying, "What's the difference between the privy and the bedroom?" This continued for another two days, and he died there in the privy. But his disciples lied to outsiders, saying, *(this is from the Record of Sir Qiu, compiled by Li Haoran[3])* "Our Master went to the Baoguang Hall to pray for blessings and passed away there that very day, after which a strange perfume filled the room." Everyone knew the truth, yet they still clung to the story.

All their biased claims were like this. People at the time made up a ditty about it:

> A hand-span of a body, nothing but skin and bones,
> Eternal Spring one morning turned into autumn;
> Pissing and shitting, he died on the privy,
> One Way flowed in, but two ways flowed out.

This ditty is excellent proof of what I say *(these are the words of [Mao Xicong,] the Fourth Patriarch of the [Authentic] Great Way school).*[4] This was on the ninth day of the seventh month of the *dinghai* year (1227.08.22).

《長春真人西遊記校注》序

王國維

《長春真人西遊記》二卷，題「門人真常子李志常述」。[1]

案：志常字浩然，道號通玄大師。[2]

長春將歿，命門人宋道安提舉教門事，尹志平副之。未幾，道安以教門事付志平。太宗十年戊戌，志平年七十，又舉志常自代。憲宗即位，以志常領道教事。戊午歲卒。凡主全真教事者二十有一年。

　　至元間，釋祥邁撰《辨偽錄》，載志常掌教時侵占各路寺院四百八十二處，又令令狐璋、史志經等集《老子化胡成佛經》及《八十一化圖》，謗訕佛教。少林裕長老以聞。憲宗召少林及志常廷辨於和林萬安閣下。志常論詘，遂令毀《化胡》等經及將所占寺院三十七處還付釋家。志常因此忿恚而卒。[3]

　　考：此《錄》本為僧徒攻

1　QXYJ02 Preface, 1a–2a.

2　See Marsone 2016.

3　Linghu Zhang's full signature in the Quanzhen text *The Eighty-one Transformations of Lord Lao, Illustrated* is "the Pure and Peaceful Householder of Boguan, Linghu Zhang" 薄關清安居士令狐璋. It is not clear, however, where Boguan refers to. Shi Zhijing, byname Tianwei 天緯, religious name "Master of Profound Mystery" (*Dongxuan zi* 洞玄子), held the Daoist title "Great Master Who Disseminates the Meanings of the Mysterious Perfected" (*Xuanzhen xuanyi dashi* 玄真宣義大師). After the Mongols conquered his hometown in 1214, he made his way to Yunzhong (modern Datong, Shanxi) and became a servant in a Jurchen family. In 1221 he converted to Daoism and studied with Liu Daoning 劉道寧 (1172–1246) in Hengshan. When Qiu Chuji returned from the Western Regions, Shi Zhijing and his teacher affiliated themselves with the Quanzhen sect. In 1241 he became the head priest in the Daoist Abbey of Yuntai in Shaanxi. During his time in Shaanxi, Shi Zhijing compiled a gazetteer for Mt. Hua (*Huashan zhi* 華山志). In 1251 he went with Yu Dongzhen 于洞真 to visit the court in Qaraqorum. (See Li Daoqian, 2004a, vol. 47, 148–149.) For *Scripture on Laozi's Conversion of the Barbarians and Transformation into the Buddha*, see Liu Yi 1997, 6; Raz 2014, 255–294. For *The Eighty-one Transformations of Lord Lao, Illustrated*, see EOT 606–607.

Appendix 14: *Wang Guowei's Preface to His Edition of* Changchun's Journey[1]

Wang Guowei (1877–1927)

Daoist Master Changchun's Journey to the West, two *juan*. Labeled "as recounted by his disciple, Li Zhichang."

[Wang Guowei's] note Zhichang's byname was Haoran. His Daoist title was "The Great Master Who Communicates with the Mysterious." When Changchun was on his deathbed, he ordered his disciple Song Dao'an, to supervise the affairs of the Quanzhen Daoist sect, with Yin Zhiping supporting him.[2] Soon after, Dao'an handed supervising over to Zhiping. In the tenth year of the reign of Emperor Taizong (Ögödei Qan), the *wuxu* year (1238), Zhiping entered his seventies and recommended that Zhichang replace him. When Yuan Xianzong (Möngke Qan, r. 1251–1259) ascended the throne, Zhichang was in charge of Daoist affairs. Zhichang passed away in the *wuwu* year (1258). In all, he headed the Quanzhen sect for twenty-one years.

During the Zhiyuan era (1264–1294), the Buddhist Xiangmai composed *A Disputation of Contrived and False Records of the Zhiyuan Era*. In this book, he said that while Li Zhichang was in charge of the sect, he illegally seized and occupied 482 Buddhist temples and monasteries scattered in the various circuits, and that Li Zhichang had ordered Linghu Zhang and Shi Zhijing (b. 1202) to compile the *Scripture on Laozi's Conversion of the Barbarians and Transformation into the Buddha* and *The Eighty-one Transformations of Lord Lao, Illustrated* in order to defame and ridicule Buddhism.[3] Master Fuyu (1203–1275) from Shaolin Monastery made this known to the court. Emperor Xianzong summoned the Buddhist master from Shaolin Monastery and Li Zhichang to debate in the palace hall Pavilion of Myriad Peace. Zhichang's arguments were very clumsy, so the Qan commanded the Daoists to destroy the *Scripture on the Conversion of the Barbarians*. He also ordered the Daoists to return thirty-seven of the occupied temples to the Buddhists. Li Zhichang was so indignant about this that he died.

[Wang Guowei's] investigation This *Disputation of Contrived and False Records of the Zhiyuan Era* was written by Buddhists to attack

全真教而作，於長春師弟頗極醜詆。所記全真家占居僧寺
一節，誠為事實。然自金貞祐以來，河朔為墟，巨剎精
藍，鞠為茂草，緇衣杖錫，百不一存。亂定之後，革律為
禪者不可勝數，全真之徒亦遂因而葺之，以居其人。坐以
寇攘，未免過當。雖長春晚節以後頗憑藉世權以張其教，
尹、李承之，頗乖重陽創教之旨。然視當世僧徒如楊璉真
伽輩，則有間矣。然則祥邁所記，亦仇敵誣謗之言，安可
盡信哉！

　　此《記》作於長春沒後。前有孫錫《序》，署戊子
秋後二日，正當睿宗拖雷監國之歲。而卷末有庚寅七月大
葬仙師事，蓋書成後所加入。

　　考：全真之為道，本兼儒釋。自重陽以下，丹陽、長春
並善詩頌，志常尤文采斐然。其為是《記》，文約事盡。求
之外典，惟釋家《慈恩傳》可與抗衡。三洞之中未嘗有是
作也。

　　乾隆之季，嘉定錢竹汀先生讀《道藏》於蘇州元妙觀，

4　Owing to the Jin court's withdrawal to Henan and the effect of Mongol raids on Hebei.
5　Wang Guowei is referring here to *Master Chongyang's Fifteen Discourses for Establishing the Teachings* (*Chongyang lijiao shiwu lun* 重陽立教十五論). In "Discourse No. 5:
Constructing Activities," Wang Chongyang urges his followers to give up on "ornate
houses outside the body" and "search for the precious halls within the body" (Reiter
1985, 46; for a translation of the "Discourses," see Komjathy 2006, 265–367).
6　A Tibetan monk from Hexi (Gansu), also known as Rin-chen-skyabs, a disciple of
Phags'pa and crony of the despised minister Sangha, perhaps most noted for his pillage
of Southern Song graves, including those of the Song imperial family, to provide capital
for construction of monasteries. (See ISTK 561–562, 577–578; Chen Gaohua 2006.)
7　Tolui, Chinggis Qan's youngest son, served as regent for two years before his brother Ögedei was formally enthroned. As Qubilai's father, he was later posthumously
honored with an imperial title.
8　In fact, Qiu passed away in the seventh month of the *dinghai* year (1227).

Quanzhen Daoism and vilely slandered Qiu Chuji's disciples. But the
narrative about Quanzhen Daoists forcibly occupying Buddhist temples
was indeed based on real incidents. That being said, from the Zhenyou
era (1213–1217) of the Jin onward, everything north of the Yellow River had become a wasteland.[4] Large monasteries and beautiful temples
fell into ruins and were overtaken by vegetation. Fewer than one in
a hundred monks survived. Monasteries that changed affiliation from
Vinaya Buddhism to Chan Buddhism were too numerous to count. This
allowed Quanzhen Daoists to take advantage of the situation, and they
renovated Buddhist temples to accommodate their own people. But to
charge them with stealing the monasteries is going too far. While Qiu
Chuji took advantage of his worldly influence to expand his teachings
in his later years, it is also true that both Yin Zhiping and Li Zhichang
carried the sect forward by greatly perverting the tenets on which Wang
Chongyang had founded Quanzhen.[5] However, they were not as bad
as Buddhist followers of that time, such as Yanglian Zhenjia (fl. 1277).[6]
So what Xiangmai recorded was no more than slander of a foe. How
trustworthy can what he wrote be?

This *Journey to the West* was written after Qiu Chuji passed away. Sun
Xi's preface was signed on the second day after "establishing autumn"
of the *wuzi* year (1228), during the reign of Emperor Ruizong, Tolui
(r. 1228–1229).[7] However, the last *juan* of the book recounts the grand
funeral for the Transcendent Master Qiu Chuji in the seventh month of
the *gengyin* year (1230), which was probably appended after the book
was completed.[8]

[Wang Guowei's] investigation   As a religion, Quanzhen Daoism in-
tegrated both Confucianism and Buddhism. From the time of Wang
Chongyang, both Ma Danyang and Qiu Changchun were good at poetry.
Li Zhichang was extremely talented in literature. The prose style of his
Journey to the West is concise, but he elaborated events incisively. In the
outer canons, the *Ci'en Biography* is its only rival.[9] There has never been
such a work in the Three Caverns.[10]

At the very end of the reign of Emperor Qianlong (r. 1735–1796), Master Qian Daxin (1728–1804) of Jiading, when reading the *Daoist Canon* in
the Yuanmiao Daoist Monastery in Suzhou, became the first to laud this

9   A reference to the *Biography of the Tripitaka Master of the Great Ci'en Monastery* (*Da
    Ci'en Si Sanzang fashi zhuan* 大慈恩寺三藏法師傳), a biography and travel diary of
    the renowned Tang monk Xuanzang (602–664), who went to India to bring back
    hitherto untranslated sutras.
10 The three groups of Daoist scriptures. On the term and its meaning through history,
    see EOT 33–35 and 827–832, inter alia.

始表章此書，為之跋尾。阮文達遂寫以進秘府。道光間，
徐星伯、程春廬、沈子敦諸先生迭有考訂。靈石楊氏因刊
入《連筠簃叢書》，
由是此書非復丙庫之附庸，而為乙部之要籍矣。光緒中
葉，吳縣洪文卿侍郎創為之注，嘉興沈乙庵先生亦有箋
記，而均未刊布。

國維於乙丑夏日始治此書，時以所見疏於書眉，於其
中地理、人物亦復偶有創獲。積一年許，其得若干條，遂
盡一月之力，補綴以成此注。蓋病洪、沈二家書之不傳，
聊以自便檢尋云爾。因略論作者事蹟，弁於其首云。

丙寅孟夏 海甯王國維。

---

11 Xu Song's work on *Changchun's Journey to the West* is probably included in his lost book
A Study of the Geography of the Northwest in the History of the Yuan (*Yuan shi xibei dili
kao* 元史西北地理考). See Zhu Yuqi 2015, 160. Shen Yao 1897 provides annotations to
the part of the trip east of the Jinshan mountains. See also Guo Liping 2005, 125–128.

book and wrote a postscript to it. Thereafter, Ruan Yuan (1764–1849) transcribed the book and presented it to the imperial private collection. During the reign of Emperor Daoguang (r. 1820–1850), Xu Song (1781–1848), Cheng Tongwen (*jinshi* of 1799), and Shen Yao (1798–1840) investigated this work in succession.[11] Yang Shangwen (1807–1856) of Lingshi published it in *Collectanea of the Bamboo Hut* (*Lianyunyi cong-shu*, 1847). Thereafter, this book no longer was just an appendage to the masters 子 category of the four bibliographical categories, but became an important work in the history 史 category. In the middle of the reign of Emperor Guangxu (r. 1875–1908), Hong Jun (1839–1893) of Wuxian, the Assistant Commissioner of the Ministry of War, annotated this book. Shen Yi'an (name Zengzhi, 1850–1922) of Jiaxing added notes and annotations. But neither work was published.[12]

I (Wang Guowei) started studying this book in the summer of the *yichou* year (1925). From time to time, I jotted down notes on the upper margin from other texts that I had read and made occasional discoveries about geography or historical figures recorded in this book. After a year many entries had been accumulated. I spent a month supplementing them to make these annotations. I was unhappy that the annotations by Hong Jun and Shen Zengzhi never circulated, so I researched them in my spare time. Here I discuss my contributions by way of a preface.[13]

> In the fourth lunar month in the summer of the *bingyin* year
>   (1926.05.12–06.09),
> Wang Guowei of Haining

---

12   See Xu Quansheng 2019.
13   See Chen Linnan 2008, 4–12.

Abbreviations for Oft-Cited Texts

EOT   Pregadio, Fabrizio, ed. 2008. *Encyclopedia of Taoism*. 2 vols. Routledge.

HHS   Fan Ye 范曄, Li Xian 李賢, Sima Biao 司馬彪, and Liu Zhao 劉昭. 1965. *Hou Han shu* 後漢書 [History of the Later Han]. 12 vols. Vol. 1. Zhonghua shuju.

ISTK   De Rachewiltz, Igor, Hok-lam Chan, Hsiao Ch'i-ch'ing, and Peter W. Geier, eds., with May Wang. 1993. *In the Service of the Khan: Eminent Personalities of the Early Mongol-Yüan Period (1200–1300)*. Harrassowitz.

JS   Tuotuo (Toqto) 脫脫 et al., comp. 1974. *Jinshi* 金史 [History of the Jin]. Zhonghua shuju.

QCJJ   Qiu Chuji 丘處機. Zhao Weidong 趙韋東, ed. 2005. *Qiu Chuji ji* 丘處機集 [Collected Writings of Qiu Chuji]. Qi Lu shushe.

QXYJ01   Li Zhichang 李志常, comp. *Changchun zhenren xiyouji* 長春真人西遊記 [Daoist Master Changchun's Journey to the West]. ZTDZ vol. 34, 480b–501c.

QXYJ02   Li Zhichang 李志常, comp. Wang Guowei 王國維, ann. 1983. *Changchun zhenren xiyouji* 長春真人西遊記 [Daoist Master Changchun's Journey to the West]. 1st ed. 16 vols. Vol. 13, *Wang Guowei yishu* 王國維遺書 [Manuscripts Left by Wang Guowei after Death]. Shanghai guji chubanshe.

QXYJ03   Li Zhichang 李志常, comp. Shang Yanbin 尚衍斌 and Huang Taiyong 黃太勇, anns. 2016. *Changchun zhenren xiyouji jiaozhu* 長春真人西遊記校注 [Collation of and Notes to Daoist Master Changchun's Journey to the West]. Zhongguo minzu daxue chubanshe.

QXYJ04   Li Zhichang, comp. Dang Baohai 黨寶海, ed. and trans. 2001. *Changchun zhenren xiyouji* 長春真人西遊記 [Daoist Master Changchun's Journey to the West]. Hebei renmin chubanshe.

QXYJ05   Gu Baotian 顧寶田 and He Jingwen 何靜文, trans. and anns. 2008. *Xinyi Changchun zhenren xiyouji* 新譯長春真人西遊記 [Daoist Master Changchun's Journey to the West, Newly Translated]. Sanmin shuju.

QXYJ06   Li Zhichang 李志常 comp. Ji Liu 紀流 et al., anns. 1988. *Chengjisihan fengshang Changchun zhenren zhi mi* 成吉思汗封賞長春真人之謎 [The Puzzle of Chinggis Khan's Favorable Treatment of Daoist Master Changchun]. Zhongguo lüyou chubanshe.

QYW   Li Xiusheng 李修生, ed. 1999. *Quan Yuan wen* 全元文 [The Complete Yuan Prose]. 61 vols. Vol. 6. Jiangsu guji chubanshe.

YS   Song Lian 宋濂 et al., comps. 1976. *Yuanshi* 元史 [History of the Yuan]. Zhonghua shuju.

ZHDZ   Zhang Jiyu 張繼禹, ed. 2004. *Zhonghua Daozang* 中華道藏 [The Zhonghua Edition of the Daoist Canon]. 49 vols. Huaxia chubanshe.

ZTDZ   Zhang Yuchu 張宇初 and Zhang Yuqing 張宇清, comps. 1988. *Zhengtong Daozang* 正統道藏 [Daoist Canon of the Zhengtong Reign]. 36 vols. Wenwu chubanshe.

Bibliography

Editions

Li Zhichang 李志常, comp. *Changchun zhenren xiyouji* 長春真人西遊記 [Daoist Master Changchun's Journey to the West]. ZTDZ vol. 34, 480b–501c.

Li Zhichang 李志常, comp. Wang Guowei 王國維, ann. 1983. *Changchun zhenren xiyouji* 長春真人西遊記 [Daoist Master Changchun's Journey to the West]. 1 ed. 16 vols. Vol. 13, *Wang Guowei yishu* 王國維遺書. Shanghai guji chubanshe.

Li Zhichang 李志常, comp. Shang Yanbin 尚衍斌 and Huang Taiyong 黃太勇, anns. 2016. *Changchun zhenren xiyouji jiaozhu* 長春真人西遊記校注 [Collation of and Notes to Daoist Master Changchun's Journey to the West]. Zhongguo minzu daxue chubanshe.

Li Zhichang 李志常, comp. Dang Baohai 黨寶海, ed. and trans. 2001. *Changchun zhenren xiyouji* 長春真人西遊記 [Daoist Master Changchun's Journey to the West]. Hebei renmin chubanshe.

Li Zhichang 李志常, comp. Ji Liu 紀流 et al., anns. 1988. *Chengjisihan fengshang Changchun zhenren zhi mi* 成吉思汗封賞長春真人之謎 [The Puzzle of Chinggis Khan's Favorable Treatment of Daoist Master Changchun]. Zhongguo lüyou chubanshe.

Gu Baotian 顧寶田 and He Jingwen 何靜文, trans. and anns. 2008. *Xinyi Changchun zhenren xiyouji* 新譯長春真人西遊記 [Daoist Master Changchun's Journey to the West, Newly Translated]. Sanmin shuju.

Qiu Chuji 丘處機. Zhao Weidong 趙葦東, ed. 2005. *Qiu Chuji ji* 丘處機集 [Collected Works of Qiu Chuji]. Qi Lu shushe.

Translations into European Languages

Bretschneider, Emil. 2001. *Mediaeval Researches from Eastern Asiatic Sources: Fragments Towards the Knowledge of the Geography and History of Central and Western Asia from the 13th to the 17th Century.* 2 vols. Vol. 1. Munshiram Manoharlal.

Waley, Arthur. 1931. *The Travels of an Alchemist: The Journey of the Taoist Ch'ang-ch'un from China to the Hindukush at the Summons of Chingiz Khan.* Hedley Brothers.

Works Cited

Allsen, Thomas. 1994. "The Rise of the Mongolian Empire and Mongolian Rule in North China." In *The Cambridge History of China: Alien Regimes and Border States, 907–1368*, edited by Denis Twitchett and John Fairbank, 321–413. Cambridge University Press.

Allsen, Thomas. 1997. "Ever Closer Encounters: The Appropriation of Culture and Apportionment of Peoples in the Mongol Empire." *Journal of Early Modern History* 1 (1): 2–23.

Allsen, Thomas. 2019. *The Steppe and the Sea: Pearls in the Mongol Empire*. University of Pennsylvania Press.

Ames, Roger, and Nakajima Takeo. 2015. *Zhuangzi and the Happy Fish*. University of Hawai'i Press.

Andrews, Peter A. 1999. *Felt Tents and Pavilions: The Nomadic Tradition and Its Interaction with Princely Tentage*. Melisende.

Anon. 1988. "Daode zhenjing jie 道德真經解 [Explanation of the Authentic Scripture of the Way and Its Power]. In ZTDZ vol. 12, 659–695.

Anon. 2017. "Longmen diecui" 龍門疊翠 [The Levels of Verdure at Longmen]. Meiri toutiao 每日頭條. https://kknews.cc/travel/rq35a2v.html (accessed February 7, 2021).

Atwood, Christopher P. 2004a. *Encyclopedia of Mongolia and the Mongol Empire*. Facts on File, Inc.

Atwood, Christopher P. 2004b. "Validated by Holiness or Sovereignty: Religious Toleration as Political Theology in the Mongol World Empire of the Thirteenth Century." *International History Review* 26 (2): 237–256.

Atwood, Christopher P. 2016. "Buddhists as Natives: Changing Positions in the Religious Ecology of the Mongol Yuan Dynasty." In *The Middle Kingdom and the Dharma Wheel: Aspects of the Relationship between the Buddhist Saṃgha and the State in Chinese History*, edited by Thomas Jülch, 278–321. E. J. Brill.

Atwood, Christopher P. 2020. "Three Yuan Administrative Units in Marco Polo: Kinjin Talas, Silingjiu, and Kungčang." *Journal of Song-Yuan Studies* 49: 417–442.

Atwood, Christopher P. 2021. *The Rise of the Mongols: Five Chinese Sources*. Hackett Publishing.

Barthold, W. 1977. *Turkestan Down to the Mongol Invasion*. E. J. W. Gibb Memorial Trust.

Biran, Michal. 2005. *The Empire of Qara Khitai in Eurasian History*. Columbia University Press.

Biran, Michal. 2007. *Chinggis Khan*. Oneworld.

Biran, Michal. 2015. "The Mongols and Nomadic Identity: The Case of the Kitans in China." In *Nomads as Agents of Cultural Change*, edited by Reuven Amitai and Michal Biran, 152–181. University of Hawai'i Press.

Bokenkamp, Stephen. 1997. *Early Daoist Scriptures*. University of California Press.

Boyle, J. A. 1964. "The Journey of Het'um, King of Little Armenia, to the Court of the Great Khan Möngke." *Central Asiatic Journal* 9 (3): 175–189.

Broadbridge, Anne. 2018. *Women and the Making of the Mongol Empire*. Cambridge University Press.

Broughton, Jeffrey. 2004. "Bodhidharma." In *Encyclopedia of Buddhism*, edited by Robert Buswell. Thomson Gale.

Buell, Paul D. 1979. "Sino-Khitan Administration in Mongol Bukhara." *Journal of Asian History* 13 (2): 121–151.

Bussio, Jennifer. 2017. "Neither Dust nor Gold: A Comprehensive Study of the Dadao School from 1115–1398." Ph.D. dissertation, School of International Letters and Cultures, Arizona State University.

Cai Meibiao 蔡美彪. 1955. *Yuandai baihua bei jilu* 元代白話碑集錄 [Vernacular Stele Inscriptions of the Yuan]. Beijing kexue chubanshe.

Chen Dezhi 陳得芝. 2005. *Meng Yuan shi yanjiu conggao* 蒙元史研究叢稿 [Collected Studies on Mongol-Yuan History]. Renmin chubanshe.

Chen Dezhi 陳得芝. 2015. "Liu Yu *Chang De xishi ji* jiaozhu" 劉郁《常德西使記》校注 [An Annotated Edition of Liu Yu's *Account of Chang De's Embassy to the West*]. *Zhonghua wenshi luncong* 中華文史論叢 1: 67–108.

Chen Gaohua 陳高華. 2006. "Zailun Yuandai Hexi sengren Yanglian-zhenjia" 再論元代河西僧人楊璉真加 [A Reconsideration of the Yuan Period Hexi Buddhist Monk Yanglian-zhenjia]. *Zhonghua wenshi luncong* 中華文史論叢 82 (2): 159–180.

Chen Linnan 陳林男. 2008. "Qinghua guoxue yanjiuyuan shiqi de Wang Guowei xueshu lunshu" 清華國學研究院時期的王國維學術論述 [A Discussion of Wang Guowei's Academic Research While at the Qinghua Research Institute for National Culture]. *Wenyi lilun yanjiu* 文藝理論研究 2: 4–12.

Chen Shidao 陳師道. Mao Guangsheng 冒廣生, ed. 1995. *Houshan shi zhu bujian* 后山詩注補箋 [Supplementary Notes to Chen Shidao's Notes to His Poetry]. 2 vols. Zhonghua shuju.

Chen Yuan 陳垣. 1988. *Daojia jinshi lüe* 道家金石略 [Daoist Inscriptions on Metal and Stone]. Wenwu chubanshe.

Chen Zhengxiang 陳正祥. 1968. *Changchun zhenren xiyouji de dilixue pingzhu* 長春真人西遊記的地理學評註 [Geographical Evaluation and Annotation of the *Account of the Perfected Changchun's Journey to the West*]. Chinese University of Hong Kong Geographical Research Center.

Chen Zhengxiang 陳正祥. 1994. *Zhongguo youji xuan zhu* 中國游記選注 [An Annotated Anthology of Chinese Travel Accounts]. Nantian shuju youxian gongsi.

Chen Zhixu 陳致虛. 2004. *Taishang dong xuanling bao wuliangdu renshangpin miaojing zhujie* 太上洞玄靈寶無量度人上品妙經注解 [Annotations to and Explications of the Wondrous Scripture of the Upper Chambers of the Numinous Treasure of Limitless Salvation from the Cavern of Mystery of the Most High]. In ZHDZ vol. 3, 616–666.

Cleaves, Francis Woodman. 1955. "The Historicity of the Baljuna Covenant." *Harvard Journal of Asiatic Studies* 18 (3–4): 357–421.

Confucius (Kongzi). Edward G. Slingerland, trans. 2003. *Analects*. Hackett Publishing.

Dai Liangzuo 戴良佐. 1984. "Dushancheng guzhi takan ji" 獨山城故址踏勘記 [Record of the Onsite Survey of the Old Site of Dushan City]. In *Yuanshi ji beifang minzu shi yanjiu jikan* 元史及北方民族史研究集刊 [Historical Studies of the Yuan and the Northern Peoples], edited by Nanjing daxue Yuanshi yanjiu shi 南京大學元史研究室. Nanjing daxue chubanshe.

Dardess, John W. 1972–1973. "From Mongol Empire to Yüan Dynasty: Changing Forms of Imperial Rule in Mongolia and Central Asia." *Monumenta Serica* 30: 117–165.

Davis, Richard L. 2009. "The Reigns of Kuang-tsung (1189–1194) and Ning-tsung (1194–1224)." "The Reign of Li-tsung (1224–1264)." In *The Cambridge History of China*. Vol. 5, Part 1: *The Sung Dynasty and Its Precursors, 907–1279*, edited by Denis Twitchett and Paul Jakov Smith, 756–912. Cambridge University Press.

De Rachewiltz, Igor. 1962. "The Hsi-Yu Lu 西遊錄 by Yeh-lü Ch'u-ts'ai 耶律楚材." *Monumenta Serica* 21: 1–128.

De Rachewiltz, Igor. 1966. "Personnel and Personalities in North China in the Early Mongol Period." *Journal of the Economic and Social History of the Orient* 9 (1–2): 88–144.

De Rachewiltz, Igor. 2004. *The Secret History of the Mongols: A Mongolian Epic Chronicle of the Thirteenth Century*. 2 vols. E. J. Brill.

Despeux, Catherine. 2018. *Taoism and Self-Knowledge: The Chart for the Cultivation of Perfection*. E. J. Brill.

Dickens, Mark. 2020. "Tarsā: Persian and Central Asian Christians in Extant Literature." In *Artifact, Text, Context: Studies on Syriac Christianity in China and Central Asia*, edited by Li Tang and Dietmar W. Winkler, 9–42. LIT Verlag.

Dunnell, Ruth. 2010. *Chinggis Khan: World Conqueror*. Longman.

Fang, Linggui 方齡貴. 2001. *Gudian xiqu wailaiyu kaoshi cidian* 古典戲曲外來語考釋詞典 [A Dictionary of Foreign Terms in Classical Opera]. Yunnan daxue chubanshe.

Farquhar, David. 1990. *The Government of China under Mongol Rule*. Franz Steiner Verlag.

Franke, Herbert. 1994. "The Chin Dynasty." In *The Cambridge History of China*. Vol. 6, *Alien Regimes and Border States, 907–1368*, edited by Herbert Franke and Denis Twitchett, 215–320. Cambridge University Press.

Fu Ma 付馬. 2019. "Tang Yuan zhi jian sichouzhilu shang de Jingjiao wangluo ji qi zhengzhi gongneng" 唐元之間絲綢之路上的景教網絡及其政治功能 [Nestorian Networks along the Tang-Yuan Silk Road and Their Political Utility]. *Wenshi* 文史 3: 181–196.

Fu Ma 付馬. 2020. "Buddhist and Christian Relay Posts on the Silk Road (9th–12th cc.)." *Central Asiatic Journal* 63 (1–2): 239–256.

Garcia, Chad D. 2012. "A New Kind of Northerner: Initial Song Perceptions of the Mongols." *Journal of Song-Yuan Studies* 42: 309–342.

Goossaert, Vincent. 2001. "The Invention of an Order: Collective Identity in Thirteenth-Century Taoism." *Journal of Chinese Religions* 29 (1): 111–138.

Graham, A. C., trans. 1960. *The Book of Lieh-tzu.* Columbia University Press.

Guo Liping 郭麗萍. 2005. "Daoguangchao xibei shidi xueren xueshu jiaoyou shulüe" 道光朝西北史地學人學術交遊述略 [Scholarly Circles among Historical Geographers of the Northwest during the Daoguang Reign]. *Taiyuan shifan daxue xuebao* 太原師範大學學報 2: 125–128.

Guo Wu 郭武. 1998. "Quanzhen dashi Li Zhichang zhuanlüe" 全真大師李志常傳略 [A Biographical Sketch of the Quanzhen Master Li Zhichang]. *Zhongguo Daojiao* 中國道教 1: 41–45.

Hamilton, James. 1958. "Autour du manuscrit Staël-Holstein." *T'oung Pao*, 2nd series 46 (1–2): 115–153.

Hightower, James R. 1984. "Han Yü as Humorist." *Harvard Journal of Asiatic Studies* 44 (1): 5–27.

Hsiao Ch'i-ch'ing (Xiao Qiqing). 1978. *The Military Establishment of the Yuan Dynasty.* Harvard University Press.

Huang Taiyong 黃太勇. 2015. "'Sanxian tu' de liuchuan lichen ji qi lishi jian-zheng" 《三仙圖》的流傳歷程及其歷史見證 [The Circulation History of the *Portrait of the Three Transcendents* and the History That It Witnessed]. *Xungen* 尋根 2: 87–92.

Huang Taiyong 黃太勇. 2016. "Chengjisihan xuanchai Liu Zhonglu shengping shiyi" 成吉思汗宣差劉仲祿生平拾遺 [Supplemental Information on the Life of Liu Zhonglu, Chinggis Qan's Imperially Commissioned Envoy]. *Yuanshi ji minzu yu bianjiang yanjiu jikan* 元史及民族與邊疆研究集刊 31 (1): 80–86.

Hucker, Charles O. 1985. *A Dictionary of Official Titles in Imperial China.* Stanford University Press.

Idema, Wilt L., and Stephen H. West. 2016. *Record of the Three Kingdoms in Plain Language.* Hackett Publishing.

Jackson, Peter. 2005. "The Mongols and the Faith of the Conquered." In *Mongols, Turks, and Others*, edited by Reuven Amitai and Michal Biran, 245–290. E. J. Brill.

Jackson, Peter. 2009. *The Mission of Friar William of Rubruck.* Hackett Publishing.

Jia Jingyan 賈敬顏. 2004. *Wudai Song Jin Yuan ren bianjiang xingji shisan-zhong shuzheng gao* 五代宋金元人邊疆行記十三種疏證稿 [Elucidations of Thirteen Frontier Travel Accounts of the Five Dynasties, Song, Jin, and Yuan]. Zhonghua shuju.

Juvaynī, 'Ata-Malik, and J. A. Boyle, trans. 1997. *The History of the World Conqueror*. University of Washington Press.

Kamalov, Ablet. 2007. "The Uyghurs as Part of a Central Asian Commonality: Soviet Historiography on the Uyghurs." In *Situating the Uyghurs between China and Central Asia*, edited by Ildiko Bellér-Hann, M. Cristina Cesaro, Rachel Harris, and Joanne Smith Finley, 31–48. Ashgate Publishing.

Katz, Paul. 1999. *Images of the Immortal: The Cult of Lü Dongbin at the Palace of Eternal Joy*. University of Hawai'i Press.

Komjathy, Louis. 2006. *Cultivating Perfection: Mysticism and Self-Transformation in Early Quanzhen Daoism*. E. J. Brill.

Landa, Ishayahu. 2020. "Loyal and Martial until the End: The Qonggirad Princes of Lu 魯 in Yuan Political Architecture." *Monumenta Serica* 68 (1): 137–167.

Laozi. Moss Roberts, trans. 2019. *Dao de jing: The Book of the Way*. University of California Press.

Laozi 老子. Chen Guying 陳鼓應, comm. and trans. 1983. *"Laozi" zhuyi yu pingjia* 老子注譯與評價. Zhonghua shuju.

Laufer, Berthold. 1919. *Sino-Iranica: Chinese Contributions to the History of Civilization in Ancient Iran with Special Reference to the History of Cultivated Plants and Products, Anthropological Series*. Field Museum of Natural History.

Li Daoqian 李道謙 (1219–1296). 2004a. *Ganshui xian yuan lu* 甘水仙源錄 [Record of Adepts Who Attained Transcendence (after the Revelation) at Ganshui]. In ZHDZ vol. 47, 113–212

Li Daoqian 李道謙 (1219–1296). 2004b. *Zhongnanshan zuting xianzhen neizhuan* 終南山祖庭仙真內傳 [Inner Biographies of the Transcendents and Perfected Ones of the Ancestral Court in the Zhongnan Mountains]. In ZHDZ vol. 47, 77–106.

Li Fang 李昉. 1961. *Taiping guangji* 太平廣記 [Wide-Ranging Records from the Taiping Xingguo Era]. 10 vols. Vol. 1. Zhonghua shuju.

Li Jidong 李繼東 and Zhao Ruimin 趙瑞民. 2006. "Longshan shiku diliuku 'piyunzizan' shushi ji zaoxiang ticai de taolun" 龍山石窟第六窟「披雲自贊」疏釋及造像題材的討論 [An Interpretation of the 'piyunzizan' Inscription and Sculptural Elements in the Sixth Cave of the Longshan Caves]. *Wenwu shijie* 文物世界 6: 12–14, 20.

Li Ting 李庭 (13th c.). 1999. "Gu xuanshou Shaanxi deng lu daluhuachi Jiagu gong muzhiming" 故宣授陝西等路達魯花赤夾谷公墓誌銘 [Grave Epitaph of Sir Jiagu Tangwudai, the Imperially Commissioned Former Darughachi (Governor) of Shaanxi Province and Other Routes]. In QYW vol. 2, 55.161.

Li Yangzheng 李養正. 2020. *Xinbian Beijing Baiyun Guan zhi* 新編北京白雲觀志 [A Newly Edited Gazetteer of the Beijing White Cloud Monastery]. Zongjiao wenhua chubanshe.

Ligeti, Louis, decipherer, and G. Kara, ed. 1990. "Un vocabulaire Sino-Mongol des Yuan: Le *Tche-Yuan yi-yu* [A Chinese-Mongolian Word List of the Yuan: Transliterations of Mongol Words in Chinese of the Zhiyuan Reign period]." *Acta Orientalia Academiae Scientiarum Hungaricae* 44 (3): 259–277.

Lin Meicun 林梅村. 2016. "Daluosicheng yu Tangdai sichouzhilu" 怛邏斯城與唐代絲綢之路 [Daluosi City and the Tang Era Silk Road]. *Zhejiang daxue xuebao* 浙江大學學報 46 (5): 39–53.

Liu An (179–122 BCE). Sarah Queen, John Major, Andrew Meyer, and Harold Roth, trans. 2010. *The Huainanzi*. Columbia University Press.

Liu Qi 劉祁 (1203–1259). 1983. *Guiqian zhi* 歸潛志 [Record of Returning to Retirement]. Zhonghua shuju.

Liu Xiao 劉曉. 2004. "Chengjisihan gongzhu huanghou zakao" 成吉思汗公主皇后雜考 [A Research Note on Chinggis Qan's Princess-Empress]. *Minzu yanjiu* 民族研究 5: 15–21.

Liu Xiao 劉曉. 2008. "Meng Yuan zaoqi xingfa yongyu 'andaxi' xiaokao: bing lun 'duan'anzhu' yu duanmozui de guanxi" 蒙元早期刑罰用語'按答奚'小考——並論'斷案主'與斷沒罪的關係 [A Short Note on the Early Mongol-Yuan Penal Term 'andaxi' and the Relationship of the Term 'duan'anzhu' to the Punishment of Confiscation of Chattel]. *Zhongguo shehuikexueyuan lishi yanjiusuo xuekan* 中國社會科學院歷史研究所學刊 5: 229–241.

Liu Yi 劉屹. 1997. "Towards a New Understanding of *Huahujing* (The Scripture of Transforming the Barbarians) from Dunhuang." *International Dunhuang Project News* 7: 6.

Liu Yiming 劉一明 (1734–1821). *Xiyou yuanzhi* 西遊原旨 [The Fundamental Significance of the Journey to the West]. Manuscript with preface dated 1758. https://ctext.org/library.pl?if=gb&res=81330 (accessed Aug. 22, 2021).

Liu Yingsheng 劉迎勝. 2011. *Chahetai hanguo shi yanjiu* 察合台汗國史研究 [Studies of the Chaghadai Qanate]. Shanghai guji chubanshe.

Liu Yingsheng 劉迎勝. 2022. "'Tuoba' yu 'Taohuashi' ('Taoguanzhu') liang-ming guanxi xintan "拓跋"與"桃花石"("條貫主")两名關係新探 [A New Exploration of the Relationship between the Names 'Tuoba' and 'Taohuashi' ('Taoguanzhu')]." *Xibei minzu yanjiu* 西北民族研究 3: 22–46.

Luo Zhufeng 羅竹風 et al., eds. 1994. *Hanyu da cidian (fulu, suoyin)* 漢語大詞典 (附錄索引) [A Great Dictionary of the Chinese Language (with Appendices and Index)]. Hanyu da cidian chubanshe.

Marsone, Pierre. 2001. "Accounts of the Foundation of the Quanzhen Movement: A Hagiographic Treatment of History." *Journal of Chinese Religions* 29 (1): 95–110.

Marsone, Pierre. 2016. "La carrière du patriarche Yin Zhiping 尹志平 et ses mystères [The Career of Yin Zhiping and His Enigmas]." *Cahiers d'Extrême-Asie* 25: 31–46.

Muraoka Hitoshi 村岡倫, and Nakata Yuko 中田裕子. 2020. "Mongoru seibu ni okeru tōzai bunka kōryū no kyoten: 2017 nen Haerzen-Shiregu iseki chōcho no hōkoku to sono ato モンゴル西部におけ東西文化交流の拠点——2017 年 Harzan-Shilegi の遺跡調査の報告とその後. [A Base for East-West Cultural Interchange in Western Mongolia: The 2017 Harzan-Shileg Site Survey and What Followed]. In Japanese with English Abstract. *Ryūkoku Daigaku Kokusai Shakai Bunka Kenkyusho kiyō* 龍谷大学国際社会文化研究所紀要 22 (6): 93–120.

Ning, Qiang. 2008. "Imperial Portraiture as Symbol of Political Legitimacy: A New Study of the 'Portraits of Successive Emperors.'" *Ars Orientalis* 35: 96–128.

Nugteren, Hans, and Jens Wilkens. 2019. "A Female Mongol Headdress in Old Uyghur Secular Documents." *International Journal of Old Uyghur Studies* 1 (2): 153–170.

Pan Yungao 潘運告, ed. 1999. *Xuanhe huapu* 宣和畫譜 [The Xuanhe Era Catalog of Paintings, (12th c.)]. In *Zhongguo shuhua lun congshu* 中國書畫論叢書. Hunan meishu chubanshe.

Pelliot, Paul. 1959. *Notes on Marco Polo*. 3 vols. Vol. 1. Imprimerie nationale.

Peng Daya 彭大雅 (13th c.), Xu Ting 徐霆 (13th c.). Xu Quansheng 許全勝, ed. 2014. *Heida shilüe jiaozhu* 黑韃事略校注 [An Annotated Edition of *A Sketch of the Black Tatars*]. Lanzhou daxue chubanshe.

Polo, Marco (1254–1323?). Henri Cordier (1849–1925), ed. Amy Frances Yule and Henry Yule (1820–1899), ed. 1903. *The Book of Ser Marco Polo the Venetian Concerning the Kingdoms and Marvels of the East*. 2 vols. Vol. 1. Murray.

Pu Huiquan 濮惠泉. 2008. "Yuandai duliangheng liangqi de shouci zhongda faxian ji qi yiyi" 元代度量衡量器的首次重大發現及其意義 [The Important Discovery of a Yuan Period Measuring Vessel and Its Significance]. *Zhongguo kaogu wang* 中國考古网 [Chinese Archaeology Net]. http://www.kaogu.cn/cn/kaoguyuandi/kaogusuibi/2013/1025/34743.html (accessed July 12, 2022).

Qian Daxin 錢大昕 (1728–1804). 1989. "Ba *Changchun zhenren xiyouji*" 跋長春真人西遊記 [Colophon to the *Account of the Perfected Changchun's Journey to the West*]. In *Qianyan tang quanshu* 潛研堂全書. Shanghai guji chubanshe.

Qin Zhi'an 秦志安 (1188–1244). 2004. *Jinlian zhengzong ji* 金蓮正宗記 [Biographies of the True Lineage of the Golden Lotus]. In ZHDZ vol. 47, 29–53.

Qiu, Yihao. 2020. "Ja'far Khwāja." In *Along the Silk Roads in Mongol Eurasia: Generals, Merchants, and Intellectuals*, edited by Jonathan Brack, Michal Biran, and Francesca Fiaschetti, 140–157. University of California Press.

Rashīd-ad-Dīn, Fadlallāh, and Wheeler M. Thackston. 1998. *Jami'u't-tawarikh: A History of the Mongols*. 3 vols. Vol. 1. Harvard University, Dept. of Near Eastern Languages and Civilizations.

Raz, Gil. 2014. "'Conversion of the Barbarians' [Huahu 化胡] Discourse as Proto Han Nationalism." *Medieval History Journal* 17 (2): 255–294.

Reiter, Florian. 1985. "Ch'ung-yang Sets Forth His Teaching in Fifteen Discourses." *Monumenta Serica* 36: 33–54.

Reiter, Florian. 2004. "Zhongnanshan zuting xianzhen neizhuan" 終南山祖庭仙真內傳. In Schipper and Verellen 2004, vol. 2, 1140.

Schipper, Kristopher, and Franciscus Verellen, eds. 2004. *The Taoist Canon: A Historical Companion to the "Daozang."* 3 Vols. University of Chicago Press.

Shen Yao 沈垚 (1798–1840). 1897. *Xiyouji Jinshan yi dong shi* 西遊記金山以東釋 [Explanation of the Area East of Jinshan in *Journey to the West*]. N.p.

Shiraishi Noriyuki 白石典之. 2012. "Gyujihaku saikō" 魚兒濼再考 [Reconsideration of the Location of Lake Yuerpo in the Early Mongol-Yuan Period]. *Nihon Mongoru gakkai kiyō* 日本モンゴル学会紀要 42: 23–38.

Simon, Walter. 1967. "Obituary: Arthur Waley." *Bulletin of the School of Oriental and African Languages* 30 (1): 268–271.

Sloane, Jesse D. 2014a. "Mapping a Stateless Nation: 'Bohai' Identity in the Twelfth to Fourteenth Centuries." *Journal of Song-Yuan Studies* 44: 365–402.

Sloane, Jesse D. 2014b. "Rebuilding Confucian Ideology: Ethnicity and Biography in the Appropriation of Tradition." *Sungkyun Journal of East Asian Studies* 14 (2): 235–255.

Song Lian 宋濂 (1310–1381). 1939. "Shu Liu zhenren shi" 書劉真人事 [Penning an Account of the Perfected One Liu]. In *Song xueshi quanji* 宋學士全集, 15.1045. Shangwu yinshuguan.

Song Zizhen 宋子貞 (1186–1266). 1999. "Zhongshu ling Yelü gong shendao bei 中書令耶律公神道碑 [Spirit Way Epitaph for His Highness Yelü (Chucai), Secretariat Director]." In QYW vol. 1, 171–172.

Starostin, S. A., A. V. Dybo, and O. A. Mudrak. 2003. *An Etymological Dictionary of Altaic Languages*. E. J. Brill.

Stephenson, F. R., and K. K. C. Yau. 1992. "The Total Solar Eclipse of A.D. 1221 and the Rotation of the Earth." *Astronomy and Astrophysics* 260 (1–2): 485–488.

Sugiyama Masaaki 杉山正明. Huang Meirong 黃美蓉, trans. 2011. *Damo: youmumin de shijieshi* 大漠：遊牧民的世界史 [The Great Steppes: The Nomadic Peoples in World History]. Guangchang chuban.

Tao Zongyi 陶宗儀 (1329–1410). 1959. *Chuogeng lu* 輟耕錄 [A Record When Resting from Plowing]. Zhonghua shuju.

Tong Laga 通啦嘎. 2007. "Lun 'Yuandai baihua' yu Meng Yuan yingyi ti" 論"元代白話"與蒙元硬譯體 [On "Yuan Period Colloquial Language" and Word-by-Word Translation of the Mongol Yuan Period]. *Neimenggu shifan daxue xuebao* 內蒙古師範大學學報 36 (2): 63–65.

Wang, Jinping. 2018. *In the Wake of the Mongols: The Making of a New Social Order in North China*. Harvard University Asia Center.

Wang Shiren 王世仁. 2013. "Jin Zhongdu lishi yange yu wenhua jiazhi" 金中都歷史沿革與文化價值 [Historical Evolution and Cultural Value of Jin Zhongdu]. *Zhongguo jianzhu shi lun huikan* 中國建築史論彙刊 8 (2): 289–300.

Wen, Zuoting. 2020. "Born of the North Wind: Northern Chinese Poetry and the Eurasian Steppes, 1206–1220." Ph.D. dissertation, School of International Letters and Cultures, Arizona State University.

West, Stephen H. 1977. "Jurchen Elements in the Northern Drama *Hu-t'ou-p'ai* 虎頭牌." *T'oung Pao*, 2nd series 63 (4–5): 273–295.

West, Stephen H. 2005. "Autumn Sounds, Music to the Ears: Ouyang Xiu's '*Fu* on Autumn's Sounds.'" *Early Medieval China* 10–11 (2): 73–99.

Wu Cheng 吳澄 (1249–1333). 1999. "Tianbao gong bei" 天寶宮碑 [Stele for the Palace of the Precious Treasure]. In QYW vol. 38, 370–372.

Xiangmai 祥邁 (13th c.). 1988. *Bianweilu* 辯偽錄 [A Disputation of Contrived and False Records]. In *Taishō shinshū Daizōkyō* 大正新脩大藏經, vol. 52, no. 2116. Taishō shinshū Daizōkyō Kankōkai. Also available at CBETA Online. https://cbetaonline.dila.edu.tw/zh/T52n2116_p0751a05 (accessed Aug. 22, 2021).

Xiao Jinming 蕭進銘. 2003. "Qiu Chuji nianpu yu lüezhuan" 丘處機年譜與略傳 [A Chronology and Brief Biography of Qiu Chuji]. *Dandao wenhua* 丹道文化 28 (3): 221–229.

Xiao Qiqing (Hsiao Ch'i-ch'ing) 蕭啟慶. 2007. *Nei beiguo er wai Zhongguo: Meng Yuan shi yanjiu* 內北國而外中國：蒙元史研究 [Identifying with the Northern Lands and Excluding the Central Lands: Studies of Mongol-Yuan History]. 2 vols. Vol. 1. Zhonghua shuju.

Xiong Mengxiang 熊夢祥 (14th c.). 1983. *Xijin zhi jiyi* 析津志輯佚 [A Compilation of Surviving Fragments from the Xijin Gazetteer]. Beijing guji chubanshe.

Xu Quansheng 許全勝. 2019. *Shen Zengzhi shi di zhuzuoji kao* 沈曾植史地著作輯考 [Studies of Shen Zengzhi's Writings on Historical Geography]. Zhonghua shuju.

Xue Zongzheng 薛宗正. 2009. "Ashina Xian shengping ji kao" 阿史那献生平輯考 [A Compilation of Sources on the Life of Ashina Xian]. *Xinjiang daxue xuebao* 新疆大學學報1: 41–49.

Xuanzang 玄奘 (7th c.). Li Rongxi, trans. 1996. *The Great Tang Dynasty Record of the Western Regions*. Numata Center for Translation and Research (Berkeley).

Yang Bojun 楊伯峻. 1979. *Liezi jishi* 列子集釋 [Collected Explanations of *Liezi*]. 2 vols. Zhonghua shuju.

Yang, Shao-yun. 2018. "Journeys to the West: Kitan and Jurchen Travelers in Thirteenth-Century Central Asia." https://denisongis.maps.arcgis.com/apps/MapJournal/index.html?appid=e0fe47ae592c4cab8930bbb37ce41269.

Yang Xiong 揚雄 (53 BCE–18 CE). Zhang Zhenze 張震澤, ann. 1993. *Yang Xiong ji jiaozhu* 揚雄集校注 [An Annotated Edition of the Collected Works of Yang Xiong]. Shanghai guji chubanshe.

Yang Zhijiu 楊志玖. 1985. *Yuanshi sanlun* 元史三論 [Three Essays on the History of the Yuan]. Renmin wenxue chubanshe.

Yao Congwu 姚從吾. Sechin Jagchid, informant. 1971. "Zhang Dehui *Lingbei jixing* zuben jiaozhu" 張德輝《嶺北紀行》足本校注 [A Complete Annotated Edition of Zhang Dehui's *Notes on a Journey North of the Mountain Ranges*]. In *Yao Congwu xiansheng quanji* 姚從吾先生全集, 285–303. Zhengzhong shuju.

Yao, Tao-chung. 1986. "Ch'iu Ch'u-chi and Chinggis Khan." *Harvard Journal of Asiatic Studies* 46 (1): 201–219.

Yao, Tao-chung. "Buddhism and Taoism under the Chin." 1995. In *China under Jurchen Rule*, edited by Hoyt Cleveland Tillman and Stephen H. West, 145–180. State University of New York Press.

Yelü Chucai 耶律楚才 (1189–1243). 1981. *Xiyou lu* 西遊錄 [Record of a Journey to the West]. Edited by Xiang Da 向達. Zhonghua shuju.

Yelü Chucai 耶律楚才 (1189–1243). Fang Xie 方謝, ed. 1986. *Zhanran jushi ji* 湛然居士集 [Collected Works of the Lay Buddhist Who Attained Clarity]. Zhonghua shuju.

Yelü Chucai 耶律楚才 (1189–1243). 1988. *Xuanfeng qinghui lu* 玄風慶會錄 [A Record of the Felicitous Encounter with the Mysterious Wind of Daoism]. In ZTDZ vol. 3, 387–390.

Yin Zhiping 尹志平 (1169–1251). 2004a. *Baoguang ji* 葆光集 [Collected Works from the Hidden Light Studio]. ZHDZ vol. 26, 753–783.

Yin Zhiping 尹志平 (1169–1251). 2004b. *Qinghe zhenren beiyou yulu* 清和真人北遊語錄 [Collected Sayings from the Perfected Qinghe's Journey to the North]. In ZHDZ vol. 26, 725–753.

Yuan Haowen 元好問 (1190–1257). Di Baoxin 狄寶心, ann. 2012. *Yuan Haowen wen biannian jiaozhu* 元好問文編年校注 [Collected Prose Works of Yuan Haowen, Annotated and Arranged Chronologically]. 3 vols. Vol. 2. Zhonghua shuju.

Yuan Haowen 元好問 (1190–1257), ed. Zhang Jing 張靜 (13th c.), ann. 2018. *Zhongzhou ji jiaozhu* 中州集校注 [An Annotated Edition of *Collected Writings from the Central Plains*]. 9 vols. Vol. 7. Zhonghua shuju.

Yule, Henry. 1913–1916. "The Travels of John de Marignolli, 1339–1353." In *Cathay and the Way Thither: Being a Collection of Medieval Notices of China*, 209–269. Hakluyt Society.

Yuwen Maozhao 宇文懋昭 (13th c.). Cui Wenyin 崔文印, ed. and ann. 1986. *Da Jin guozhi jiaozheng* 大金國志校證 [A Critical Edition of *Record of the Great Jin State*]. Zhonghua shuju.

Zhang Fang 張方. 2012. "Meng Yuan shiqi Wangwushan Quanzhenjiao huodong shulüe" 蒙元時期王屋山全真教活動述略 [Quanzhen Daoist Activities on Mt. Wangwu during the Mongol Yuan Period]. *Yichun xueyuan xuebao* 宜春學院學報 10: 60–62, 91.

Zhang, Xushan. 2010. "On the Origin of the 'Taugast' in Theophylact Simocatta and the Later Sources." *Byzantion* 80: 485–501.

Zhao Gong 趙珙 (13th c.). Wang Guowei 王國維 (1877–1927), ann. 1968. *Mengda beilu jianzheng* 蒙韃備錄箋證 [A Critical Edition of *A Comprehensive Account of the Mongol Tatars*]. In *Wang Guantang xiansheng quan ji* 王觀堂先生全集. 50 vols. Vol. 12. Wenhua chuban gongsi.

Zhong Xingqi 鍾興麒, ed. 2008. *Xiyu diming kaolu* 西域地名考錄 [Geographical Names of the Western Regions]. Guojia tushuguan chubanshe.

Zhu Yuqi 朱玉麒. 2015. *Xu Song yu "Xiyu shuidao ji" yanjiu* 徐松與《西域水道記》研究 [Studies of Xu Song and His *Waterways of the Western Regions*]. Beijing daxue chubanshe.

Zhuangzi 莊子 (4th–3rd cc. BCE). Burton Watson, trans. 1968. *The Complete Works of Chuang-tzu*. Columbia University Press.

Zhuangzi 莊子 (4th–3rd cc. BCE). Guo Qingfan 郭慶藩 (1844–1896), ed. 1995. *Zhuangzi jishi* 莊子集釋 [Collected Explanations of the *Book of Zhuangzi*]. Zhonghua shuju.

Zuo Qiuming 左丘明 (ca. 502–422 BCE). Du Yu 杜預 (222–285), ann. Lu Deming 陸德明 (d. 630), ann. Kong Yingda 孔穎達 (574–648), sub-ann. 1973. *Chunqiu Zuozhuan zhushu* 春秋左傳注疏 [Annotations and Sub-annotations to the *Zuo Commentary to the Spring and Autumn Annals*]. Yiwen yinshuguan.

Index

Abuhan Mountains xxxvii, 49, 109,
   163 n.xlvii
Alixian 27, 39, 81, 85, 97, 101, 105, 106
   n.29, 107, 113, 119, 120 n.59, 125,
   161 n. xxviii, 171–173, 189, 205
Almaliq 60 n.104, 61, 63, 107, 165
   n.lxvi
Altai Mountains (Jinshan) xliii, 45
   n.84, 51, 53, 63, 65, 73, 109, 111,
   123, 164 n.xlvii, 234 n.14
Amu River (Amu Darya) 71, 81,
   82 n.136, 83, 96 n.14, 99, 166
   n.lxxv, 167 n.lxxviii
Authentic Great Way sect 159 n.i,
   228 n.4, 229

Baideng 9, 119
Baiyun (White Cloud) Monastery
   153, 159 n.iii, 170 n.xxvi
Baljuna Covenant xxxv
Balkh 96 n.15, 99
Baoguang Hall 151, 229
Baoxuan (Precious Mystery) Hall 16
   n.24, 17, 133, 143, 151, 170 n.xxvi
Beiting Protectorate (Tang dynasty)
   xxxix, 57
Besh-Baliq xxxix, 57, 165 n.lvii–lviii
Bianliang (Kaifeng) xxx–xxxi, 132
   n.86
Bichurin, Nikita Yakovlevich xlvii
Bodhidharma 28 n.54, 29, 183
Bo'orchu xlviii, 81, 83, 167 n.lxxxi
Bretschneider, Emil xxix, xlvi

calcium carbonate dust storms 109,
   111
catfish 166 n.lxxiv

Central Plain (Zhongyuan) xxxviii,
   xxxix, xlii, xliv, 32 n.61, 35, 43,
   61, 164 n.xlviii, 207, 215
   in contrast to Samarkand 79
   in contrast to Amu River 83
   in contrast to local agricultural
      products 83
   in terms of contrasting lifestyle 93
   as a site of arrogance and indul-
      gence 175
   and Daoism 215, 225
Chaghadai (The Second Prince) 61,
   63 n.107, 77, 93, 107
Changbala (Jambaliq) 59, 165
   n.lxiii
Changsong (Long Pine) Range 43,
   163 n.xl
Chaoyuan Monastery 23, 25, 27, 33,
   119, 121, 159 n.iv
Chen Shike (Chen Xiuyu) 19, 154
   n.19, 133, 169 n.xvi
Chinqai (Tian Zhenhai) xxxviii, 47,
   49, 51, 53, 59, 65, 69, 73, 81, 85,
   99, 101, 163 n.xlv
Chinqai City (Balaghasun) xxxvi–
   xxxvii, 45, 47, 163 n.xlv
Chinggis Qan xxvii, 3, 13, 51,
   and Qiu Chuji 127
   and Li Zhichang xxxvi
   and Yelü Chucai xxxv
   and rise of Mongols xxviii,
      xxxi–xxxiv
   consorts and wives xxxi, 45, 163
      n.xli–xlii
   headquarters of 71, 85
   instructions to Qiu Chuji's han-
      dlers 29, 49, 187

Chinggis Qan (*continue*)
  rescripts to Qiu Chuji 126 n.69,
    127, 175–8, 183–5, 189, 191
  special favors to Quanzhen School
    xxvii, xxxiv, 107, 126 n.70, 187
  western campaign against
    Khwarazm xxxiii, 60 n.104, 84
    n.141–42
Christians xxxiv
See also Tarsa
Cinnabar Fields (*Dantian*) 22 n.36,
  131 n.82
Cistanche 110 n.41, 111, 168 n.viii
clothing xlii, 143, 155, 211, 215, 223
  of Muslims 93, 95
  of steppe people 61, 103
coral 89
cotton 60 n.105, 61, 93, 95, 101
Cuiping Pass 35, 162 n.xxxi
danishmand (scholars) 92 n.6, 93, 95

Dashi: see Qara Khitai
Dashi Linya: see Qara Khitai
Daihai, Lake 116 n.52, 117
desert monitor lizard 83
Dexing xxxii n.17, 9, 17, 21, 107, 121,
  123, 153, 159 n.ii, 169 n.xiii, 179
Donglai: see Laizhou

Eastern Xia 65, 166 n.lxx

Fanghu Chamber 142 n.104, 143

Gailipo 35
Gan Ji 214 n.6, 215
Gaochang: see Qocho
Gengsang Chu 222 n.17
Golden Tablet retreat 34 n.64, 35,
  120 n.60
grapes 55, 65, 71, 73
Great River Post Road 108 n.34, 109
Great Snowy Mountains: see Hindu
  Kush

Guangcheng, Master 222 n.16, 223
Guo Dequan 109, 113

Hangzhou (Lin'an) xxxi
Haotian Monastery 7
He Zhijian (Zhiqing) 113, 203
Headdress
  Muslim 93
  woman's *gugu* 41
Heavenly Lake: see Sayram, Lake
Hela: see Qara
Hela-Bahai 107, 171–73, 205
Helaxiao 45, 163 n.xliv
Hezhongfu: see Samarkand
Hezhou: see Qocho
Hindu Kush (Great Snowy
  Mountains) xl, xliii, xliv, 69, 77,
  79, 81, 85, 95, 209
Huizong (Song emperor) 132 n.86,
  207, 219, 221
Hülegü (Prince), xxviii
Hulun Nur 39

Ili River 107, 165 n. lxv–vi, 166
  n.lxix
Iron Gate 43, 81, 83, 87, 96 n.11, 97,
  167 n.lxxxi
Islam 59 n.102, 67, 93, 94 n.8–9, 95
Island of Gemlike Flowers 129, 130
  n.80, 133, 149, 169 n.xvii, 201
  Mount Shoule on 133

Ja'far Khwāja 127, 129, 169 n.xv
Jambaliq see Changbala
Jia Chang 121, 191
Jiagu, Lady 47, 113, 163 n.xlvi
Jiagu Tongzhu 117, 168 n.xi
jiao (Daoist ritual) 10 n.8, 11, 15–17,
  21, 33, 111, 121
  cosmic efficacy of 135, 139, 145
  Noumenal-Treasure Purification
    jiao 155
  Yellow Register *jiao* 137

Jin dynasty (Jurchen Jin) xxix–xii,
    xxx–xxxi, 3, 12 n.9, 65, 98 n.17,
    190 n.xxv, 175, 221, 225, 233
    and Qiu Chuji 6 n.3, 7, 179
    battles with the Mongols lxiii, 34
    n.63, 224 n. 17–18,
    former officials of xxxiv–v, 13, 159
    n.iv, 160 n.x, xxi, 220 n.13, 221
    former princess of Jin, then
    consort to Chinggis 45, 47, 163
    n.xli
    former palaces of 129, 169 n.xvii
    northern border wall of 35
Jinshan: see Altai Mountains
Ju Zhiyuan 113, 155, 203
Juyong Pass 9, 17, 125

Kaifeng: see Bianliang
Kemkemji'ut prefecture 111, 168
    n.vii.
Kereit xxxv, 169 n.xv
Kerulen (Luju) River 39, 47, 73, 91
Kesh 83, 97
Khangai Range 45 n.84
Khojand River (Khojand-müren)
    69, 103
Khwarazm xxxiii, 65, 166, n.lxxi
Khwarazm-shah: see Muhammad,
    Sultan
Kishliq Darqan xlviii, 105, 168 n.iv
Kitan xxxi, xxxv, xlix, 43, 71, 160 n.xii,
    163 n.xxxix, 166 n.lxxii, 208 n.1
    See also Qara Khitai
Kong Zhitong 229
koumiss 41, 99
Kou Qianzhi 216 n.10, 217

Laizhou (Donglai) xxxi–xxxii, 7, 9,
    209
Laozi (Most High Lord) 12 n.13, 13,
    14 n.18, 15, 29, 31, 79, 183, 192
    n.2, 193, 207, 215, 217
Li Boxiang 59

Li Shiqian 19
Li Zhichang xxviii–xxix, xxxiv–xxx-
    vii, 5, 100 n.20, 113, 151, 153, 164
    n.xlviii, 168 n.vi, 203, 228 n.3,
    231, 233
Lin Lingsu 207, 219, 220 n.13, 221
Liu Chuxuan 162 n.xxx, 215
Liu Min 125, 169 n.xiv
Liu Yu 224 n. 19, 225
Liu Zhong 19, 160 n.xvii
Liu Zhonglu (Liu Wen) xxvii,
    xxxii, xxxiv–xxxv, xxxviii, 7,
    9, 11, 13, 17, 49, 81, 85, 93, 101,
    153, 155, 171–172, 177, 179, 205,
    209, 213
    description of travels from
    Chinggis's *ordo* to Shandong 9
Longgang 123
Longmen River 121
Longyan Temple 31
Longyang Monastery 3, 17, 19, 21,
    29, 31, 33, 107, 121, 123, 159 n.ii,
    169 n.xiii
Lugou Bridge 11, 12 n.9
Luntai 57, 59, 165 n.lx

Madame Yuan: see Qinsheng
Ma Yu 149, 162 n.xxx, 215
melons xliv, 58 n.101, 59, 91, 92 n.2,
    93, 95, 99
Meng Zhiwen (Zhiyuan) 113, 164
    n.xlviii, 202 n.i, 203
Menggudai (Mengguda) 107, 171–73,
    205
minaret 66 n.113, 72 n.119, 94 n.9, 95
Mongols (accompanying or encoun-
    tered by the travelers) 7, 39,
    41, 89 n.149, 99, 103, 105, 111,
    171–3, 205
Möngke Qan xxxvi, 231
Muhammad, Sultan xxxiii, 65, 67,
    70, n.118, 71, 73, 84 n.141, 101,
    182, n.6, 166 n.lxxi, 182, n.6

muezzin 95
Naiman xliii, 9, 51, 53, 67, 163
    n.xxxix, 166 n.lxxiii
neidan ("inner elixir") xxx, 115, 131
    n.82–3, 169 n.xviii

Ögödei (The Third Prince) xxxvi, 51,
    63 n.107, 97, 231
onions
    cultivated 55
    wild 39, 43, 45
ordo 8 n.5, 9, 13, 27, 33, 39, 45, 91,
    163 n.xli
    of the Princesses 39, 45
Otegin (Temüge-otchegin, Wochen,
    Prince) 27, 39, 161 n.xxviii

Palladius (Pyotr Ivanovich Kafarov)
    xlvii
Pan Dechong 113, 203
Plain of White Bones xxxviii, xliii,
    35, 53, 61, 165 n.lxii
Prince Shao of Wei: see Wanyan
    Yongji

Qaju 99, 167 n.iii
Qara (Hela) 13, 29, 73, 77, 125
Qara Böde (Hela-bode) 85, 167
    n.lxxxiii
Qara Khitai xlix, 43, 64 n.110, 65,
    67, 79, 89, 95, 163 n.xxxix, 166
    n.lxxii–lxxiii
Qatun xxxi, 39, 45, 163 n.xli–xlii
qi 25 n.45, 88 n.145, 113, 115 n.51, 117,
    161 n.xxiii, 208 n.iv, 211, 217,
    219, 223
Qi Zhiqing 113, 203
Qingshe: see Yidu
Qingzhou: see Yidu
Qinsheng, Lady (Madame Yuan) 47,
    163 n.xlvi

Qionghua dao: see Island of
    Gemlike Flowers
Qiu Chuji
    and appearance of cranes 11, 17,
        125, 155
    construction of memorial hall for
        153–5
    death 151, 229
    dietary needs 77
    early career 7
    fulfillment of Ma Yu's prophecy
        for 149
    funeral and interment ceremo-
        nies for 153, 155, 157
    illness on return trip 113, 115
    meetings with Jin consorts in the
        steppes 47
    names for 7, 85
    relations with Jin court xxx, xxxii,
        6 n.3, 7
    request to Chinggis to delay
        journey 13
    sermons to and conversations
        with Chinggis Qan 85, 97, 99,
        101–03, 105, 209–27
    visits with Chinese inhabitants on
        the steppe 47, 103, 107–11
Qiuyang Monastery 123
Qixia Monastery 49, 109, 164 n.xlix
    Changchun and Yuhua congrega-
        tion of 109, 168 n.vi
    troubles among congregants 111
Qocho 55, 165 n.lvii
Qubilai Qan xxxiv, xlvi, 232 n.10

Ramadan 67 n.115, 92 n.7, 94 n.8
Ruoshui (Weak River) 18 n.29, 19

salt sources 41, 35, 71, 96 n.12, 97, 225
Sairam (Sayram) City 66 n.112–13,
    67, 107

Samarkand xxxiii, xxxv–vi, xliii–iv,
    xlvi, 43, 55, 69, 70 n.118, 71, 77
    n.131, 78 n.134, 79, 82 n.135, 85,
    89, 91, 94 n.9, 97, 99, 101, 103,
    163 n.xxxix, 166 n.lxxvi, 167
    n.lxxviii, 199
  agricultural products of 91
  description of city 71
  description of gardens in 79
  description of inhabitants 93
  description of local products 93
Sanguan 123
Sayram, Lake ("Heavenly Lake") 61,
    63, 105, 109, 165 n.lxv
Sendeb: see Shimo Xiandebu
Shaolin Monastery 231
Shimo Xiandebu 13, 125, 160 n.xii,
    193, 199
Shi Xu 19
Shizong (Jin emperor) 159 n.vi, 194
    n.5, 225, 227
Sleep (demon of sleep) 73, 151
  and Quanzhen religion 25 n.46,
    215
  and dreams 111
  and abstinence 219
Solar Eclipse of 1221 39, 73, 162
    n.xxxvi
Song Dao'an 49, 109, 111, 113, 151, 153,
    164 n.xlviii, 203, 231
Song Defang 35, 119, 120 n.60, 121,
    151, 162 n.xxxii, 203
Sultan of Khwarazm: see
    Muhammad, Sultan
Sun Xi 5, 19, 159 n.iv, 233
Sun Zhijian 113, 203
Sun Zhou 19, 160 n.xvi

Tabgach 61, 166 n. lxviii
Taihang Mountains xxxviii, 35, 63
Talas River 65, 166 n.lxix
Taliqan 84 n.139, 96 n.15, 99

Tan Chuduan 162 n.xxx, 215
Tangut
  ethnicity: 71, 107, 161 n.xxviii, 163
    n.xlii, 167 n.lxxxiii, 171, 173
  state of Xia (Xixia) xxxiii, 114
    n.47
Tarsa 59, 165 n.lxi
Temüjin xxxii
Tengri xxxii
Tengri möngke kün 85
thunder 40, 102 n.23, 103, 147
Tianchang Monastery xxvii, 3, 15, 16
    n.24, 125, 127, 135, 143, 147, 159
    n.iii,
  Qiu Chuji's appointment as abbot
    of 193, 195, 199
  Eight Congregations of 109, 111,
    127, 168 n.vi, 169 n.xvi
  repair of 143
Tiancheng 119
Tian Shan Mountains (Yinshan) 31,
    45, 55, 57, 59, 61, 63, 65, 79, 91,
    95, 109
Tolui 232 n.10, 233
Tuanbaliq 97
Tudan, Lady 47, 163 n.xlvi
Tula River 43

Uyghur 12 n. 14, 43, 45, 54 n.95, 99,
    56 n.96, 58 n.100, 69, 168 n.vii,
    175
  as overall reference to Muslims
    66 n.114, 84 n.141
  bandits 85
  commanders in the Mongol army
    71
  language xlix
  monks 57, 59,
  script 93, 103
  town or city 53, 55, 57, 59, 65, 67,
    69, 73, 97
  troops 70 n.118, 83, 84 n.141, 87

Waley, Arthur xxix–xxx, lxvii–lxviii,
Wang E 164 n.xlviii, 168 n.vi
Wang Gou 19
Wang Guowei lxvii, 163 n.xli, xliv,
    172–3, 231–5
Wang Juchuan 13, 27, 131, 157, 160
    n.xiii, 195–7
Wang Rui 19, 160 n.xx
Wang Zhe (byname Chongyang)
    xxx, 7, 18 n.31, 76 n.129, 85, 174
    n.2, 199, 232 n.8
Wang Zhizai 19
Wang Zhiming 113, 147, 151, 203
Wang Zuan 215, 216 n.9
Wanyan Loushi 220 n.14, 221
Wanyan Yongji xxxii
wights xl, 51, 55, 111
Wild Fox Ridge xxxviii, 30 n.58,
    31, 34 n.63, 35, 91, 121, 162
    n.xxxi
Wu Deming 19, 139, 141
Wu Zhang 19, 160 n.xviii

Xia Zhicheng 113, 203
Xiangmai 229, 231, 233
Xingchan Monastery 229
Xuande Prefecture xxxv, 23, 67, 119,
    121, 162 n.xxxi, 169 n.xiv, 191

Yanjing (Zhongdu, modern Beijing)
    xxvii–xxviii, xxxi–xxxii, xxxiv,
    xxxvi, 3, 9, 11, 13, 17, 31, 33,
    34 n.63, 125, 127, 133, 135, 157,
    159–60, 162–3, 167 n.i, 169, 179,
    193, 199, 213,
Yan Liben 15, 160 n.xiv
Yang Agou 84 n.143, 85, 87, 107
Yang Biao 19
Yanglian Zhenjia 232 n.9, 233
Yang River 119

Yang Zhijing 113, 203
Yellow Emperor Xuanyuan 216 n.12,
    217, 223
Yelü (Yila) Ahai xxxv, 71, 99, 101
Yelü (Yila) Chucai xxix, xxxiv–vi,
    100, 160 n.xvii, 161 n.xxi, 165
    n.lx, 167 n.i, ii, 174 n.1, 207, 208
    n.1–3, 209
Yelü (Yila) Tuhua xxxv, 23, 119
Yidu 9, 11
Yin Qianyi 121, 169 n.xiii
Yinshan: see Tian Shan Mountains
Yin Zhiping 9, 25 n.46, 67, 83, 113,
    115, 119, 151, 153, 160 n.xi, 163
    n.xlvi, 169 n.xiv, 170 n.xxvi,
    203, 231, 233
Yu Zhike 113, 203
Yu'erpo (Fish Lake) xlii, 37, 41, 162
    n.xxxiv
Yuxu Monastery 3, 13, 19, 125
Yunzhong 117, 119, 168 n.xii, 230 n.4
Yuyang Pass 115
Yuzhou 123

zhai rituals 23 n.38
Zhang Daoling 214 n.8, 215
Zhang Lin 9, 11, 160 n.x
Zhang Rong 107, 168 n.v
Zhang Tiandu 17, 160 n.xv
Zhang Zhisu 113, 151, 203
Zhang Zhiyuan 113, 203
Zhang Ziyin 145
Zhangzong (Jin emperor) 12 n.9, 47,
    113, 163 n.xlvi, 194 n.5, 203
Zhao Fang 19, 160 n. 21
Zhao Jiugu (Daojian) 51, 67, 107, 111,
    121, 164 n.li
Zhao Zhongli 19, 160 n.xix
Zheng Zhixiu 113, 203
Zhi Zhongyuan 143, 170 n.xxiii